Doing Life
with Mandela

MY PRISONER, MY FRIEND

To:
Winnie Atterbury-O'Keefe

Enjoy reading my book!

Christo Brand

 20/02/2023

Doing Life with Mandela

MY PRISONER, MY FRIEND

Christo Brand
with Barbara Jones

**Updated edition with
added material**

EDITED BY ANDREW RUSSELL

BLUE EAR BOOKS

Published in 2022 by
Blue Ear Books
7511 Greenwood Ave N, Box 400
Seattle, WA 98103
USA

www.blueearbooks.com

www.christobrand.co.za
Email: info@christobrand.co.za
Instagram and Twitter: @christobrand60
Facebook: Christo Brand

ISBN: 978-0-6397-1846-0

Contents

Foreword:
My Uncle's Unlikely Friendship
ZOHRA KATHRADA AREINGTON

It is an honour to be asked by Andrew to contribute this foreword to the second edition of Christo's book.

I was born in a small town called Schweizer Reneke in the North West province. My dad was Ismail Kathrada, brother of Kathy, as we fondly called Nelson Mandela's close associate and fellow political prisoner Ahmed Kathrada. I did my primary schooling there and had to leave home after finishing Standard 5, as there were no high schools for non-whites in Schweizer. I finished my high school in Lenasia. I married Alie Areington in April 1984 and moved to Port Elizabeth. We have two sons. Later we relocated to Johannesburg.

In 2011 I was interviewed by Shan Balton, the CEO of the Ahmed Kathrada Foundation. The Foundation was looking at employing a full-time personal assistant for Kathy, and I joined in February 2011. I thoroughly enjoyed my time at the Foundation under Shan's leadership. I worked with Kathy and the Foundation up until his passing in March 2017. Alie and I remain with the Foundation and do voluntary work for them. I won't walk away from the Foundation. It does exceptionally good work, which I believe will continue the legacy of Kathy, and it is well managed by an excellent board of trustees.

When I was a child, my dad always spoke of his brother, who had been sent to Robben Island prison and was serving a life sentence there. My dad promised me that when I turned 18 he would take me to visit Kathy. At the time, one had to be 18 to visit political prisoners. My dad spoke of the 1964 Rivonia Trial, which led to the imprisonment of Mandela, Kathrada, Sisulu, and others who were convicted of sabotage and sentenced to life imprisonment.

On my 18th birthday, 25 May 1979, I was on the ferry to Robben Island. I was quite nervous, as it was my first time meeting Kathy. I was taken to a cubicle where we were separated by glass, and there was a telephone on each side. As we sat across from each other, separated by this thick glass, we clearly understood that there would be no hugging, so we just sat there staring and crying at each other, lost for words. After we settled down we just spoke, as there was so much to talk about. This was also my first time meeting Christo Brand. I was allowed to visit Kathy again, and I went to Robben Island a few times. After Kathy was transferred to Pollsmoor we had our first contact visit, no glass separating us, and Christo was there.

In October 1989 Kathy, Sisulu, and others were released. What a joyful time in history for the families and for the country at large. As I spent time with Kathy, making up for lost time, as there was much to talk about, he often spoke of his friendship with Christo. They remained friends throughout the years, and Kathy always mentioned how Estelle would bake a cake for him twice a year, on Kathy's birthday and for Christmas. Estelle carried out this tradition for years, until the passing on of Kathy. Kathy and Christo kept in touch regularly, and I used to think how wonderful it was for two people to enjoy this kind of relationship, when one had been a prisoner and the other a warder. I once posed that question to Kathy and he replied, 'In life one has to forgive and move away from bitterness and hatred, and only then will we be able to live in peace and harmony with each other.'

Even since Kathy's passing, Christo and Estelle remain family friends. Alie and I visit Christo and Estelle when in Cape Town, and they do the same when in Joburg. We cherish this friendship that Kathy has started and will definitely see it through our lifetime.

PROLOGUE

Nelson Mandela spent his boyhood in the green and golden hills of South Africa's Eastern Cape. There he ran wild with his friends in the village of Qunu. He has told of the happiest years of his life – shooting birds out of the sky with a catapult, gathering fruit from the trees, catching fish with a bent hook and drinking warm milk straight from the cow.

Just like me, he sometimes looked after flocks of sheep and would go home to his family's little house after playing till dusk, to eat supper and listen to his mother's stories around the fireside.

As a young boy, he had no immediate knowledge of apartheid. In his small, safe world there was no obvious menace. His childhood was secure in the rural Xhosa community where he belonged.

I also knew nothing of the cruel racial boundaries in our country as I grew up. My father was a farm foreman in a fertile part of the Western Cape. All my young life I played with black and mixed-race children who lived on the farm with us in Stanford, many miles from the city.

Looking back, Mandela and I both enjoyed childhoods full of innocence and charm, although many years apart. We were both brought up in the Christian tradition, our lives ruled by strict but loving parents who taught us right from wrong. All that mattered was home and family, with rewards for good behaviour and punishment for bad.

He and I, in contrasting worlds, came to know in our different ways the full cruelty of the apartheid laws, and those worlds collided only many years later when we both found ourselves on Robben Island, the bleak maximum security prison where he was serving life and I was his warder.

I was 19 years old when I came face to face with Nelson Mandela. He was 60. Until that day I had never heard of him, or his African National Congress, or the deeply held reasons that meant that he and his comrades were prepared to die for their cause.

I found a man who was courteous and humble, yet at the same time the powerful leader of many of the political prisoners serving time on Robben Island. If he was outside where they could see him, they would set up a chant – 'Amandla! Power to the People.' They would sing and shout and make the power fist salute. He could not acknowledge them, those were the rules. He had to walk by, and would often only be able to acknowledge them by giving just the slightest nod in their direction.

He was their charismatic leader, their reason for being on the island, yet most of them never even met him once. Those were also the rules.

Mandela, both a dignified prisoner and at the same time a great leader of men, set my young mind racing. I saw his respect for my job and his understanding that I had to make him keep to a harsh regime if we were both to survive. I saw him scrubbing floors, emptying his toilet bucket, cleaning the exercise yard – sometimes on his knees – and, along with a few fellow prisoners, tending a little garden where he grew chillies and vegetables to give variety to the terrible prison food.

He addressed me, a mere boy, as Mr Brand. I called him Mandela. Together, across our different worlds, over time, we somehow came to be friends who were able to show each other kindness and consideration.

After 18 long and difficult years on Robben Island, Mandela was transferred to Pollsmoor Prison on the mainland in a government attempt to break down the ANC's High Command. I was there with him and his comrades.

Later, he moved again, to Victor Verster Prison, where he was given private quarters as he continued the tentative talks he had recently begun with government leaders during his time in isolation at Pollsmoor. He was emerging as the key figure in negotiations to end South Africa's darkest days. Over several tortuous years, the reconciliation process slowly picked up speed. Again, I was with him throughout that time.

On the day of his release, it was decided he should walk free out of the prison gates with his wife Winnie beside him and no warders in sight. So I watched that extraordinary moment on TV at my home, with a lump in my throat and tears in my eyes. Unbelievably, I told myself, our journey together was over.

But Mandela called me a few weeks later. He wanted to catch up with me again. I have been in his life ever since, there at most of the important moments and honoured to still be considered part of his extended family today.

He wrote of his 'long walk to freedom', and I walked some of that road with him, an incredible journey that defines my life today, as well as his.

In truth, my life began so much later than his. A white Afrikaans boy born into the very culture that created Mandela the revolutionary, I'd had no idea it was going to lead me to him.

CHAPTER 1

I grew up on a small farm just outside Stanford, a quaint village set in a mountain valley, two hours' drive from Cape Town, the big city. A river meandered through it and the Atlantic Ocean was nearby. Our farm was called Goedvertrouw, which means 'good trust' in Dutch.

We had our own little school on a nearby farm and that's where I was sent at five years old.

Come rain or shine, every morning I had to walk five miles to the nearest bus stop. But often one of the farmworkers, an African man we called Chocolate, would walk with me to the bus stop or sit me on the front of his bicycle and give me a lift if his bike was in good repair. We never knew Chocolate's real name. He was just always there. He had no relatives and his whole life was spent working on the farm or helping my mother in the house.

Our family was always hard up with little money and no luxuries. But we had a rich home life: we may not have had a lot but what we had was good. There were roast potatoes with butternut, marrow and pumpkin with breadcrumb stuffing and fresh peas. I hardly knew the taste of meat but it didn't matter. After supper, we would take the candles outside to the stoep – we had no electricity – and my father would take out his violin and Chocolate his guitar and the music and merriment would ring out into the dark night.

The days started early and sometimes went on until midnight, especially when the winter rains caused havoc with the crops or the fences. I would sometimes go out in the dark with my father and Chocolate, holding the torch for them, while they fixed fences in the driving rain. In the Boland area of the Western Cape, there would be icy cold winters where the washing froze on the line and your hands went numb and blue. By contrast, the summers were stiflingly hot and you could hardly breathe. My upbringing was that of a typical Christian Afrikaner. I had been baptised into the Dutch Reformed Church and we went to services every Sunday, with a nap in the afternoon. During daylight hours in the school holidays and at weekends, I would be out all day roaming the farm with my friends, the children of the African and mixed-race workers.

During school hours, however, my fellow students were exclusively white. Although I can honestly say I hardly noticed the division at the time, in term-time, our tiny two-classroom school was for the white children of farmers and their managers and foremen. The coloured and African children went to a different school at the bottom of the hill.

Before and after school, though, all of us would meet at the bus stop together and often light a fire right there on the dusty ground if it was cold and we had long to wait for the bus. But we never talked about why there was segregation at our schools. We were small kids – innocents, I suppose – and it was just a fact of life.

The only time I played with white children at home was when my mother's sisters and their families visited us from Cape Town at weekends. My cousin and I would go out early in the morning and Chocolate would accompany us while we hunted rabbits and pigeons.

Then, one day, Chocolate completely disappeared. To this

day I do not know what happened but he was probably arrested for being somewhere without a pass. The pass laws for blacks and coloured people were notorious. They were contemptuously known as 'dompas', the stupid pass, and they ruled the lives of non-whites.

My father tried to find out what happened to Chocolate but nothing came of it. We just accepted it as part of an African's life in those days. Men like him would have come from a large, poor family, living in a shack with no water or electricity or sanitation. He may have lost his parents to malnutrition or tuberculosis, and gone wandering to look for work. He had no belongings and no education, and his birth would not even have been registered so he had no ID papers. He would have considered himself fortunate to find any sort of work or home, having been taken in by my parents.

Chocolate would be classified as an unskilled labourer despite his ability to fix everything on the farm and to teach a child like me how to fish and hunt, and mend fencing and tend animals. He would have no employment record and would have fallen through the system like so many Africans who had no value to the apartheid state.

He was obliged to carry a 'dompas' with him wherever he went and would be required to produce it for random police stop-and-search squads to prove that he was allowed to be wherever they had encountered him. But Chocolate had no 'dompas': officially he didn't even exist.

If he was stopped by police outside of our farm, especially at night-time, he would find himself in a police cell where his life was literally of no interest to them. Many hundreds of thousands of black South Africans 'disappeared' during those years. It was not practical, and not safe, to make too many enquiries. Poor Chocolate was just another casualty of apartheid. We missed him but we were living in a police state and had limited rights ourselves. My father would have asked at our local police station, but would not have been surprised at their lack of interest. To them he would have been just another itinerant African with no real name.

The apartheid system in South Africa was one of the most cruel examples of legitimised racism anywhere in the world. Inspired by the notion of white supremacy brought to South Africa by its first 'conquerors', the Dutch, who were then closely followed by the British, the Afrikaans-speaking National Party set up these laws of segregation when it came to power in 1948.

For decades, black South Africans had been slaves, or servants, or low-paid workers serving the white interlopers' best interests. They had already been disenfranchised by the time the apartheid laws were introduced, and the Native Land Act of 1913, brought in by the British, had deprived them of land ownership. Now they were put at the mercy of further crippling restrictions, with dozens of separate Acts of Parliament being passed to rule their lives and ensure their wretchedness.

As well as the much-hated pass laws, the Reservation of Separate Amenities Act of 1953 introduced the notorious 'whites-only' official notices that went up in every public place, including airports and even cemeteries. Black people were forbidden to use the same beaches, buses, park benches, hospitals, schools or public toilets as white people. The Prohibition of Mixed Marriages Act and the Immorality Act prevented the formation of sexual relationships between different races. And, perhaps cruellest of all, the Bantu Education Act meant that black people were schooled only as preparation for a lifetime as labourers, thus ensuring white dominance for future generations. As

Hendrik Verwoerd, Minister of Native Affairs and the architect of apartheid, once said: 'There is no place for the Bantu [black person] in the European [white] community above the level of certain forms of labour... What is the use of teaching a Bantu child mathematics when it cannot use it in practice?'

Non-whites could not live in a city unless they were employed there and were ordered to carry passes everywhere they went. Millions were forcibly removed from their homes under the Group Areas Act which designated specific, poor, areas for blacks and coloured people.

This inequality did not go unprotested, of course, but the state's response was predictably brutal. By 1960, uprisings against the pass laws reached their peak when police opened fire on demonstrators in the township of Sharpeville, shooting dead 69 black people – many in the back – in what became known as the Sharpeville Massacre. As a result, the government declared the first State of Emergency in South Africa, during which time all civil liberties were suspended and the police could detain suspects at will without any appeal to the courts. All public meetings containing three or more people were banned.

A decade later, in 1970, the situation became still worse for the black population when the Bantu Homeland Citizen Act was passed. This law was designed to strip black South Africans' citizenship from them, forcing them to become citizens of ten so-called 'homelands' – areas of unproductive, unwanted land many miles from the white-dominated cities. This resulted in more than three million people being forcibly resettled.

I know now that the outside world was raging against these terrible strictures, but as a boy growing up in the Western Cape countryside in a non-politicised family I had no knowledge of it whatsoever. Chocolate was a constant presence in my daily life and I knew many other African and mixed-race men who were the heads of their families and whose homes I was always welcome to enter, just as they were welcome to enter ours. I realise now how rare that was and I value it.

It would have been impossible for city residents to have any one-to-one knowledge of a man like Chocolate, or for their children to be playing with black children. It was only possible for me because my parents lived in a house tied to their work on the farm, the same as the black and coloured workers.

I had no awareness of any of this at the time, of course. I simply remember the many childhood friendships I made without any hint of racial tension on either side. When my grandfather bought me a bicycle, for example, the African children would steady it for me and run after me to help me learn how to pedal it and make sure I didn't fall. We shared a lot of things, playing near the river and catching fish. Sometimes we would wrestle and have play fights, after which we would all swim naked in the river and be friends again.

One day, a young coloured boy came to live with us and my parents gave him his own room in the attic. His name was Pikky. Somehow he got left behind on the farm when some seasonal fruit-pickers left, so my mother brought him up.

Pikky used to help my mother in the kitchen and also worked on the land. When I came home from school, I would plant onions or potatoes with him. He was with my family until he was about 15 and then, just like Chocolate, he disappeared and we never saw him again. It was very painful for me because he had been like the brother I never had. We'd shared so much together.

Despite my grief for this loss, I did not ask questions and my parents did not speak of it. Nothing was ever explained to me about the circumstances of people like Chocolate or Pikky. But they had been treated like family when they were with us, and it is only now when I think back that I see how unusual that was.

In fact, looking back, my parents were exceptionally kind to all the people around us, whether they were black, white or coloured. On Fridays, payday, my father would take all the workers to the town 20 miles away to do their shopping. On the way, he would give lifts to workers walking from other farms until our pickup truck was packed full.

Despite his generosity, my father could be very strict and I learned the hard way that he would not tolerate me disrespecting older people, of any colour. One day, he heard me shouting at an elderly black worker on the farm when we were trying to get the cows into a kraal. I was using bad language and my father was furious. He took a sjambok – a whip – to me and all the time he was telling me that older people deserved our respect. The colour of their skin was no matter: it could not come off and anyway they were all human beings just like us. Our farmworkers reciprocated my parents' respect and were kind and caring towards me. One of my earliest memories is of wandering off at the age of about three, and getting lost while playing in a canal. I was always out playing somewhere or at the river, fishing with the other children. All our workers turned out to help my parents find me.

However, these settled times did not last. In 1972, when I was just 12, all those nights out in the cold and rain took their toll on my father and he developed pneumonia. He was really sick and couldn't work in the fields. The farm owner, a white man, decided to evict us. So, at one stroke, we lost both our home and our livelihood. We were experiencing the mercilessness that millions of black people also suffered.

We were forced to move to the city and we were stuck there for a whole year, living in a room in the backyard of my uncle's small family home in Parow Valley, a white middle-class suburb of Cape Town. My father, mother and I lived in one cramped room. I slept on a mattress on the floor and I yearned for the green, open spaces of the veld, and the farm fields.

Once my father recovered, he started working on the railways, and a year later we moved to Epping Garden Village, another suburb of Cape Town, which is now called Ruyterwaght. It had been designated for white railway workers. We owned our own house for the first time and today I have inherited it and extended it and live there with my own family.

It was a different sort of life in Ruyterwaght. My father was at home every night now instead of mending fences or rounding up sheep on the farm. But I was missing my friends and all our playtime on the farm. I had no one to go fishing with and I had no black friends any more. I was at an all-white school and I was noticing that public toilets in the city and on the railway station were marked differently for whites and blacks. I still didn't fully understand apartheid, but I was starting to see small differences that I'd not perceived before.

I was soon completing my schooling in the city and gained quite a reputation as the fastest sprinter in my year. I took up target-shooting too. But our family's financial deprivation continued, and I decided to try to make some pocket money for myself in my spare time.

By the age of 15, I was working at the weekends with a builder who paid me about 8 rand a day – about the equivalent of £5 – to help build his house. I mixed cement, carried loads of bricks and helped him install electricity, working long hours, from six in the morning till six at night. During the week, after finishing my homework, I went door-to-door selling pots and pans and mixing bowls. One of our neighbours worked at a stainless steel factory, and he offered me 25 per cent of all the sales I could make on the products he would give me. I took samples around to show people, along with a catalogue with prices, and they could see that the factory prices were cheaper than those in the shops.

I did quite well, and soon I could afford to buy a secondhand Suzuki 50cc motorbike to make it easier for me to do deliveries. I was still only 16 then. By 17, I had bought an old Ford Cortina, which needed its engine overhauled and gearbox replaced.

My social life revolved around going to braais – barbecues – where we cooked meat and fish caught locally. I was becoming a fully-fledged Afrikaner boy immersed in the white community around me.

In 1976, when I was 16, there was a national scare among the white population about the possibility of a violent black uprising. During two terrible days in the Soweto township, in the heart of Johannesburg, police had shot dead more than 100 black students who had been protesting at the country's racist education system. Many children died, and the violence had escalated around the township.

Everyone was worried the uprising would spread. All of us older students were called out to guard our school at night because the teachers believed black people were going to burn it down. We took turns to patrol the school yard alongside the principal and teachers, who had firearms with them at the ready. Despite our state of paranoia, the feared mob didn't arrive.

After school, I had to face conscription, national service. From 1967, all white South African males between the ages of 17 and 65 years old had to become members of the South

African Defence Force (SADF) or the South African Police (SAP). At first, conscription lasted only nine months, but by 1977, due to increased fighting in Namibia and Angola, it had increased to two years. Afterwards, you would have to attend a camp up on the borders for a month each year for eight years.

I had friends who had died in military camps on the borders of South Africa, and I had been to their funerals. I didn't want to die like them, and I didn't want to join the police force with its reputation for brutality.

Two of my cousins were sent to a military prison in Phalaborwa because they refused to take up arms and do their national service. I was very close to both boys; we were very good friends. Their mother, my aunt, described to me how they were being treated, telling me how they were being forced to do hard labour for five years, and given the same status as common criminals.

I decided my best option was to train as a prison warder or guard. If you served for at least 13 years, you could not be called up to the police or military or be forced to attend the annual border camps. It was looked on as a low-class job with a low salary, but I listened to recruiting officers who came to our school and I reckoned it was the answer for me. I signed up as soon as I could and soon found myself in a prison at Kroonstad, a large town south of Johannesburg in the Orange Free State.

With me was a friend from my schooldays who was only there because of an amazing set of circumstances. He had desperately wanted to be in the prison service, but he knew he would probably fail the medical. Somehow, I had managed to persuade the sergeant in charge of recruitment that he should give my friend a chance. We were sworn in together for the start of training, but the medical check-up was looming and I was worried.

In those strange, lawless days, the prison service actually conspired with me to get him in. The doctor, who was coming from Worcester some way away, was unavailable for some reason on the morning of the medical. His name was Dr Brand, and because I shared the same surname I was told I would have to impersonate him to get the process going.

Today, I both laugh and shudder when I think of it. All I can say is that a whole lot of trainees who would never have qualified after their medicals managed to go on to enjoy long careers in the prison service. My old school chum was not the worst of it: I 'passed' one guy who was completely deaf in one ear. There was another whose eyelids were partially paralysed so he couldn't keep his eyes open for ten seconds at a time.

Despite our lack of fitness for service, our training at Kroonstad was extremely tough, consisting of three months of doing drills, target-shooting with the army, undertaking strenuous physical exercises and studying criminal law. We were paid R70 a month and received a very unpleasant taste of life around hardened criminals.

We were on permanent alert, with inspection drills carried out at a few moments' notice. The alarm would sound at any time of night or day, and we trainees would have to be dressed and ready for inspection within five minutes. We could be pulled up and charged for the slightest offence: an overall in which the seams were not perfectly straight, a spot on the floor, or a bed not made with perfectly straight edges.

To fool the system, we would sleep on a mat on the cement floor so the bed would never have to be made. We never wore shoes in our room, because it took more than two hours to polish the floors. Our days would start at 5.00 a.m. with a two-hour exercise drill, whatever the weather, whether it was freezing cold or boiling hot. Even dripping with sweat, we would sit on the cold cement floors rather than flop on the bed and risk making it untidy.

On winter mornings, the water would freeze in the taps and we had to break blocks of ice with our bare hands, before assembling a complex handgun or rifle with our fingers still numb and sore.

It was torture, and we were always hungry. When we were assigned to clean up the officers' mess after a function, we would grab all the leftover bread and take it back to our room to devour it. Perhaps it was designed to give us an insight into the way prisoners felt when ordinary liberties were taken away from them.

Sometimes we were called at night to search the prison, looking for knives, drugs, and other illegal objects. Often, there were fights to the death between gang members. There would be blood in the cells and we had to shoot teargas inside before we went in, taking dogs with us.

One day a prisoner in solitary confinement, a murderer, called out to a trainee warder with me to ask the time. The warder showed him the time on his watch. The next moment, the prisoner grabbed his wrist through the bars and pulled off the watch. By the time we got the keys out to open the cell, he had put it in his mouth and swallowed it in one go. There was no doctor on duty that night to have his stomach pumped, so we made a report and that was the end of it.

I saw some desperate things at that time. Prisoners would cut their own tendons with a razor blade to make themselves unable to work. Others injected themselves with Brasso, which led to gangrene and eventually amputation of their legs.

Once, there was a fight between two groups of gangsters. We always tried to separate them, but one warder made a mistake and the gangs – some thirty men in all – had met up in the passageway. I was there, along with just two other warders, with no dog-handlers to help us. We blew our whistles and ran in with batons, to avoid a bloodbath.

They attacked us by using metal prison mugs with their socks pushed through the handles to make it easier to beat us. They had taken shower taps and hidden them inside their socks too. After an intense struggle, we managed to push the smallest group into an empty cell and defuse the situation.

But that wasn't the worst of it. Sometimes, a gang leader would force one of his underlings to attack a warder with a razor blade. He had to draw blood to prove himself. The prisoners would target the youngest warders; they could see we were wearing trainee uniforms.

At the end of training, I had chosen to apply to be posted to Robben Island, because my family home was in Cape Town and that was the nearest prison. I knew it was a remote and hostile place, buffeted by the wind and sea, and feared and reviled by all who had been there, but I believed that life could not be any worse than at Kroonstad. I was wrong.

As soon as I applied for the post, all of my family and friends were checked out by Special Branch. I had had to fill in my friends' names and addresses, and they were all visited on more than one occasion and quizzed about their political background or membership of any organisations. I hadn't even been able to warn my family or friends about getting visits from Special Branch, as I hadn't been told myself. Some of my friends thought the police must be investigating me for a serious crime. Anyhow, they found no interest in politics in my life, so I was accepted.

My ignorance of history had made me an ideal candidate, and, when I heard that I was going to be guarding the most dangerous criminals in South Africa's history, I believed it. The prisoners I would be looking after there, I was told, should have received the death sentence but managed to evade it and that's why they were on Robben Island, the most isolated place possible.

Later, once I had met Mandela and the other political prisoners, the police began asking my friends if I talked about him or his comrades. I came to realise that I was also being followed and monitored by the security police when I was home on leave in Cape Town.

On my first trip to the island, we had a nightmare boat ride from Cape Town in bad weather. The ferry rolled and dipped so fiercely that I spent the whole time vomiting. My first impression of the island was that it was a grim and isolated place where the sea crashed savagely against the rocks. When I arrived on a typical Cape winter's day with gale force winds and driving rain, it seemed so bleak that I found myself marvelling at those first Dutchmen who chose to come ashore in the 17th century. We must have looked like lambs to the slaughter to the older warders watching us disembark. One of our first jobs was to serve wine to the sergeants in the big hall. Then they forced us to drink the brackish water from the island's borehole, laced with cheap wine. Once we were drunk, they piled us into a pickup truck and drove us to the back of the island. There were six of us in the vehicle. They switched off the engine and told us to get out. From there, we had to push-start the engine, then we heard them start it up and drive off, with the old-timers shouting and swearing at us out of the windows.

It was dark and raining, with no street lighting. Back at our quarters, they were waiting for us again. They made us run around in circles, a hundred laps each to show how fit we were. They were so drunk. Some of us fell into the bushes and hid there together. We didn't even care if there were poisonous snakes or rats. We were cold, wet and exhausted. They came looking for us again, but we crept back inside and spent the night on the floor underneath our beds, and they gave up.

It was the old warders' idea of a cruel joke, an initiation into the ways of Robben Island.

The next day, the head of the prison welcomed us and introduced himself. He told us we would be working with the biggest murderers and rapists in the country. They were worse than the criminals we had previously met, and were so evil that they were in for life. In fact, the men I would be charged with looking after would be neither rapists nor murderers, though they were seen as a bigger threat to the nation than either.

On our first morning, we new recruits were divided up and placed with senior warders. Then I was told I was going to work in B Section. This was where seven of the eight men known as the Rivonia Trialists were held. I would be working with some of the most notorious prisoners in South Africa.

CHAPTER 2

The terrorism trial in which Nelson Mandela and seven others were sentenced to life imprisonment took place at Rivonia, a suburb of Johannesburg. That had been the location of their main hideout, Liliesleaf Farm, where several were arrested. Mandela was already in solitary confinement in Pretoria Prison at the time, serving five years for leaving the country without a passport and inciting workers to strike. At Rivonia, in June 1964, he was found guilty of sabotage and sent with six of the other convicted men to Robben Island. The only white man found guilty, Denis Goldberg, was sent to Pretoria Central Prison, which had a whites-only security wing for political prisoners.

Before his prison term in Pretoria, Mandela, posing as a gardener at the farm, had been leading an armed campaign to sabotage the apartheid government's worst efforts to marginalise, dispossess, and oppress black people. Radicalised while still at university, where he was threatened with expulsion for standing up for student representation, Mandela had recognised the effectiveness of mass action when he witnessed township marches against the pass laws and raised rents.

By now, Mandela was committed to the African National Congress (ANC), a political party founded in 1912, dedicated to bringing all Africans together as one people to fight for their land and freedom. Since the 1950s, the ANC had been organising a defiance campaign of civil mass resistance in order to put pressure on the government to end apartheid. In the immediate aftermath of the Sharpeville Massacre, Mandela proposed setting up a military wing of the ANC to further continue the struggle. In the face of apartheid's brutality, he declared: 'The time comes in the life of any nation when there remain two choices – submit or fight.'

In 1961, therefore, Mandela was selected as first Commander-in-Chief of the ANC's armed wing, Umkhonto we Sizwe – Spear of the Nation – and set about a campaign of sabotage. Tracked by police and intelligence operatives, he went underground to elude capture.

Liliesleaf Farm was his team's secret headquarters, where they worked under cover of darkness. But the ever-vigilant security police had noted their movements and were following them. On the afternoon of 11 July 1963, armed police arrived in a laundry van and drove through the farm gates. They rounded up everyone on the premises and trapped others one by one as they arrived. It was a government coup hailed loudly as a huge success on national radio that night. The key members of the armed wing of the ANC had been stopped in their tracks as they plotted the overthrow of the apartheid government. Detailed plans and quantities of armaments had been gathered up as evidence. There was no doubt of their guilt.

Realising this, and knowing the consequences, Mandela and his comrades could only hope to use the trial as a public platform for their cause. As he walked up the steps to the dock, Mandela turned to the crowd and raised his clenched fist. 'Amandla!' he shouted, and the response from his supporters was deafening.

Mandela refused to be cross-examined and instead gave a

four-hour speech from the dock to explain who he was and why he and his comrades had felt compelled to turn to violence to defeat the apartheid government. He admitted that Umkhonto we Sizwe had carried out acts of sabotage on government installations, but he maintained they had always tried to avoid casualties. Mandela also said that he hoped to live by his ideal of a free nation for all South Africans, but that if necessary he was prepared to die for it. His lawyers had advised against that declaration, believing he was almost inviting execution.

The renowned author Alan Paton, who wrote *Cry, the Beloved Country*, also came forward to give a speech in mitigation. He begged for clemency, telling the judge that he believed sparing Mandela and his fellow accused would be the only way for South Africa to have a future.

In truth, the defendants had no hope, and fully expected to receive the death sentence for the prosecution's long list of offences, which included conspiring to overthrow the government, obtaining funds for revolution from abroad, ordering munitions, recruiting for guerrilla warfare, and inciting foreign military units to invade and sabotage of government installations. All the trialists had agreed to face the hangman if they were sentenced to death, rather than appeal.

Thus, when life sentences were handed out in the packed, hushed courtroom, one of Mandela's comrades – Denis Goldberg – shouted out, 'Life! Life is wonderful!'

Mandela and his fellow ANC leaders were transferred to Robben Island, where they were always referred to as the 'Rivonians'. Mandela was to spend the next 27 years in prison, 18 of which would be spent on the island.

During my prison service training, I had been familiar with the sort of criminals who ran in gangs and had facial scars and tattoos. When I was sent to B Section on Robben Island where Nelson Mandela and the others were kept, I was puzzled by their appearance and quiet manners.

I asked the sergeant in charge: 'What are these criminals here for?'

He told me they were not common criminals, but that they were terrorists who were trying to overthrow our country.

He told me they would not steal anything from us. You could leave your money or food on a table in the section with the door open and they would never take it. They were only hungry for news, he said. They were not getting newspapers or any information about what was going on in the outside world.

He reassured me they were not hardened criminals, ready to murder, rape, or harm. But nonetheless they were determined to blow up our lives, to eliminate white people and take over the government.

I duly worked up a hatred towards these men. I decided to just do my job, locking up the prisoners and having minimum contact with them.

But when I came into the section I saw prisoners, old guys, standing up to greet us. I had never heard of Mandela at that time. I looked at all these men and saw no tattoos, no marks of the notorious 26s or 28s prison gangs. I went through to the cells, and I asked a sergeant if he was afraid of them.

He said: 'No, man, they won't harm you. They're relaxed, they're here for life.'

He told me about the Rivonia trial, but it meant nothing to me. As far as I was concerned, they were just terrorists sitting in prison. I wasn't really aware of their political beliefs.

However, I came to see how disciplined they were with their studies, with cleaning and polishing their surroundings, not like in a criminal prison where everything is dirty. Everything here was in place; it was clean and the cells smelled fresh.

I was also surprised when the first of the Rivonians, Andrew Mlangeni, greeted me in Afrikaans. I was surprised at both the greeting and his use of our language. Nonetheless, we were strictly forbidden to fraternize, so for a long time I only experienced these polite greetings and clipped discussions about their letters and visits. There was no conversation.

Then, one day, I had to escort Mandela to the visitors' centre, about 300 metres away. It was the first time I had seen him on his own. He was a quiet, dignified man with an imposing bearing, tall, slim and fit from his daily exercise regimen and immaculate in his prison uniform.

I was very surprised that he didn't try to talk any politics with me or ask me about the outside world. All he wanted to know was where I came from, whether my parents were still alive, and to ask if I had any brothers and sisters.

He would say, 'Oh, that's good,' when I told him about my upbringing. He was happy to hear that I had a close family. I told him I had grown up on a farm and didn't know much about the city, but that we had moved to the city and my father was working on the railways.

This was the first time we had talked. On B Section, no conversation was allowed with the prisoners. It was only possible while he was walking slightly ahead of me and no one could overhear us in the open air.

We carried on talking as we walked. He asked me what sports I took part in, so I told him about my jogging and that I enjoyed playing badminton. He was smiling and nodding, saying exercise is good for your health and morale. He then asked me if I was studying. I replied that I was studying criminal procedures for the prison service to get myself a promotion.

His manner was fatherly, concerned. He told me to please say hello to my parents when I next saw them. He also asked me about girlfriends, to which I replied that, yes, I had a few. He seemed to disapprove of this, saying I must take my time and choose the right one for me. On the way back to B Section after the visit, Mandela thanked me for our nice conversation and hoped we could talk together again one day when we were alone.

This first exchange was a revelation to me. All my ideas about Mandela up till then revolved around the uprisings, the bombings and burnings going on in South Africa, and the attempts to overthrow the government. And here he was talking about my family and other down-to-earth personal matters. He seemed genuinely concerned – a new experience for me, this concern for me as a person, not just a warder. It was impossible not to be drawn to him, this powerful leader of men facing a lifetime of hard labour and isolation, seemingly without bitterness or anger.

I was one of four guards who had daily contact with Mandela. We would try to keep him busy. All the time he was on Robben Island, I tried to treat him like the other prisoners but when I was alone with him he drew me in. I found myself listening to him and respecting him more and more for his views. Gradually, I became very involved with him. There were little ways in which I could bend the rules to make his life easier but I had to be careful. I knew that everything that happened on the island was being watched and reported.

I had learned not to tell my family anything about my job. Once, I was home for the first weekend off after three months and my uncle visited. He asked me if I had seen a man called

Nelson Mandela. I told him he was just one of the prisoners there, and that I couldn't talk about any details. My uncle said he was asking because he was wondering if Mandela was long dead. In South Africa, no one had heard anything about him after he was given a life sentence in 1964. The authorities had done a thorough job in making him disappear. The last thing they wanted was for his revolutionary ideas to take hold among the black majority.

Similarly, if we were at a function on the island with outsiders, people would ask us about Mandela and we would say nothing. One night, a warder who had been drinking was talking about Mandela. The next day, he was removed. He was transferred away from the Rivonians for four years. That was difficult for us, actually, because we needed him. He was the only one who could speak Xhosa.

The language issue was in fact part of the reason I had been chosen for the job. I was one of a group of young warders who had been sent to the island because we had a good educational standard and we could speak English – which the prisoners could understand – as well as Afrikaans. There were 21 of us, a larger-than-usual contingent because it had recently been decided to change the criteria for warders. Before our time, new recruits were selected for Robben Island for their physical size; they were needed to break the prisoners and intimidate them, scare them. But they could not communicate well because they only spoke Afrikaans, and often the prisoners could not understand instructions.

However, despite the fact we had been brought in for our communication skills, any white person suspected of becoming too close to black or coloured people was automatically under suspicion.

One day, three of us – warders Smuts, Terreblanche and I – were called into the prison office to be questioned by some government representatives. We were nervous about it, suspecting trouble.

The commanding officer of the prison wanted to know how we felt about working with Mandela. Smuts was called in first and asked what he thought of him. He told me afterwards that he had said: 'Mandela is a politician. He is a man of politics, fighting for his people.'

The government representatives were very upset about this, and they all jumped up and told him he would no longer work on B Section. They practically chased him out of the office. Smuts told me all this while Terreblanche was in there for his interrogation, so when my turn came I was ready for that question.

Sure enough, when I went into the office, the conversation soon turned to what I thought of Mandela. I just shrugged casually and said: 'Oh, I think Mandela should have been hanged that time. He just gives us all a hard time and puts in unnecessary complaints. I don't think he should even have been brought here.'

They liked that. They said I should carry on the good work. I shouldn't fight with the prisoners, but just do my work according to the rules. You had to have no political motivation if you wanted to work in B Section.

My reward for such perfect answers to their questions was to be moved into the Censor's Office, where ironically I was to learn more about Mandela and his so-called highly dangerous comrades and to discover their humanity. Rather than uncovering their terrible secrets, I was simply learning to feel even more drawn to them. The government had overlooked the effects of isolation on a small group of men such as ours, with warders and prisoners similarly unable to escape. Ironically, it meant that our relationships with the prisoners became more important to us.

It was the small, human connections between us that created the first bond. I used to watch Mandela working in his little garden where he had planted onions, tomatoes, spinach, and aubergines. The water from the island's borehole was very sour so he used to put out buckets to catch rainwater for the garden. It was the way he tended his plants and took refuge in his garden that first drew me to him. He told me that he also came from a farm community. I found myself talking to him about how to protect his plants from insects and from the terrible south-easter winds that plagued Cape Town and the island. I brought him some netting, and together we worked out how to keep the most tender plants away from the worst of the weather. How could you not be drawn to a man with great dignity and humility who would willingly take instructions from a teenage boy to get down on his knees and clean up pigeon droppings from the passage behind his cell?

'Mr Brand,' he said to me, 'the manure will be very good for my garden. I'm glad to be doing this.' Another time, he was in a legal consultation with a young Indian lawyer, Priscilla Jana. I was sitting outside the room acting as a sentry. Regulations meant that prisoners should be able to consult their lawyers without a warder overhearing them, but of course the rooms were all bugged anyway.

This time, I looked in the small viewing window to check all was well and I saw Miss Jana had gone round to Mandela's side of the table. I went in to tell her that was not allowed, and I saw she was handing him some chocolates. I had to take them off her and she was very angry, furious and shouting at me. I told her I would keep the chocolates and hand them to her in the office as she left the prison.

Mandela told her to calm down. He said: 'This man is only doing his job. He knows what he is doing. I can go without chocolates.'

He was protecting me, he understood how things worked. Maybe he knew perfectly well that I would keep some of the chocolates and give them to him later without the lawyer knowing. It was better for no one to know that rules were being broken.

If I lost my job, Mandela would lose an ally within the prison. And by then we had a small history of secrets between us, sealing our understanding of each other – just little things I had done, little relaxations of the rules, that had made his life more comfortable.

Then there was an incident where I took a risk so great, and achieved something so dear to him, that it formed a bond between us for life.

On a rainy winter's day when the wind was howling around the island, Mandela's beautiful wife Winnie came to visit him. She was a banned person under the Suppression of Terrorism Act and she had been forced to leave Johannesburg and live hundreds of miles from there in a white Afrikaans area called Brandfort in the Orange Free State. For many years, she had been allowed only very limited prison visitation rights – just one thirty-minute visit in his first year on the island – though this had gradually increased over the years. Now, to get to see her husband for thirty short minutes once every three months, she had to receive an invitation from him, apply for a permit to the prison, then go to her local magistrates to have the permit stamped.

Most visitors supported each other in a large group and drove to Cape Town, sometimes overnight, to stay at Cowley House, a charity-funded lodging house set up for the families of prisoners, in the city and from there take the trip to see their loved ones. After the prison visit, they would return to Cape Town on the ferry and stay overnight again at their lodgings, able to share their news and enjoy the friendship of those in a similar situation.

For Winnie, it was different. She lived under a strictly monitored curfew and could only leave her home between 6 a.m. and 6 p.m. So she took a flight to Cape Town, alone, to board the ferry to Robben Island, then flew back. Because of her husband's status, there would always be a large number of journalists at the embarkation point to see her leave and return. They were hungry for news of Mandela, despite a total ban on anything being published about him or his fellow Rivonians in South Africa. His sympathisers in England and America got to know much more about his prison years than any of his supporters in his own country.

On the day of Winnie's visit, as the white prison officers and their wives and families went inside the ferry boat – the *Susan Kruger*, named after the wife of the Minister of Prison Services, Jimmy Kruger – the black visitors, as always, had to sit on the top deck, exposed to the wind and rain, or else downstairs in the cold, bleak hold of the ship. Winnie had wrapped herself in a huge blanket against the weather, knowing the 45-minute journey would be hellish.

However, the warm covering also served a dual purpose. Only her handbag had been checked at the embarkation office in Cape Town's waterfront; no one had looked inside the blanket. When she arrived on Robben Island, I was there to collect her and the other visitors. I accompanied the group on foot, and when we reached the visitors' centre I watched her take off the blanket. I was astonished to see there was a baby hidden inside. It was Zoleka Mandela, the daughter of Zindzi, who was Nelson and Winnie Mandela's child.

Now this was a serious breach of the rules. Political prisoners were not allowed visits from their own children and were even forbidden to set eyes on the children of warders whose families lived with them on the island. A particularly cruel regulation meant they could not see any child under the age of 16 for the whole length of their sentence.

An ANC prisoner, the academic Neville Alexander, has written about hearing a child's voice only once in ten years on Robben Island. He said: 'We all stood dead still and everyone was waiting for the moment when we would actually glimpse that child. And of course it wasn't allowed.'

A fellow prisoner, Patrick Lekota, who later became Minister of Defence, wrote to his daughter about how there was terror that one could die on Robben Island without ever being able to make contact with one's child.

Mandela told me that when he worked in the limestone quarry there would sometimes be the distant sound of the warders' children playing in nearby bushes. 'We immediately stopped, wanting to enjoy it,' he said. 'But the warders would come at us shouting and make us start shovelling again.'

Now I was faced with this extraordinary situation. Winnie was holding out a baby to me. What on earth was I meant to do?

I told her: 'Mrs Mandela, you must leave the baby with other visitors in the waiting room while you see your husband.'

Winnie, although she was a fighter and was in many ways living out her own wretched sentence under constant harassment from the apartheid police, knew better than to fight prison rules. She might find the visit to her husband was disallowed altogether. So she went into the visitor's booth alone. She and Mandela as usual greeted each other as lovingly as possible by each putting a hand up on the glass panel that separated them. I sat behind Mandela, listening in to their conversation on the warders' phone. I saw his face as she told him that she had brought their four-month-old granddaughter Zoleka and had somehow managed to get her all the way to the prison. He looked at me, standing behind him, supervising the visit. 'Please, Mr Brand,' he said. 'Is it possible to see the baby? Please let me see this little child.'

I told him it was impossible, that I would lose my job. After a few minutes, a warrant officer came into the passage. Mandela tried again, pleading with both of us. But we told him it was against the rules, that there was no way we could allow it.

He asked again, saying perhaps he could watch as his wife left carrying the child. We said, 'No, impossible.' But by now the warrant officer and I were exchanging looks. It was a flesh-and-blood moment when your heart told you it was only human to find a way around the cruelty. At the end of the visit, I told Mandela to stay in the visiting booth and I would call his wife back so he could ask her to apply for a Christmas visiting permit. I knew the microphones were off so I went around to Winnie in the waiting room, where she had the baby back in her arms. She took R200 in cash out of her handbag – a small fortune and much more than my monthly salary.

She said: 'Please, sir, please, Mr Brand, let my husband see the baby for a few seconds.'

I told her: 'Ma'am, I cannot take your money. Please put it away. This is a bad situation for both of us but you have to realise I can't help you, I'm sorry.' She looked downcast, but I went on: 'Ma'am, could I please hold the baby for a moment? I've never held an African child.' It was the only thing I could think of at that second.

I told her she could have a moment with her husband to talk about applying for a permit at Christmas. I ushered her back into the booth on her side and locked her in, then quietly closed the door to the passageway.

The window in front of Mandela was by now also closed, so I walked through the passage on his side of the booth and held out the baby to him. He took her and held her and he just said, 'Oh', and I saw tears in his eyes as he kissed the baby. We both stood there in silence, and after about 30 seconds he knew he must hand her back to me.

Neither of us said it but we knew this had to be a secret, even from his wife.

When I returned to Winnie with the baby, she begged me again. 'Please, Mr Brand, just let me show him this little child for one moment.'

I refused her sternly and turned away. It was not safe to let her know what I had done. My job was in danger, and Mandela's privileges would have been cancelled if anyone knew about the breach of regulations.

Journalists were waiting for Winnie when she reached Cape Town on the ferry, and she told them how cruel we were. She had smuggled their grandchild to him but they wouldn't let her show her husband, even from a distance.

On the way back to the cells, Mandela walked close enough to tell me: 'Thank you, Mr Brand. I know you can lose your job for that. Now it's a secret between us, just you and me.'

Later, I was called into the prison office to explain how a

child had been brought to the island. I said we hadn't shown Mandela the baby, and then I had to write a report to our head office in Pretoria to inform them of the incident, and a second report to the security police assuring them that this would not happen again, that no baby would be allowed in next time.

This moment that passed between us, this silent understanding from man to man, meant everything to him. We became allies for life, without referring to that day again all the time he was in prison.

CHAPTER 3

Robben Island is an unmistakable landmark from any point in Cape Town. It can be seen from the glamorous beaches and shopping malls, from the spectacular peaks of the Table Mountain range, and at many points along the Atlantic Ocean waterfront. After dark, the single beam from its lighthouse is a blur on the choppy sea, visible for miles around.

It sits in the inhospitable Atlantic Ocean, seven kilometres from the mainland, a wretched monument to the centuries of misery it has seen.

The island, a flat oval about 11 kilometres in diameter, was once a leper colony where unfortunates were sent to die. Later, it was a quarantine station housing sick animals. But its natural God-given purpose must surely have been as a prison. A low-lying, windswept place tantalisingly in sight of land, but from where escape was virtually impossible.

In the late 19th century, Mandela's own ancestors, a group of Xhosa chieftains, were imprisoned there by the British after the skirmishes that ensued when the settlers forced 20,000 tribal people out of the Eastern Cape. Their leader, Chief Maqoma, died on Robben Island, and many of his descendants campaigned to have the place renamed after him. On a day of wild weather, you can almost hear their ghosts wailing.

Violent surf constantly pounds its shores, the scene of many shipwrecks. In the late 17th century, a Dutch galleon, the three-masted *Dageraad*, carrying gold coins to Indonesia for the salaries of Dutch East India Company employees, sank there literally without trace, and remains inaccessible to this day. From a hoard of seventeen chests of gold worth tens of millions of pounds, only a few coins have ever washed ashore, with some ducats and silver pieces-of-eight found in rock pools. Ironically, its isolation makes Robben Island a safe and sheltered haven for more than 100 bird species, among them African penguins and breeding colonies of seabirds like the crowned cormorants, Caspian terns and black-crowned herons that circle the shoreline.

More sinister are the three quarries. Robben Island maximum security prison itself was built from the dark grey-black slate hacked out by its first inmates. A stone quarry on the eastern side of the island is where the first Dutch settlers used their slaves to harvest slate that built Cape Town's castle. A plaque today commemorates their work.

The limestone quarry, which almost cost Nelson Mandela his sight and his general health, lies at the centre of the island. For 13 years, he broke rocks from the sunken cliffs here every day, the white limestone reflecting direct sunlight. The constant southeast wind would whip up choking dust clouds, burning the prisoners' eyes and entering their throats.

The convicts would be accompanied by dog-handlers and armed warders on the 500-metre route-march to the quarry each morning. They would then be forced to break down rocks and mix it with seashells for use in constructing roads across the island.

The prisoners were not allowed sunglasses, so they attempted to fend off the glare with homemade contraptions of netting and bent wire. Mandela's eyesight suffered for the rest of his life, with eye-drops making little impact. A strict rule of his after his release was the banning of flash photography.

By the time I arrived to work at Robben Island, the older men, like Mandela, had successfully campaigned to stop these outdoor work groups after the age of 60, but they recalled them bitterly. Mandela would tell me of the horrendous hard labour of those days in the quarry, and the lesser horror of his later duties hauling kelp – Cape seaweed – from the sea and the beaches, to be processed and exported as fertiliser. In Afrikaans, we called it bambous.

There were some advantages to the beach work, though, he said. Few officers were around, and the warders were more relaxed. Sometimes, they would be able to set traps to catch rabbits and guinea fowl. They would make a fire on the spot and eat it. They would also pick limpets off the rocks and sometimes eat them raw.

Other small transgressions could also take place in the more relaxed conditions. One day when they were working with kelp on the northern beach, it was agreed that two prisoners could get into the seawater to catch crayfish while a warder guarded the rest of the work group. They lit a fire and cooked and ate the crayfish, prisoners and warders together. This fraternizing would have been greatly frowned upon by the authorities. It was a small, conspiratorial defiance of the rules.

Another day, the prisoners found a seal on the beach and immediately saw it as a rare source of meat. They killed it with a spade and one of the warders lent them his knife to skin it and clean it out, providing that he could share the meat with them. They lit a fire then and there on the beach and cooked it. The red meat was tender, Mandela told me. It tasted like lamb in so far as they could recall the taste of any meat. They cooked and ate in a little group alongside their warders, and imagined the barbecues they would enjoy once they were back home again. Each and every one of them believed they would be out of prison one day, with a life to look forward to.

It made me smile sadly to hear them talking of the future. They were all inside forever; they were never going to have a real life again as far as I could see. Political prisoners were allowed no reduction of their sentences for good behaviour and they could not apply for parole. They were in prison for their whole term. Mandela himself was serving life – and he and his comrades, the High Command of the banned ANC, were old already.

I used to tell him: 'Why don't you relax and take things easier? You don't need to waste your money sending postal orders to buy books and university courses, and doing studies for a future career. You're having your life now. This is it. Why not take books from the prison library and enjoy them, instead of driving yourself with all these exams?'

It was true: Mandela was consumed with studying, and used every spare minute to further his knowledge. He believed education was, in his words, 'the future of our country', even telling us that we guards should be studying. The way he saw it, if you have education, if you have degrees, if you have knowledge – even if it's about motor mechanics – for as long as you are alive, they can't take it away from you. He wanted us to have careers, to be thinkers, to lift up our lives for ourselves and our families. He made us think about that, mostly by his own example.

He put pressure on his own people to study and had this great dream that Robben Island could have its own university. Many of the prisoners began to study with the warders without the authorities knowing, and they would exchange books. We worked together well, and I even saw prisoners help warders with their assignments.

Mandela's mantra to his fellow captives was that 'Your years in prison will go faster if you enhance yourself with education'. That way, he would say, when they all came out, they would be better educated and would qualify for better work.

The opportunities for education for black people on the outside were very limited, he said. If you studied here in prison, you could keep your mind alert and also avoid trouble. Through his persuasive arguments he converted some of his less-educated comrades into great thinkers armed with degrees. Among the prisoners there were doctors, lecturers, and schoolteachers, and they all helped each other. It was like an informal university where the men educated each other.

But Mandela was up against a lot of opposition in his determination to study. He needed to organise money for books and assignments to be sent in from university correspondence courses. He would apply to see a lawyer, then pass him a list of names of those who needed funding. Money came in from the church and charitable organisations, the South African Educational Trust, and supporters on the outside. The government tried to stop this by stipulating that money could only be sent in by their families.

Mandela himself was determined to learn Afrikaans and take exams in the language. He believed it would give him an edge. He had already received a certificate in 1964 in Afrikaans-Nederlands, but he wanted to take those studies further, and so he enrolled every year to take written exams. Unfortunately, he failed his practical Afrikaans every time. I began to help him by always talking to him in Afrikaans and by reading his 'homework' before it was sent off to a school on the mainland, where mistakes would come back underlined in red. Of course, the teachers had no idea it was Nelson Mandela's handiwork they were marking.

His first essay assignment was to write about a day on the beach. So he wrote about a day on Robben Island where he was working outside, hauling the seaweed plants out of the sea and cleaning them off the rocks on the beach, then hanging it on railings so it could dry before being chopped up, bagged, and exported as fertiliser. On this particular day, he had slipped on the sharp rocks and gashed his foot badly.

I had to hand the essay back and tell him to do it again. It was too long. He was only allowed 450–500 words, and so I had to tell him he needed to shorten it. We didn't talk about his day on the beach.

After a year of talking to me only in Afrikaans, he finally passed the exam. This was a victory that clearly gave him enormous pleasure.

Before I arrived, Mandela had fought long and hard for the right to study in prison, continually writing to the Minister of Justice until it was agreed that certain subjects were to be allowed. Political science and military history were of course banned, and Mandela was warned that if he persisted in studying law it would be a waste of time for him. There were several attempts to have him struck off as a lawyer when he was in prison, but he fought and won. He and his fellow activist Oliver Tambo – the leader of the ANC since 1967 – had represented hundreds of black defendants in their time as partners in a Johannesburg law firm, and Mandela dreamed of returning to that work one day.

Tambo was living in Zambia, running the ANC in exile. To many of the Rivonians, he was their only hope, keeping their organisation alive until it was ready to come into power in South Africa. But he and other political prisoners were not allowed to be quoted publicly within the country; their voices could not be heard. Without the oxygen of publicity, the government hoped that the ANC would quietly wither away and die.

Mandela, meanwhile, was obsessively applying to UNISA, the University of South Africa, to take their correspondence courses, and all of the political prisoners in B Section did the same. Sometimes, I would be on the mainland, sitting in the UNISA office for hour after hour waiting to register them. I also had to pick up the study books they all needed from government-approved bookshops in Cape Town.

The right to study was one I knew Mandela valued extremely highly. This had been used against him earlier, before I started working on the island. He had once lost his study privileges for four years, when the original manuscript he had written for his autobiography *Long Walk to Freedom* had been found hidden in cocoa tins buried in his garden. The punishment was the most severe they could think up.

Now he needed more time to gain his exams, and he appealed to UNISA. Mandela made himself busy every day applying for something, or demanding more blankets, better food, or more visits. His policy was to make himself and his comrades noticed, to keep themselves alive and alert.

It struck me that all of these old guys were really serious about advancing themselves, and were never going to give up. Even when they failed exams, they enrolled again and again, or appealed to have them remarked. Occasionally, one of Mandela's subjects would be remarked and he would get through when he had previously failed. He wasn't a natural student, and he admitted to me that it became more difficult as he got older.

I was gradually coming to realise what he and his comrades were fighting for, what they had risked their lives for, what they had given up their freedom for. It was impossible not to notice the impact that Mandela had made when I was out in the 'real' world. We were all living in a police state, and there was no freedom of speech, but occasionally I would see some graffiti in Cape Town before the authorities cleaned it off. Always the same words: 'Free Nelson Mandela', painted on a bridge or a wall. People all over South Africa were thinking of him. People all over the world were thinking of him.

And when we had to take him and his group outside once a week for recreation – when they would spend an hour just kicking a football around on the deserted air strip – we would hear hundreds of other prisoners clamouring for him. 'Amandla! Amandla!' We would hear them shouting and chanting, though they could hardly recognise their leaders from 200 metres away. They would never meet Mandela face to face. Yet they became hysterical at the very sight of him in the distance.

Mandela could not really acknowledge them; he would just give a slight nod towards them. Anything more and the men from B Section would not be allowed outside the prison buildings again.

Even in prison, Mandela had a sense of purpose and drive. As much as the prison regulations ruled every minute of his life, he also had his own rules, his own discipline. His day would start early – all part of the hardship – but he worked to turn it to his advantage, using every minute to try to go forward with his life, always fighting for the future, never looking back on his 60-plus years and accepting that it might all be over.

An ear-splitting clanging would start up all over the prison at 5 a.m. We used metal pipes with a chain inside to make the maximum noise, a horrible grinding sound, to wake up all the prisoners in their icy cells.

The cells were as cold as fridges, all year round. They were made of cement and unpainted. Overnight they would freeze. Prisoners slept on the floors with two mats, one hard sisal mat and another softer one. They had three blankets with no extra ones allowed, even in winter. Requests to the prison office for more blankets would be turned down. Occasionally, some of them would persuade a warder to feel sorry for them and one of us would give them an extra blanket on condition it was handed back early the next morning before inspection.

I would see Mandela doing exercises in his cell at 5 a.m., usually for an hour. He would have been cold all night, so he would be doing sit-ups to warm himself up. He was a tall man, and the two mats issued to him were too short. When he lay back, his head would be touching one wall, his feet the opposite wall.

I would see him running on the spot, doing push-ups and sit-ups, everything you could do on your own in the cell. He would wear black or white, or black and red, gym shorts donated by the Red Cross, and a sleeveless running vest.

He was over 60 years old but to me he looked very fit, lean and wiry. He was slender and you could see his muscles. At this time in the morning, he would not have had anything to eat, just a few sips of warm water from the coffee flask he had bought himself through the prison tuck shop, and was allowed to keep in his cell.

At 6 a.m., the bell rang again and prisoners had to get ready for inspection. Like all the others, Mandela had a cleaning pack that he kept in his cell. In the mornings, he would take a piece of old prison blanket out of it and polish the floor until it shone. The floor was cement, but prisoners were given liquid polish to rub into it. It had to look like a mirror when it was finished, and be clean enough to eat off. He would also need to fold up his mattress and bedding and put them tidily in a corner. All this would take about an hour, then maybe he would look through his study books while he waited for inspection.

At 7 a.m., the warders reported for day shift. We started with parade in the courtyard. We had to stand to attention, present ourselves for inspection, then stand at ease. We had strict rules about being clean-shaven with short haircuts, the same rules we imposed on the prisoners.

The prisoners were also inspected every morning to see if they were properly dressed and that their uniforms were neatly ironed. As they were not allowed access to irons, their only way to achieve that was to sprinkle water on it, rub it hard with a prison mug, and then press it overnight underneath their sleeping mats on the cement floor.

Then it was time to say the daily prayer. It was always the 'Our Father'. When it came to the line 'give us this day our daily bread', I would feel bad for the prisoners who could hear us. The black prisoners never had any bread. It was given only to the mixed-race and Indian prisoners.

Discrimination in South Africa at that time was multi-layered. So, although all of these men were being punished for their beliefs, some were being punished more cruelly than others. For example, Mandela and the other black Africans were at first issued only with khaki shorts and sandals, with no shoes or socks. They wore a canvas khaki jacket of which three buttons had to be fastened during inspections. They had protested for several years that they were cold and also humiliated by wearing boys' clothes, and by the time I arrived on the island they were beginning to be allowed long trousers and socks.

This racial discrimination extended even to food allowances. Black prisoners had 12 ounces of maize-meal porridge with no sugar or salt in it for breakfast, and a mug of black coffee. The coloureds and Indians had 14 ounces of porridge and bread, and coffee.

After the parade, the day-shift warders entered the sections and counted the prisoners with the night shift. The master key was used to open the cells. B Section was about 50 metres inside the one-storey prison building, on the left-hand side. It was accessed by a metal door cut into the solid wall and controlled by a series of locking and unlocking procedures in a sequence to be strictly followed. Each warder carried the key to B Section on a leather strap held in place under the epaulette of his uniform. His single black metal key would open all the cell doors in that section. The night-shift warders held different keys to the day-shift.

Once the prisoners had been counted, the numbers were written on an official record so that they tallied. Some prisoners may have been taken to the hospital section, or some to the harbour with escorts for the ferry trip to the mainland for a Cape Town hospital. We needed to know at all times how many prisoners were physically on the island, so these records were an important security measure to prevent escapes.

At 7.30 a.m., when the cells had been opened, the prisoners could take their toilet buckets to the community toilet to empty them. They washed them out under the showers and put them in the courtyard to dry in the sun. During this cleaning, the prisoners would talk intensely. They knew very well that we didn't want to be near them during this unpleasant task, and it was a chance to exchange news. In general, though, we had to observe the prisoners closely throughout the morning rituals, even when they were using the community toilets. The stalls were designed so that you could see their heads and their feet.

The prisoners were given a disinfectant like Jeyes Fluid to clean the buckets. They were steel half-drums with a lid on. Once, for several days at a time, Mandela went to a neighbouring cell where fellow prisoner Eddie Daniels was quite sick. He took his toilet bucket out for him, cleaned it, and dried it in the sun.

All of these actions, without a word being exchanged, were making us realise the extent of the comradeship, the solidarity, between these guys. We had never seen this before.

Prisoners would then use the communal showers. The water was just lukewarm, with no soap provided – though the water was so hard that soap did not work anyway. They used shampoo bought in bulk from the tuck shop, having pooled their money allowance to buy it. They didn't complain. Years before I came to the island, the conditions were even harsher. There was no warm water, and prisoners would be forced to line up naked in the courtyard to be hosed down with cold water by the warders. I heard that one time a group of drunken warders got them all out of bed in the middle of the night to stand in the freezing cold while they hosed them down, cackling with cruel laughter while they searched through all of their cells. Some of the more unlucky prisoners were kept in their cells, and the guys outside had to listen to them being beaten. Fikile Bam, who later became Judge President of the Land Claims Court, was reduced to tears at the sounds. Govan Mbeki ended up collapsing, and had to be taken to hospital on the mainland. I hope I would never have gone along with that harsh treatment. I hope I would rather have resigned from the service.

Breakfast was dished up in the courtyard. In winter, the food tables would be undercover. They all queued up with a plate and a mug. One bucket held fresh water and prisoners could take two mugs each. Mandela had taught himself to tolerate the brackish water that came out of the taps from the island's bore-holes so he didn't have to take a turn at the bucket. Wherever possible, he was self-reliant, disciplined.

At 8.30 a.m., there would be duties like cleaning the courtyard, the passageways, and the recreation hall. Before I came to the island, they would be sent out in working groups at this time, either marched to the quarries accompanied by the dog-handlers, or to the beach where they hauled kelp.

However, by the time I arrived on Robben Island, the hard labour had finished for the older prisoners after years of petitioning, mainly by Mandela. They now worked in the courtyard and indoors, sewing mailbags sent over by the Post Office, repairing prison clothes, and cleaning and polishing the floors. In my time there, the authorities established a homemade washing machine, a big 44-gallon diesel drum. They put it on a stand at an angle, and somehow poured in the water and washing powder. It was made in the prison workshop. The prisoners didn't like it; it was hard work turning a steel handle for many minutes at a time. But then they came to realise it cleaned their bedding well, especially the blankets.

Mandela would also work in the little garden he had made. It was about fifteen metres long by two-and-a-half metres wide. There was topsoil to which he added pigeon and other bird droppings. Other prisoners gave him droppings from outside their cells. He taught me to look after and respect a living thing, a fruit or a flower, something alive. He would say that he just wanted to feel the soil in his hands. He managed to grow a peach tree, which bore fruit. He even planted carrot seeds, and people would bring him tomato seeds they found in their food. He would sometimes manage to get some wildflowers to grow around the edges, but he was mainly interested in growing food. He would spend half an hour there in the morning and half an hour in the afternoon. I am also a gardener, and I watched how things were growing. I encouraged him. He knew the water from the island borehole was sour, so he put buckets out to catch rainwater, and others would bring him their water from clothes-washing.

For lunch, the prisoners got samp – mealie-meal (corn) – with a meat sauce on top, or something resembling meat. They would have a mug of tea with powdered milk and a little sugar. Again, the blacks would not be given bread. A list of the amounts of food and drink given to prisoners, divided according to their ethnic origin, was posted in the kitchen. Visitors to Robben Island today can still see the originals. At all times, the black prisoners were given less than the others. Their allowance for fish or meat four times a week was five ounces. The others were given six ounces.

Comrades would share with them. Indian prisoners like Mandela's great friend Ahmed Kathrada would divide up their own bread. It was humbling to see this, yet as warders we had no power to change the rules, so all we could do was observe how they dealt with it and be privately impressed.

On someone's birthday, they would all try to make something. One prisoner would provide chillies, and maybe tomatoes and onions from the kitchen. They would make a prison cake by collecting all the leftover bread and adding water to soften it and sugar to sweeten it, and porridge or condensed milk if they had managed to save some. When they got jam, they would spread it in the middle. The porridge became stiff, and you could cut it like a cake. Sometimes they could persuade the prisoners working in the kitchen to give them an egg to put in the cake and then bake it in the oven for a short time.

They also made birthday cards. They would use paper from a notebook, and draw and colour it in using leftover paint. Everyone would sign it and write small messages and sing 'Happy Birthday'.

There were other small occasions when the rules were relaxed, for warders and prisoners alike. Sometimes from the shore you could see huge flocks of gulls catching fish in the sea, with fishing dinghies circling around out there in the distance. Boats were not allowed to come nearer than one nautical mile to Robben Island, but you could see there was plenty of fish close to the island on days like that.

So, on occasion, we warders would all decide that we fancied an afternoon fishing. The head of prison would call in the section committees representing the prisoners and tell them the warders would like to go fishing that day, and that it would mean locking the prisoners up at noon. We would give them their lunch and supper at the same time. They always agreed, knowing they could ask for something special in return.

For example, they might want to play a soccer tournament on a Saturday, with teams of prisoners from different sections playing against each other. We would agree on that in return for our day's fishing, and we would also bring back some of our fish to the kitchen for it to be cooked for them. We had a good relationship of give and take.

I came to realise how important these little glimpses of common humanity were to the prisoners. One day, long after I had left the prison service, I met the family and lawyers of a former prisoner on their way to the beach at Robben Island. Wilton Mkwayi, a prominent trade union leader who served many years with Mandela, died in 2004, some 15 years after his release, and had left a request with his family to take his ashes back there.

They told me how he had been the unofficial cook, arranging an extra drum of fresh water to be taken with the work group so he could rustle up wonderful fish stews they all enjoyed, warders and prisoners alike – small, pleasurable moments during a long period of pain. It was a measure of how much those moments of humanity had meant to him during the years of harshness and desperation that he had asked for his ashes to be scattered there.

I know many prisoners have come over on the ferry after their release – maybe to show their families the hardship they suffered. But I don't know any other prisoners who wanted it to be their last resting-place.

CHAPTER 4

Life was harsh on Robben Island, but gradually I began to cope. In a way, the environment was like the farm I grew up on. Few roads, many trees, and unpolluted air, far from the city. In my free time, I went with my friends among the warders on fishing trips to our favourite spots on the island. If there was a northwest wind blowing, we would choose the stone quarry side; if it was a southeaster, we went to the harbour side.

We caught galjoen and white stompneus or hottentot fish, and sometimes yellow-mouth fish. We cooked them on the braai or, if I had weekend leave, I would take some back to my family.

There was seafood too, crayfish and abalone, both delicacies in their way. Once a month, we organised a dinner-dance in the recreational hall to raise money for the warders' club. It sounds strange now, but smart people from big companies and banks, and even hospital staff, would pay for tickets and arrive in black tie and ball gowns. There would be a live band and a party atmosphere.

Dog-handlers and warders patrolled the whole area so that people could not wander around. But just a kilometre or so away were the prison cells holding what the government insisted were the country's most dangerous men.

If I worked a day shift, I would always find a group of my

fellow warders to go jogging with. We would set up quite a pace covering the entire 11 kilometres of the island.

But despite these distractions it was still a prison, and I felt continually isolated. I was supposed to have home leave every other weekend, but often that would be cancelled when we were put on standby because of the threat of uprisings.

From the start, I longed for leave, but the rules and regulations followed me all the way home, and time off was very spasmodic. It felt like we young warders were prisoners there, too, just not kept in cells.

After we'd locked up the prisoners at 4 p.m., I'd go to my bedroom and there would be nothing to do. We got television only years later, and I wasn't married when I was first on the island, so I was alone. We got bored. We tired of seeing each other's faces, and some of the warders started drinking. It was not a healthy environment for any of us.

The prisoners, too, suffered from the boredom of the daily routine, though they did their best to vary it and to keep themselves active. Prisoners weren't allowed to sleep during the day; they were locked out of their cells. After lunch they would play tennis in the courtyard, or squash. We would have proper matches with homemade certificates presented to the winners. They were like the birthday cards they made by hand – just a piece of notepaper or card coloured with whatever bit of leftover paint they could find, with the winner's name printed on it and an ornamental edge drawn around it.

They were all keen to keep fit, and they would jog around the courtyard, all of them in or around their sixties, all believing they would get out one day and have another life, and so they must stay fit for that.

Some of them were good guitar players. There was one of our political prisoners, James Mange, who played great jazz.

He started teaching other prisoners, and they sang some songs together in Xhosa. We had a warder called Burger who was a good guitarist too, so he joined in. Mandela would just watch, listening. It was relaxing soft music and actually a strange sight, when I look back, seeing this little makeshift band of musicians enjoying themselves in that grim place.

On rainy days, the prisoners would stay indoors in the recreation hall. There were card games, chess, poker, table-tennis, and dominoes. They were not allowed to just sit around and talk. They had to keep themselves busy, or one of us would want to know what was going on.

In the hall, there were boxes and boxes of old magazines like the Afrikaans version of *Farmers Weekly*, and *Time* magazine and *Reader's Digest*, censored of course to take out any political content. The prisoners had set up their own library in an empty double cell. They appointed themselves a librarian, and there was a warder who would let them in two at a time. They had a card to record what books they were borrowing. A warder would sit there throughout to make sure there was no political plotting.

Books came from the provincial public library in Cape Town. Sometimes they requested certain books, and these of course would always be checked first to ensure there was no political content or sex scenes. Everything was mercilessly censored.

Supper was about 4 p.m. It was porridge again, same as in the morning. Coloureds and Indians got two slices of bread with their porridge, along with soup for coloureds and Indians, and a watery African drink for the blacks. It was hot water that was supposed to have powdered maize and yeast in it, but was really just a mug of tasteless cloudy-looking water.

After supper, we started counting them in for lock-up time. The night shift started at 4 p.m. Prisoner totals had to tally and be handed in again.

Once a week, a government doctor came over from Cape Town. He would prescribe medication or refer a prisoner to the hospital section of Robben Island. We had a dental surgery in a clinic away from the prison, and a visiting dentist. Every fortnight, there was also a visiting psychiatrist.

By the late eighties, after I had left Robben Island, I heard that several newly arrived prisoners were getting very sick, and the doctor drew blood and discovered they were HIV positive. They were immediately separated from the others and transferred off the island.

Despite the regular visits from medical professionals, there were occasions when prisoners would die in our care. One of my more unpleasant tasks was to take the corpses of prisoners from the island by ferry boat to the government mortuary at Maitland, on the mainland. There I would fingerprint the prisoner and formally release him to his family.

Once, I found a family removing the dead man's prison uniform and dressing him instead in a fine suit. They put a hat and sunglasses on him and somehow got him into the back seat of their old car. They propped him up, did up the seatbelt, and drove off with him to the Eastern Cape for burial in his home village. It was a journey that would take them a whole day. I could not imagine how they managed that, the car already crammed full with family members.

Luckily, Mandela never seemed to get really sick at this time. He would perhaps have cough medicine occasionally, but that was all. A medical officer visited the section every morning. He would hand out the tablets for that day, whatever had been prescribed by the doctor.

The prisoners had some limited opportunities to buy things for themselves, too. The prison tuck shop was inside the main building. Prisoners could receive money only from their families. They were never paid for the hard labour tasks like working in the quarry or sewing mailbags.

All the money that came in was registered under the prisoner's name. Once a month, they wrote a list of items they wanted from the tuck shop. Mandela could buy pens, writing pads, sugar, coffee, tinned food, toothpaste, some spices, and cigarettes or biscuits. He bought cigarettes to give to prisoners who had used up their quota and could not buy for themselves, and would swap them for toothpaste. His favourite biscuits were the popular South African Ouma rusks, to dip in tea or coffee. The cash limit for one month was just enough for small items. He would also buy Blue Pantene hair oil to give his hair a slick look, and Vaseline for use as a body lotion and for his hands and face. He was a handsome man who cared about his looks, particularly when he had a visitor. He would never go to the visitors' centre in a prison uniform that wasn't perfect.

On Fridays, there were films in the recreation hall. We covered the windows with blankets, standing on each other's shoulders to hook them up. There were no blinds.

We had a projector set up. Prisoners applied for movies through a shop in Cape Town, a precursor of video shops. They would send out a list of what they wanted to see, with the different sections taking turns to pay for the movies.

I remember B Section asked for *Roots*, which was a typical sort of choice for them. The Cape Town library also sent free movies, mostly short documentaries, on educational matters like nature, and medical matters and diseases. They were like Discovery Channel documentaries.

On Sundays there would be church services from different denominations, and Mandela always insisted everyone should attend. Sometimes, three different denominations would give services on one day, and they would go to all of them. Mandela wanted everyone to respect the fact that a priest had made the effort, but also it was important for them to welcome anyone from the outside world. They enjoyed Holy Communion because it meant they got a sliver of bread and a sip of grape juice.

Years later, Mandela told me there was a priest who always brought a newspaper in his bag when he came to the island. He would arrive before 9 a.m. and stay the whole day until 4 p.m. He would talk to the prisoners and leave his bag lying around. During prayers and sermons, the warders would sometimes get bored and hot in the summer sun. That was when their attention might wander and a prisoner could sneak to the priest's bag and take the newspaper.

Once a prisoner said he would like to take prayers, and told everyone to close their eyes while he spoke. That was another chance for one of them to get to the priest's bag for the paper. Although breaches like these were fairly harmless, other prisoners made bolder plans. Attempts to escape were rare, but were taken very seriously when they occurred.

The only known and documented escape in the island's history was when the Khoi chieftain Autshumato, sent there in 1658 by Dutch settlers who accused him of stealing cattle and goods, took to a rowing-boat and made it back to the mainland. He had previously worked as a trade interpreter for the settlers, and when he landed in Table Bay they gave him his old job back, presumably impressed by his achievement. That was a man you would surely want to meet.

In my time at Robben Island there was only one unexplained escape, and I like to think he made it, but that would make him unique. He was a 'trusty' – someone who was allowed to walk freely around the island. He was in for non-payment of maintenance to his ex-wife.

Two weeks before he was due out on parole, he stole a warder's paddle-ski. Despite the bad weather and rough seas, he disappeared into the raging waves, leaving his prison clothes behind on the rocks. The paddle-ski later washed up on shore. He had been a life-saver at Cape Point, so he was a good swimmer with good knowledge of rough sea conditions. I think and hope that he might have been rescued by a passing fishing trawler. Anyhow, he was never seen again. No warders were punished or demoted for his escape, because he was a 'trusty' and was therefore not being supervised.

Earlier, though, I had seen terrible scenes at Belville Prison, just outside Cape Town, when I was there on a visit. A working party of 12 prisoners were marching out towards their job on the land. One of them attacked a warder with a spade, and they all ran off.

A warder from the guards' observation post started shooting them down. He shot nine of them dead. The others lay flat and survived.

The warder was rewarded with a medal for bravery. I saw those nine bodies, and that one warder who had been up in his observation post within incredibly easy range being lauded as a hero.

On Robben Island, it was virtually impossible to escape. But warders in the Censor's Office, listening in to the cells in B Section, reported one night that they heard locks being opened. They suspected a key lost years earlier might be being used to unlock cells.

Over the next few nights, they listened in to some talk

about an escape plan. Extra bugging devices were put in the cells, and for the next week one of the officers put himself on permanent night shift to monitor the situation. Dog-handlers were instructed to increase their patrols. Prisoners were of course aware of this development and could be heard discussing the extra patrols.

Then a group of warders was sent in with hammers to test all the walls to listen for anything suspicious. Nothing was found. Years later, I discovered that Eddie Daniels was behind that failed escape plan. He was a coloured guy who was a teachers' union leader serving 15 years for terrorist activities. He was released in 1979 and later admitted that he had intended to get Mandela out. He published a book, *There and Back*, in which he showed plans of the prison that he had drawn at the time, and explained his daring idea. Due to the international economic sanctions that many countries had imposed against apartheid, there had been no foreign container ships allowed to dock in Cape Town, so all fresh vegetables, fruit, and other small cargoes were regularly flown by helicopter from Cape Town to the container ships out at sea.

No flights could go over Robben Island. But in bad weather the helicopters could fly over for safety reasons. Eddie planned that, on a Friday afternoon, when most prisoners were inside watching a film, and half of the warders were off-duty and on the mainland, Mandela would ask for permission to work in his garden.

Eddie would organise a helicopter carrying a basket, as if to take supplies. It would change course suddenly to fly over the island, then drop down into B Section and pick up Mandela. By the time prison authorities had scrambled, Mandela would be deposited safely at the American consulate in Cape Town.

It was a good plan on paper but, of course, it would have carried huge risks had it been attempted. In the end, Eddie had informed the ANC in exile in Lusaka, Zambia, of the plan, and they put a stop to the attempt, fearing that it would be too great a risk to Mandela's life.

There were always fears among the prison authorities that he could escape en route to hospital on the mainland. I accompanied him several times when he had annual medical check-ups, like all prisoners of his age. He had regular eye tests and visits to an ear, nose and throat specialist. No one was going to neglect Mandela's regular check-ups. Pro-apartheid supporters were saying openly that 'the only thing worse than a free Mandela would be a dead Mandela'. Better to take care of his health than have him die a martyr.

When the time came for the journey, he would be put in the back of a white prison van. I sat with him on a side bench, and I and other warders were locked in with him. In advance, all the roads would be cleared of traffic and people, with police roadblocks around the building where the medical clinic was.

Once inside the building, I would go ahead of Mandela to clear the waiting-room area of books and newspapers, which might have his picture in them, and he would not be allowed to communicate with anybody or even to greet the receptionist. I would be with him inside the clinic while the doctor examined him. On these occasions, I would be armed with a 9mm handgun and other warders were outside carrying machine guns.

One time, we took him to a clinic where the doctor said he must have chest X-rays immediately. He arranged for Mandela to go to a building opposite, across Adderley Street, the main shopping street in Cape Town. It was full of shoppers, and there had been no time to put up roadblocks.

There were four of us, wearing our khaki uniforms, all armed. Mandela walked along next to me in leg chains that ran from his ankles up the inside of his trousers. They were effective restraints against a prisoner ever trying to make a run for it. I locked the chains at his ankles, and he had to hold them up himself at his waist or he wouldn't be able to walk at all. We made our way up the street, and I saw a coloured guy rushing towards us. I recognised Dullah Omar, one of the lawyers who came regularly to Robben Island. He had his head down, carrying a briefcase, probably late for court. I pushed Mandela into the nearest shop until Omar had passed.

No one recognised him. Some street vendors handed us free bananas and apples for our prisoner. But nobody realised it was Mandela. He nodded at them and said thank you. It was touching to see these guys, who had nothing themselves, reaching out to help a stranger.

Back on the island, of course, financial gifts were allowed only from family members. All money sent in by families was strictly processed on the island, even though it was often tiny amounts. An official note of each prisoner's money was kept with the rest of his belongings in a cloth bag stamped with his prison number and kept in a walk-in safe in the reception office. Mandela's prison number, now world-famous, was 46664. It meant that he was the 466th prisoner to be admitted to the prison in 1964. At the time I was with him on Robben Island, neither of us would ever have believed that one day thousands of t-shirts would be made bearing his number.

Money sent in by family members or their lawyers would be recorded and kept in a government bank account, with a small cash flow available for prisoners' tuck-shop purchases, stamps for letters, and other costs.

Mandela would have to pay to sign up for a correspondence course for his law degree. He took this very seriously. He would identify a study book he needed, then enquire about the price and write postal orders for the payment. It might take two months to arrive. When it did, the study officer would receive it, check if it was relevant or too political, then refer it to the Censor's Office.

When he was first imprisoned, Mandela would have to sit on the cement floor in his cell when he was studying, using a small bench as a table. By the late seventies, he was allowed to have a study table, so he could use the bench to sit on. He was allowed to buy a desk clock to time his studies in preparation for exams. There were other ways for the prisoners to spend their money too. When the prisoners were allowed to watch a movie, as they were once a week, it had to be jointly paid for by the inmates. The younger prisoners wanted action movies and the older guys like Mandela usually wanted something more serious, though he was also fond of the *Rocky* movies because he had been a keen boxer and he liked Sylvester Stallone's character. Sometimes, we would watch religious and musical movies and educational material sent by the South African government libraries.

The films, of course, had to be seen by the warders first. We had to make notes of any racial issues, or violence or politics, or love and sex scenes, or the film would not be cleared for the prisoners to watch. If a whole film was rejected, it would be sent back and their money wasted. I remember requests for Pink Floyd's *The Wall* didn't stand a chance.

If we found inappropriate scenes, we would physically cut the tape then roughly Sellotape the two ends together. The storyline would jump all over the place, with unfinished sentences and dialogue that didn't make sense.

But there were no complaints. It was a period when the prisoners could be together, whispering between themselves without being overheard.

And it was often genuinely enjoyable. We would sit there, prisoners and warders together, laughing our heads off at a Laurel and Hardy movie, able to forget where we were for just an hour or so. It was a lifeline for all of us.

On other evenings after lock-up, I would play music for them if I was on night shift. Their section committee would give a list of music they wanted to hear. Their families had sent in records to the prison, and they had a list of what had been sent in.

B Section would take turns to choose the music, as would the other sections. I was like a DJ. Mandela and B Section's favourite was always jazz by black musicians. I would play the music until 7 p.m., piped through the sound systems into speakers in the cells, followed by the censored news of the day for about 20 minutes. Then they might listen to a previously recorded programme, maybe a soccer or boxing match, or a debate programme – but never politics. They could press a button to interrupt, tell me I was playing the wrong records, or complain they were sick and needed medical attention. There were always complaints if I played Afrikaans music, my favourite. They considered that an insult.

Of course, this was also the period in which they might want to study. Mandela told me he became so used to the music in the background that when he wrote his exams he sometimes had to try to remember music he'd heard to find the answer.

By 9.00 p.m., everything was shut down and, even though the lights stayed on in the cells all night, prisoners were not allowed to study after that. They could apply in writing for special permission to study till 11.00 p.m., but only if they were preparing for exams.

Given the system of wires going into their cells, they must have known that they were also being bugged throughout the day and night. In fact, the recording bugs were fed down into the light fittings in each cell from the ceiling. One day, I found a secret door into the roof space where they were connected. But Mandela and his comrades were mellow – they knew the rules, they knew how the system worked. They just worked around it.

In the late seventies, though, some new inmates joined the prison, and the atmosphere subtly changed. In 1976, South Africa's Soweto student uprising hit the headlines all over the world. Young, aggressive activists, some of them still teenagers, began to arrive on the island. It would take two or more years for their trials to come to court. They would have been on remand, and many of them tortured, before they arrived on Robben Island.

I was sent to the mainland to collect a group of about 30 guys. I had to handcuff them and put on leg chains. They looked frightened and young. I put them in the hold of the ferry boat so they could not see out. Some of them were very seasick.

I talked with the men as we walked to the prison. One guy, Vusumzi Mgongo, could speak Afrikaans. He said to me: 'Where are you taking us? Are you taking us to our leaders?' I told him no, you are going to reception and then you'll be in observation for a month. After that, we'll get reports from security police and we'll give you work that suits your experience. Some of them had been cooks or builders, and we could find appropriate work for them. Security police would also interrogate them to find out who their leaders were, so that we could split them up. I did not tell him that.

They ended up in C Section, next to Mandela. They would whisper from cell to cell at night, trying to tell him about the Soweto uprising.

This blood-soaked period of shame in our country resulted in the death of more than 600 people, most of them youths who staged a peaceful mass protest against schools teaching them in the Afrikaans language. The world watched in horror as television footage showed running battles in the streets of Soweto where police brutally beat the protestors and shot many in the back. An emotive black-and-white photograph showed a youth carrying the dead body of his fellow student, 13-year-old Hector Pieterson, one of many innocent young victims. Mandela had first heard about the uprising a year or so after it had occurred from prisoner Eric Molobi, but now he was hearing about it for the first time from those who were there.

Men from both sections tried to put messages in the dirty dishes for the prisoners in the kitchen to smuggle through. They were desperate for real information, for numbers and names, and for knowledge that the ANC had not been crushed.

Another tactic for passing messages was to slit a tennis ball with tiny cuts and insert notes with news that the ANC was still active, still strong in the country. The new inmates would give their names so that the organisation could identify them and their allegiances.

The new prisoners were hostile towards all the prison officers. They stabbed a warder with a knife, and they were charged and put into isolation. They were harder people than Mandela. Mandela sent back messages saying they should not use violence. The warders were just doing their job. They didn't want attacks; it wouldn't help their situation. All energy must go into furthering the anti-apartheid cause.

But the tensions kept bubbling up. In 1981, when I had been on the island for three years, the whole prison, except for B Section, went on hunger strike. The prisoners were demanding better mattresses, longer hours out of their locked cells, more blankets and visits, and better food and more fresh water.

The prison authorities had promised to take up their demands, but after a week nothing had happened. So the prisoners handed in a letter saying they were going on hunger strike.

B Section knew nothing about this. After six weeks, Mandela got to hear about it. He asked for permission from the head of prison to meet a delegation from the committee members of each section. He wanted to persuade them to stop. Mandela felt strongly that hunger strikes could be counterproductive, although he declared that when he felt there was no other redress he would bow to the majority and not only join in but lead the protest himself.

On this occasion, he met with the disgruntled prisoners and they described their demands to him. Mandela told them: 'We are prisoners, we should look after our health and not put ourselves in extra danger. We don't want to die here for the sake of a few petty things.'

The prisoners listened to Mandela and some other leaders and stopped the hunger strike. They had made their point, and after a while they got sponge mattresses and other conditions improved. Mandela was proving he was always the leader, always the diplomat.

Another time, there were complaints about some rotten fish. The head of prison offered to eat it in front of them and, although they still refused to eat it themselves, they calmed down and agreed to go into their cells without making trouble. In truth, the prisoners had every right to feel angry

75

about their conditions, although they had in fact improved in recent years. In the early seventies, before my time, there had been incidents where a prisoner was told to dig a hole to bury himself in, as a punishment for some wrongdoing. He was buried up to his neck, and when he pleaded for water the warders urinated on him.

Later, by the time I was there, this sort of sadistic behaviour had been stamped out – but not out of kindness. The government just didn't want to encourage martyr status for the political prisoners. They had also clamped down on torture techniques, and the truth was that there was no new information to get out of Mandela and his comrades anyway. They had been on the island for years.

But there was torture of a more subtle kind: the censoring of letters and newspapers and radio reports. The control of visits, the keeping away of their families. Stopping all contact with the outside world. Damping down the power of people like Mandela. Making him disappear from the public's mind.

I was to learn all about the censor methods when I was transferred to the Censor's Office.

CHAPTER 5

My own personal prison – the single warders' quarters – was 20 minutes' walk away from Mandela and his friends in B Section. In winter, I was hunched up against gale-force winds and slanting rain as I made my way down the rough track after work. In summer, I sweated in the searing heat.

The quarters were in a one-storey block, which was originally used as the female lepers' infirmary until 1931. As well as lepers, it also housed the mentally and chronically ill. Hardly changed since then, it was built of the same dark slate as the prison and was hellishly unwelcoming.

I remembered a family friend telling us how her aunt was sent to Robben Island with leprosy and was gone forever. There was no communication, no visits. In those days, a doctor seeing the mildest case of skin rash would diagnose leprosy and banish the patient to the island in fear of the disease spreading on the mainland.

The lepers' cemetery on Robben Island is a desolate place. I once searched through it looking for the grave of our friend's aunt. I couldn't find it. The names have nearly all disappeared through erosion.

The single warders were allocated one room between two of us, with an old cracked washbasin in one corner. We were provided with the same scratchy blankets as the prisoners had in their cells. Theirs were army-issue grey, ours were dark blue. The difference was that we could ask for more if we needed them.

The floors were covered with cheap plastic tiles glued on to cement, so it was always cold. We had a heater but sleep was difficult anyway because right outside was the island's power station where diesel engines pumped noisily day and night.

My roommate was much older than me, an unsociable type who was interested only in his time off fishing. He kept his rod and bait-pail next to his bed, and there was always crayfish and abalone in our fridge. Consequently, our room always smelled of old fish. I never complained; I had to respect his seniority.

All of us got bored with the dismal pace of life on the island. Some, like me, were still teenagers who wanted to go to parties and see girlfriends. Yet there we were – not able to see any females at all except the married warders' wives, and not even able to read in our rooms because the light was so poor.

There was no television in our quarters either so we would go to the recreation hall after dinner, where we could all watch the news together. South Africa only got television in 1976 and it was state-controlled, so we could view a censored version of the news and very little else.

You could use a public phone box to call your family or girlfriends, but the phones were bugged. One day, a warder we disliked was promoted to sergeant and he called home boasting to his parents that soon he would be a warrant officer. We overheard it all, of course, and mimicked him to his face later, sneering gleefully at his embarrassment.

Inevitably, there were practical jokes. There was often a live crayfish or a seabird put into someone's room, and you would wake up in alarm to find a shellfish clattering around the tiled floor or a bird screeching and flapping in your face, trying to get out.

Like Mandela and his comrades, I teamed up with my fellow sufferers and we devised ways to get through the tedium. After work every evening, a group of us went jogging right round the island, all 11 kilometres. Others would play rugby. Then we all showered and went to the warders' mess for dinner, and on to the clubhouse for drinks. Liquor was very cheap, and there was nothing else to do, so many warders would spend all evening in there getting drunk.

With all news of the outside world censored, and our phone conversations monitored, we felt our lives were almost as restricted as the prisoners'. But of course our suffering was nothing compared to theirs. We could leave the prison service, or catch the ferry over to the mainland on our days off. We had a freedom they might never experience again in their lives.

Soon after I started work on Robben Island, I was told I'd be filling in for someone on night shift in the Censor's Office. I had to start at 4 p.m. and wouldn't finish until 7 the next morning. We were on alert all night in case of emergencies, such as an attempted break-out or a medical crisis. We had a medically trained warder on call at all times. In addition, the dog-handlers patrolled through every section of the prison on a three-hourly basis and were constantly in touch with us through the internal phone system.

At night, there were also killer dogs running on chains all the time. They were in between the double steel-mesh fences standing three metres apart that surrounded the entire prison. The dogs were mostly Rottweilers, really vicious. Dog-owners in Cape Town whose animals were out of control would send them to us. Then they were systematically provoked to make them even madder. They could not be handled; they had to be controlled at the end of long metal poles.

The Censor's Office was considered the heart of the prison, set right in the centre of the main building, on the second floor, with a view over the whole of B Section. But there was no heart in that place. Instead, it was this department that meted out some of the worst cruelty to prisoners, namely the holding back or destruction of their letters, their all-important link to loved ones, and the ruthless censoring of daily news to make them believe their stand against apartheid was for nothing, the sacrifice of their freedom pointless. Instead of the real news, all the prisoners would get to hear about was the boring, uncontroversial stuff such as the deaths of prominent people, government appointments or road traffic accidents, or examples of the government's military successfully taking out ANC strongholds. Any show of solidarity from the outside world would be hidden from them, or destroyed.

There were more personal cruelties, too. Mandela had had his 60th birthday the year before I came to the island. When I started work in the Censor's Office, I asked what was in the boxes and boxes piled up there, with still more arriving every week. I was told that tens of thousands of birthday cards had arrived for him, mostly from abroad. Anti-apartheid activists in England alone had coordinated the posting of 10,000 individual cards. Others came from the Netherlands and elsewhere in Europe, and there were many from America. Some universities, like Michigan State, had organised batches of birthday cards, all posted individually. The stamps were pretty and colourful so some of us warders cut them off and took them home.

Each card was removed from its envelope, read carefully, and then neatly clipped back on to the outside of the envelope. They were sorted according to the country they came from.

Any letters or cards not given to prisoners for any reason were supposed to be put with their property and stored until their release. But it was too much trouble to keep Mandela's birthday cards. They were taken out and burned on the fire in our boiler-room. Years later, I wanted to tell him about them, as I felt bad for him. But he told me: 'Mr Brand, I already know all about that.' Some prisoners who had been at the dumping site on the island had found charred scraps and given them to him. He had been given only six cards on his birthday – from Winnie, from their daughters Zindzi and Zenani, from Mandela's daughter Makaziwe from his first marriage, from his son Magkatho, and from his lawyer.

I was considered efficient in the Censor's Office, so I was asked to stay on there. The office was lined with shelves and filing cabinets holding many years' worth of papers and documents. There were no computers; everything was done by hand. On one wall there were post-box alcoves where all incoming post was stored until Saturday mornings, when it would be handed out. Everything was read and reread and heavily censored.

Outgoing letters would be handed back to prisoners to rewrite if the contents had flouted the regulations. Everything had to be signed for. We kept a handwritten register of all letters they received, and all rejected letters would be stored alongside the rewritten version.

When letters arrived for the B Section guys through the post office on the mainland, they had already been examined by censors in the police Special Branch office at the embarkation point for Robben Island, and those of particular interest would have been sent on to the National Intelligence agents in their Cape Town office. They would send the letters on in a locked briefcase with a note on each one saying if the prisoner could receive them or not.

Any political content, or reference to fellow revolutionaries, or to the anti-apartheid struggle, would be completely struck out with black indelible ink.

Then we censored it again, checking for any mention of another prisoner or reference to the man's family on the outside. Whole passages would be cut out with a razor blade and the shredded remains, a pitiful thing, would be handed in its envelope to the prisoner at a Saturday-morning session in the courtyard.

It was awkward and strange to be reading a man's love letters to his wife, as I did with Mandela's letters to Winnie. I felt I was breaking into his privacy, especially because by this point I had met my future wife, Estelle, and I was busy sending love letters myself that were full of longing for my fiancée.

Of all his correspondence with Winnie, one letter stands out and is reprinted in Mandela's book *Conversations with Myself*. In it, he pours out his intense feelings for her at a time when she had been ill in bed and had not replied to recent letters from him. He wrote:

> The crop of miseries we have harvested from the heartbreaking frustrations of the last fifteen months are not likely to fade away easily from the mind. I feel as if I have been soaked in gall, every part of me, my flesh, bloodstream, bone and soul, so bitter I am to be completely powerless to help you in the rough and fierce ordeals you are going through.
>
> What a world of difference to your failing health and to your spirit, darling, to my own anxiety and the strain

that I cannot shake off, if only we could meet, if I could be on your side and squeeze you, or if I could but catch a glimpse of your outline through the thick wire netting that would inevitably separate us.

Physical suffering is nothing compared to the trampling down of those tender bonds of affection that form the basis of the institution of marriage and the family, that unite man and wife. This is a frightful moment in our life ... To a freedom fighter hope is what a lifebelt is to a swimmer – a guarantee that one will keep afloat and free from danger. I know, darling, that if riches were to be counted in terms of the tons of hope and sheer courage that nestle in your breast (this idea I got from you) you would certainly be a millionaire. Remember this always.

Mandela signs his letter: 'Tons and tons of love and a million kisses. Devotedly, Dalibunga [his initiation name]'.

In another, published in Fatima Meer's biography *Higher than Hope*, Mandela writes:

My dearest Winnie,
I have been fairly successful in putting on a mask behind which I have pined for the family, alone, never rushing for the post when it comes until somebody calls out my name. I also never linger after visits although sometimes the urge to do so becomes quite terrible. I am struggling to suppress my emotions as I write this letter.

I have received only one letter since you were detained, that one dated August 22. I do not know anything about family affairs, such as payment of rent, telephone bills, care of children and their expenses, whether you will get a job when released. As long as I don't hear from you I will remain worried and dry like a desert.

I recall the Karoo I crossed on several occasions. I saw the desert again in Botswana on my way to and from Africa – endless pits of sand and not a drop of water. I have not had a letter from you. I feel dry like a desert.

Letters from you and the family are like the arrival of summer rains and spring that liven my life and make it enjoyable.

Whenever I write to you I feel that inside physical warmth, that makes me forget all my problems. I become full of love.

Outgoing letters were not to be longer than 500 words. Mandela would often have letters returned because they were too long. He would also have letters to the Commissioner of Prisons, for example, handed back to him because they contained issues of race. This was a way of trying to limit his endless complaints and requests to the authorities.

Sometimes his love letters would be rejected by the security police on the grounds that they might be coded. He was baring his heart and soul to the wife he longed to see and hold, knowing he might never be with her again, and these letters were being discarded out of nothing but spite.

Worse, I once overheard a warder in B Section's courtyard saying to Mandela: 'There's no point in you waiting for letters from your wife. We all know she has a new boyfriend. She's sleeping with one of the Special Branch guys.'

Mandela, without a trace of anger, told him: 'Sir, I am inside here, powerless. She is a flesh-and-blood human being living in the outside world. I can't be jealous about what she is doing, or tell her what she can and cannot do.' He simply refused to show his inner anguish.

Of course, it was not just Mandela's letters that were censored – I had to look at all the correspondence to and from the other political prisoners too. One time, this caused a mystery when I noticed that a man who I knew to be illiterate had managed to put together a very articulate romantic letter to his girlfriend.

Other warders were reading identical passages from other prisoners, some of them quite sophisticated. We began to hold them back and compare them. Then we discovered an article in the *Reader's Digest*, one of the few magazines they were allowed to see, about how to write love letters. The prisoners had all been copying it.

Once, a letter to Mandela arrived from Winnie containing a photograph of their children. One child was showing a peace sign, holding his fingers in a V for Victory. We had to keep that photograph back, and he was never allowed to see it while he was on the island. All rejected letters, cards, or photographs were supposed to be put with his property and given to him on release. But he was selected for especially harsh treatment. There was correspondence he never saw.

If his quota was full, he would not be allowed to see any more letters. Once a year, he could apply in writing to see all the letters that had been held back. He could read them, in the Censor's Office, but then they were put back with his property. Mandela learned he could spend one extra rand to register his outgoing letters and then check with the post office to see if they had been delivered. By doing this, he knew what was going on, and he was able to stay one step ahead, as he always wanted to.

Like the other prisoners, Mandela was only allowed to receive correspondence from immediate family members or his lawyers. Others were automatically considered a security risk. Prisoners were supposed to give contact details of all their family members, friends, and associates, and that information was stored in our files. Ninety per cent of them only gave their immediate family members' details, not friends or comrades. They knew the security police would start harassing them if they reported their names.

However, since post would only be passed on to a prisoner if it came from a known source, that was a further restriction on their links to the outside world. If a prisoner had not registered his brother's name, for example, then if a letter came from him the prisoner would not receive it. It would be added to his property bundle and only given to him on release.

We had a few warders who could speak Xhosa, Sotho, or Zulu, and would censor letters in those languages. They also censored visits. Mandela took all his visits in English because we didn't have many Xhosa speakers and, if there was nobody available, then that could have delayed or even cancelled visits, which he couldn't bear to contemplate.

All this was harsh, but a great improvement on the restrictions when Mandela had first come to the island. Then, he and his comrades were allowed to write and receive one letter every six months. By 1975, he was allowed three letters a month, so thirty-six a year in total. By the time I was working there, in the late seventies, the yearly quota remained the same, but there was a maximum of four letters per month. Sometimes he needed to write to his lawyer and that letter would have to be included in the quota.

In addition, Mandela was allowed to receive a total of 12 birthday or Christmas cards each year, of no more than 12 to 15 words each. Anything longer was classified as a letter. All correspondence would be stamped and signed by a warder like myself to show its status, approval or rejection.

On one occasion, Ahmed Kathrada, Mandela's great friend and fellow Rivonian, had a letter held back due to its political content. He knew it had arrived and applied in writing to see it. That was the system. However, a warder in the Censor's Office had decided to burn it. When Kathrada complained, again in writing, he was told it was lost. It was a long, slow frustrating process and, at the end of it, nothing but denials.

Frequently, we realised that security branch officers were throwing away outgoing letters, as prisoners complained of no feedback or requests for visits from relatives they had invited. That was all part of the casual cruelty, encouraged by an obsessively paranoid government.

Even more important than letters from their loved ones were their visits.

In 1964, his first year on the island, Mandela had been allowed only one visit – from his beloved Winnie – and he could receive two letters. In 1965, he received two visits, in July and December. Gradually, the number of visits permitted improved slightly, year on year, and they continued to be his lifeline, at the core of his ability to survive and stay sane.

By the time I started work on Robben Island, he was allowed one thirty-minute visit every three months by one person alone. Later, that improved to one visit per month, and by the 1980s he was allowed more regular visits, two per month of forty minutes each by two people at a time. He and several of his comrades had earned privileges by their good behaviour, which meant no fights or attempts to smuggle material out, no trouble of any kind, and a cell always clean and ready for inspections.

By the time I was guarding him, he had reached A Group, gaining top privileges such as the authorisation for more visits and more letters, and permission to buy more groceries at the tuck shop.

On a Friday or a Saturday, we would tell prisoners if they were going to get a visit. Mandela would prepare himself, and by 9 a.m. he would be shaved and neatly dressed, and impatiently waiting for the visitor's arrival.

We warders would joke about them having an outing that day. They were excited and happy. But sometimes the ferry wouldn't come because the sea was too rough. Visitors would be turned back home and forced to wait for the next calm day. It was hard on Winnie because for each visit she had her ban lifted for only one day, and she would then have to reapply in writing for another date. If the sea stayed rough for two days and the ferry was cancelled, the visit would also be cancelled, and lost.

Mandela would therefore be anxious from dawn to see that the weather was clement. Only once he knew that the ferry was running and Winnie was on her way would he be calm.

Before a visit, I would escort him down the track to the visitors' centre and, if he saw a flower, a white Namaqualand daisy, he would pluck it carefully and later lay it on the shelf on his side of the viewing glass where Winnie could see it. He loved her deeply and romantically and, even though we were two big men marching in uniform down a prison track together, with dog-handlers on either side of us, I never found it amusing or foolish to see him pick a tiny flower. It was a part of him, all man and all feeling.

Armed warders would be watching us from the observation posts as we walked along. Everyone was on high alert during visitors' days. Mandela would walk slightly ahead of me, and we could talk without being overheard during that 100-metre stretch.

He would always carry a notebook and pencil with him. Every minute of a visit was vital to him, and he wanted to note it all down and reread it later. He would also take a notebook for Winnie, so that she could write down instructions about contacting lawyers or their daughters' schools.

Just before the ferry arrived, I would lock Mandela in a cell. Then I would walk over to fetch all the visitors and walk them up to the visitors' centre. They would then be locked into the waiting room.

Often they were pale and seasick and needing a toilet. I felt so sorry for them and gave them a few extra minutes to recover in the waiting room, but some of them would really struggle to get through the visit, especially knowing they had to face a rough ride back on the ferry again.

A female lawyer who came to visit Mandela one day refused to go back on the ferry, because it had made her so ill and frightened on the way over. They had to send a military helicopter for her in the end, just to get her off the island.

There was always a huge swell in the channel between Robben Island and the mainland. These days, the ferry will be cancelled at the first sign of a choppy sea for the sake of the tourists. But back then it brought essentials like food and fresh water and, most importantly for the paranoid government, sheaves of documents tracking the prisoners' every thought and action.

Winnie sometimes looked uncomfortable after the crossing,

but she was tough, and she would not miss a minute of a visit for anything in the world.

I would bring Mandela into a booth, with empty booths on either side so that no prisoner could see another man's visitors. Then I would stand behind him throughout. He and Winnie would both put their hands on the soundproof glass, no bigger than a piece of A4 paper, then pick up the phone to talk.

I was on a phone linked to theirs, so there was no privacy for them at all. They weren't allowed to mention other prisoners or people on the outside unless it was close family. I would turn off the microphones immediately if I heard any transgressions, and I would have to warn Mandela that the visit would be terminated.

Winnie would talk about money problems and would often say that she was worried about their daughters running out of control. She and Mandela were like any concerned parents. He was worried sick about the dangers of the outside world. Zenani was at boarding school in Swaziland, Makaziwe was in America, and Zindzi was in all sorts of danger living with her mother in Brandfort, because everyone knew she was the daughter of Mandela, the terrorist.

Just before I joined Robben Island, in 1977, Winnie had been banished to Brandfort, a remote Afrikaner-dominated town in the Free State, where she was given a house with no running water or electricity, or even floors and ceilings. Hardly anyone in the town spoke Xhosa, Winnie's mother tongue.

Winnie told Mandela that she and Zindzi were constantly harassed by security police. Even visitors bringing them food or money were being arrested. She was unhappy and alone. She wanted Mandela to help her by talking to his lawyer. He felt helpless, trapped on Robben Island and unable to care for his family.

Every second of those visits was important, and I found it hard to have to tell them there was only five minutes left. Sometimes Mandela would immediately ask for a further 30 minutes, knowing he could have no visit the next month.

Some warders, out of nothing but cruelty, advanced their watches to deliberately cut short visits. They would shout: 'Five minutes left!' and the devastated prisoner and his visitor would have no means of complaint.

Sometimes, Winnie would come with happy news for her husband, for example a new baby born into the family, but mostly their visits were serious and disturbing and Mandela would leave with a heavy heart. I found myself full of stress and sympathy on his behalf. This family of his was in chaos, all over the place, and he could do nothing.

On our walk back to B Section he would say it had been good to see Winnie. She wanted to cheer him up, but somehow there were always more problems. However, he would always talk about how he was going to deal with these problems; he never let them push him under. Back in B Section, he would go into the courtyard and immediately be surrounded by his friends and comrades and talk over every detail with them.

By 1980, prisoners like Mandela, Ahmed Kathrada, and Walter Sisulu had enough good behaviour privileges to be graded as 'A' class prisoners, as has been previously mentioned. This also meant that they could now receive newspapers. Mandela ordered and paid for the Afrikaans papers *Die Burger* and *Rapport*. Sisulu would get the *Cape Times* and the *South African Sunday Times*.

Other prisoners were not allowed newspapers; they were not even allowed to touch them, let alone read them. So Mandela and the two others would sit in the courtyard reading out loud, very loud, so that everyone could hear.

The newspapers were heavily censored. Any reports of police raids would be cut out with scissors, and sometimes the whole newspaper would be in shreds. There would be more advertisements than news stories. Then they would ask us what we had cut out, and of course we couldn't say. Often it was me who had censored them. The head of the Censor's Office made the decisions, and I worked with the scissors.

Nothing about the ANC or fellow revolutionary groups was allowed through, and nothing about bomb blasts or mass actions by the people. We sometimes let an article go through to show the police were defeating the ANC effectively.

We didn't have to cut out any pictures or stories about Mandela. It was already prohibited by law for newspapers to publish anything like that. He was being deliberately erased from the public's mind and memory.

Sometimes, the head of the Censor's Office would leave something provocative in for them to read. For example, at one time a group of 26 political prisoners were released from Robben Island, and 21 of them were killed in a police raid in Lesotho less than two weeks later. That news report was left in to demoralise them and make them believe the ANC had weakened.

All visits from lawyers were supposed to be confidential, and there was a great show of respect for that by putting a room aside in the visitors' centre. A warder would be posted outside, out of hearing. But of course these rooms were all bugged, and all conversations taped and sent off to the security police daily in the locked briefcases.

The prisoners all knew this and would find a way around it. Mandela would keep scraps of paper torn from a cement bag in his pocket, then start a sentence in conversation with his lawyer while just writing down crucial information, like the initials of someone he was referring to – for example, O.T. meant Oliver Tambo, the ANC leader – or a message he wanted passed on. He would slide the paper across to the lawyer to show him, then quickly put it in his mouth and swallow it before a suspicious warder rushed in to take it from him.

Over the years, lawyers could sometimes smuggle some food in, as these were contact visits with no glass panels between them and the prisoner. Dullah Omar used to bring in samosas made by his wife and was smart enough to offer them to the warders too. Ismail Ayob, another of Mandela's lawyers at the time, brought in fruit. Mandela told me excitedly how he had had his first banana for 15 years.

Mandela's legal consultations were mostly attempts to help Winnie or fellow comrades. She needed money, and she needed help to survive her banning period. It was a difficult and dark time for the couple.

CHAPTER 6

The Rivonians and their comrades had been sent to Robben Island to be crushed. They were to be physically and mentally broken as thoroughly as the limestone they were forced to hack in the quarry for 13 back-breaking years. The Africans like Mandela were literally semi-starved by being given meagre rations, less than other inmates, because they were regarded as the lowest creatures in the land. And all the prisoners were observed, monitored and bugged during every activity, no matter how personal, every conversation no matter how trivial. Yet, when I arrived on the island and met the Rivonians, 14 years into their incarceration, I did not see broken men. Instead, I saw a group of close friends who supported each other through every hardship, every illness, and every setback. They were bound together not just by their circumstances but by their beliefs. They were the strongest men I had ever met.

Yes, I and the other warders watched them naked in the showers and in the toilets. We would order them to get on their knees to clean and polish floors and passageways. We would even cut their letters and cards to shreds when we censored them, and we would take part in the government's plan to make them literally disappear from the world. The relentlessly harsh way of life was intended to strip these men of their dignity and reduce them to little more than insect status. The intention was to see them crawl pitifully back and forth between their cells and the yard until they eventually sickened and died.

But what the government in all its paranoia had failed to realise was that the ANC leadership in prison – Mandela, Walter Sisulu, Raymond Mhlaba, Andrew Mlangeni, Govan Mbeki, Elias Motsoaledi and Ahmed Kathrada – was impossible to break. Mbeki was the intellectual of the political group, and was a committed Communist. He and Mandela clashed badly at this time over ideology, and at one point didn't speak for nearly two years. Despite that, by keeping them together, the authorities had inadvertently strengthened the bonds between them.

Their hopes and beliefs were unshakeable. Here they were, mostly men in their sixties, who never doubted for a second that their cause was right and that they would eventually see a day when good would triumph over evil, and that they would be an important part of it.

Mandela had been the undisputed leader from the very start. He was assertive without ever dominating or belittling the others. He had a natural gift for leadership, using it with charm and good humour so that warders like myself were drawn in without even realising it.

Of course, there were many warders who brutally maintained the superiority of their status over the Rivonians, and revelled in intentional sadism. They would cut short food rations, harass prisoners while they ate, tear up and throw away their letters, and goad them at every opportunity. They would tell a prisoner his wife was being unfaithful or that his visitors had failed to turn up, when they had in fact been stranded on the mainland because the ferry failed to run.

In the limestone quarry, prisoners would be ordered to half-fill the wheelbarrows. The next day, they would be ordered to work faster and fill them three-quarters full, and on the following day ordered to work faster still. There was no earthly point in this; it was institutional bullying at its most ruthless.

Each prisoner carried an identity card with him at all times on pain of loss of privileges. On it was written his name and prison number, his place of birth, his crime, his sentence, his religion, and his ethnic origin. It also contained his fingerprints. Mandela's religion was Methodist and he was labelled Bantu – the generic and derogatory term for black Africans within the apartheid system. I saw the insult 'kaffir' written on some prisoners' identity cards.

I had early on decided to go a different route to this. Having been brought up in a kind environment with no racial overtones, I had a natural respect for my elders. I also saw a rare warmth between these men and a total lack of bitterness at their hopeless situation. I saw no reason to make their lives more miserable.

The fellowship between them was almost enviable. The Rivonians had the respect of all other prisoners, and I got to know them well. I like to think they feel the same way about me, having shown them what compassion I could get away with for all those years, while still locking them up in cells and dishing up the terrible prison food. Maybe they were sorry for me in my own 'imprisonment' on the island. They certainly had the capacity for that.

When the Nelson Mandela Foundation published its book *A Prisoner in the Garden* in 2005, I was incredibly proud to see a chapter about myself in which they described the relationship between Mandela and me and my family as 'one of extraordinary richness'.

In his own life story, *Long Walk to Freedom*, Mandela wrote lengthily about Robben Island – the dark years. He stated that the most important person in any prisoner's life was not the Minister of Justice, not the Commissioner of Prisons, not even the head of prison, but the warder in one's section. The officers and higher authorities would work according to the rulebook because they rarely came into direct contact with the prisoners, whereas the warders would often show more humanity.

He wrote: 'If you are cold and want an extra blanket, you might petition the Minister of Justice, but you will get no response. If you go to the Commissioner of Prisons he will say, "Sorry, it is against regulations." The head of the prison will say, "If I give you an extra blanket I must give one to everyone." But if you approach the warder in your corridor and you are on good terms with him, he will simply go to the stockroom and fetch a blanket.'

He said he always tried to be decent to the warders in B Section, as hostility was self-defeating.

'There was no point in having a permanent enemy among the warders,' he wrote. 'It was ANC policy to try to educate all people, even our enemies; we believed that all men, even prison service warders, were capable of change and we did our utmost to try to sway them... In general we treated the warders as they treated us. If a man was considerate we were considerate in return. Not all of our warders were ogres. We noticed right from the start that there were some among them who believed in fairness... Yet being friendly with warders was not an easy proposition for they generally found the idea of being courteous to a black man abhorrent.'

He wrote about one particular warder who guarded them at the quarry, forbidding them to talk to each other. Mandela described him as hostile and crude. But, as the Rivonians and other prisoners made attempts to befriend him, the warder became less wary and even began to ask questions about the ANC.

Like many of us, he would have been brainwashed by the government's propaganda during his training and would believe they were all terrorists and Communists who wanted to drive the white man into the sea. But, as the prisoners explained to him their non-racialism, their desire for equal rights, and their plans for the redistribution of wealth, he scratched his head and said: 'It makes more bloody sense than the Nats [the governing National Party].' They had made a friend, if not exactly a convert.

The ANC's leaders in prison were in fact great characters. Walter Sisulu, six years older than Mandela and also a Thembu, was undoubtedly his mentor. Sisulu had been a brilliant political networker, founding the ANC Youth League with Mandela and Oliver Tambo in 1944 and soon becoming its leading light.

He believed from the start in a more aggressive campaign against the prevailing government and was jailed seven times between 1953 and 1963. He was caught by police during the raid on Liliesleaf Farm in 1964 and served 27 years in prison. I found him amiable and easy-going, the senior trusted comrade to whom Mandela would turn in times of crisis. Mandela has written of how, after he received news of his younger son Thembekile's death in a road accident, he lay on his mat on the floor of his cell and could not talk. Walter came in and was shown the telegram. He knelt at his bedside and held Mandela's hand. Mandela said there was nothing one man could say to another at such a time.

Years later, in Pollsmoor Prison, I was working with Mandela in his garden and he looked across to Sisulu digging in some plants. He said: 'You know, if it was not for that old man I wouldn't have joined up, and I wouldn't be in this prison now. It's all his fault.' They laughed, and Sisulu carried on singing like he always did. He would be singing when washing his clothes and going about other prison tasks, and when he talked about one day being released he would say, 'I'll go singing.'

Sisulu became deputy president of the ANC in 1991. He died in 2003 and has a national botanic garden and a university named after him, among many other honours.

Mandela said in a eulogy that Sisulu's absence 'has carved a void. A part of me is gone'. He recalled how they had both decided to face the death sentence at the Rivonia trial, rather than to protest their innocence. 'I know he planned to meet the hangman with a song on his lips,' he said.

Raymond Mhlaba, another Rivonian, was a larger-than-life character. He was always friendly to me, with his loudspeaking voice and his uncontrollable laughter, which rang through the whole of B Section and sometimes even annoyed others who were trying to study.

He was the noisiest guy in the prison. It was a great joy when he became the first Robben Island prisoner in South Africa to get permission to marry. By this time – 1986 – we were all in Pollsmoor Prison in Cape Town. Mhlaba's common-law wife, Dideka, a nurse, could not receive her pension without a marriage certificate. After many years of written applications, Mhlaba was told the ceremony could go ahead.

I was on guard outside the Commander's office where Mandela and Sisulu were witnesses, wearing smart black suits hired by Mhlaba's lawyer. It was the first time I had seen them out of uniform. They looked rather handsome, with carnations in their buttonholes brought by the lawyer's wife. The bride wore a white dress and carried flowers, and there were snacks and sparkling grape juice in an adjoining room after the short ceremony.

Mhlaba was a very nervous guy, and obviously extra nervous that day. He could never take exams, he was too jittery. Getting married was a big step for him. He was able to kiss and hug his wife that day for the first time for 22 years, but the honeymoon had to wait a further six.

I felt for him as I watched him say goodbye to his bride, and then I escorted them all back to the cells, taking the rest of the snacks for the other prisoners.

Rivonian Andrew Mlangeni liked to talk to me about fishing, a pleasure denied to him, although it was a major pastime for off-duty warders. He would ask about my catch, and often I kept fish back for him when barbecuing with warder friends, sending it into his cell with that night's dog-handler.

He asked for cough medicine every day when supplies came round from the doctor. He used to joke that it was his alcohol; he was pretty well addicted to it.

I never forgot that Mlangeni was my first introduction to B Section. When I arrived, he greeted me in Afrikaans, my own language. I came to realise that because he was fluent, it had been agreed among the prisoners that he should ask for the cell nearest to the warders' office so that he could overhear our conversations.

He had been brought up in Soweto in a poor family. He became a bus driver and joined strikes, joining the ANC Youth League at an early stage and volunteering for military training outside South Africa once the armed struggle started. It was Mlangeni who told the judge at the Rivonia trial that all the apartheid government had achieved was to put leaders in jail and break up families.

He was the champion table-tennis player in B Section, and

he and I enjoyed many games. We remained friends long after Robben Island and up to this day.

Elias Motsoaledi was a born fighter; it seems inevitable that he would end up at the Rivonia trial. At 17, he was arrested for refusing to produce his pass book and sentenced to work on road-building in Pretoria. He was a working-class hero who led the fight for better wages and conditions for factory workers and helped to establish the South African Congress of Trade Unions.

Motsoaledi was a proud member of the South African Communist Party and had clashed many times in the past with ANC Youth League hotheads like Mandela and Sisulu. By the time they were on Robben Island, they realised they had a great deal in common and worked together.

I remember him mostly for his fierce antipathy towards cigarette smokers. He would call for medical treatment if anyone lit up near him, so, of course, the others would joke that they were going to their cells for a smoke and he would immediately get sick and call for help.

But he was also kind and down-to-earth. He liked to help Mandela in his garden and it became a community activity, something they could do that actually showed results. He was a Sotho speaker and a family man who lived for his wife's visits and letters.

Motsoaledi died on the day of Mandela's inauguration as president, on 9 May 1994. Mandela talked fondly of him during a speech at his funeral.

Govan Mbeki, although he came to be a giant politician – he played a major part in negotiations to reconcile black and white South Africans, and his son Thabo succeeded Mandela as president in 1999 – was the quiet man in B Section.

I remember him playing Monopoly endlessly in the recreation hall and wanting to make his own rules. He gave the impression of being very serious, although he had a quiet sense of humour underneath. Generally he didn't speak to the warders very much, although he opened up to me a lot on the day I had to escort him to see Mandela in isolation at Pollsmoor years later.

But Ahmed Kathrada – Kathy as everyone calls him – was probably my closest friend and remained so until the day he died, 18 March 2017.

He was the only Indian on trial at Rivonia, and he refused an offer to go free in exchange for giving evidence against the others. He had been an activist since the age of 12 when he joined the Young Communist League of South Africa, handing out leaflets and doing volunteer work.

He always spoke to me in Afrikaans, which I appreciated. He was a kind, gentle person, an intellectual with a huge appetite for studying. He gained his Bachelor's degrees in History, Criminology, and Bibliography on Robben Island, as well as Honours in History and African Politics. He would have gone on to gain his Master's if the authorities had allowed it. He eventually held four honorary university doctorates.

Kathy was always very close to Mandela. He was elected to Parliament in South Africa's first democratic elections in 1994, and Mandela appointed him to the political advisory post of Parliamentary Counsellor.

He found an extraordinary way of dealing with his memories of the Robben Island days. He was elected chairman of the Robben Island Council in 1994, in which post he remained until his term expired in 2006, and he still travels to the island regularly to bring visitors on private tours, often taking the ferry over and advising on the management of the island as an important cultural centre. Kathy was at President Obama's side when he visited B Section on Mandela's 95th birthday and stood for several minutes in Mandela's cell, looking silently through the bars. Kathy has witnessed many such emotional pilgrimages. He understands them but also strongly believes in the positive elements of his long imprisonment.

Of all my B Section prisoners, Kathy has maintained the most positive philosophy about his days on Robben Island. As he remarked in a speech in 1993:

> Someone has written about two prisoners looking out of their cell window – one saw bars while the other saw stars.
>
> The real picture of prison life is one of great warmth, fellowship, friendship, humour and laughter, of strong convictions, of a generosity of spirit, of companionship, solidarity and care.
>
> It is a picture of continuous learning, of getting to know and live with your fellow beings – but more importantly where one comes to know one's self, one's weakness, inadequacy and potential.
>
> By reducing prison life to cold impersonal statistics one is blotting out the deep multi-dimensional experience, feelings and interests of a vibrant community.
>
> We would want Robben Island not to be a monument to our hardship and suffering but a triumph of the human spirit against the forces of evil.

Old friends like Kathy, Mandela, Mbeki, and Sisulu shared many memories of life before Robben Island. I would overhear them reminiscing and smiling about some old times. Mandela himself has written of their gallows humour at one of the worst periods of their lives, while they were waiting to be sentenced by the Rivonia trial judge.

In *Long Walk to Freedom* he recalls how he, Kathy, and Mbeki were being guarded by a bad-tempered, red-faced police officer called Lieutenant Swanepoel. One day, while Swanepoel watched them from the door of the holding cell, Mbeki wrote a note in a secretive way. He handed the note to Mandela, who read it, then, nodding seriously, passed it to Kathy.

As Kathy took out matches to burn the note, Swanepoel burst in and grabbed the piece of paper from his hand. He left the room to read his prize.

A few moments later, he snarled at them: 'I'll get you for this!'

Mbeki had written in capital letters: 'ISN'T SWANEPOEL A FINE-LOOKING CHAP?'

Aside from the Rivonians, the leaders, there were other unforgettable prisoners. Japhta Masemola was the longest-serving political prisoner on the island, locked up there for 28 years. He was one of the key members of the military wing of the PAC, the Pan-Africanist Congress, a breakaway organisation from the ANC.

He was a man who could fix anything and everything. He could make or build things out of cardboard, pieces of driftwood, paper torn from cement bags, anything. He made furniture, bookshelves, even suitcases, for his friends. He mended other prisoners' clocks so they could time their studies in preparation for exams. He even made a sombrero hat with a wide rim for Mandela to protect him from the sun. It was made out of cardboard, coloured in with white paint. Mandela wouldn't go anywhere without it – he wore it in the limestone quarry and when he was gardening. It was among a handful of items that left prison with him when he was released years later.

Once, Masemola made a special trap to catch mice. It was so effective that he actually wanted to patent it. But someone stole the design. He went on hunger strike to protest, certain that one of the warders had taken it, but it never reappeared.

When Mandela was in Pollsmoor, he liked to take his study books and sit outside alone on the stone ledge. In cold weather he would wrap a blanket around himself, and he asked me one day if he could have one of Masemola's famous pins to secure it. I got two blanket pins from Masemola, and Mandela used it to keep his blankets together around his shoulders. I found these pins in his cell after his release and took them home, where my wife used them for our new baby. But Masemola wasn't an easy prisoner. He was difficult and short-tempered. He tried to break the speaker in his cell one day when he didn't like the music. He was so argumentative he would get into a physical fight with his own comrades.

He had been orphaned at an early age and brought up by his sister. He did his teacher's training and radicalised some of his pupils. As a result, some of them were later incarcerated with him on Robben Island.

Two days before Masemola was released from prison, in October 1989, Mandela asked to see him. Masemola was flown from Johannesburg's Leeukop Prison to Victor Verster Prison, where Mandela was by then living alone. Nothing has ever been disclosed about their conversation at that meeting.

On release, Masemola plunged himself immediately into active politics again and was rapturously received by supporters, who filled a football stadium to listen to him. The apartheid police continued to follow him and monitor him.

On 17 April 1990, when he was travelling without a

bodyguard, a truck collided with his car and killed him. The truck disappeared from the scene and has never been traced. The PAC introduced its annual Heroes' Day to honour and remember 'our great son of Africa'.

There were other notable PAC members imprisoned in B Section, including their president, Zephania Mothopeng. He was a sad sight to see in prison – an old, overweight man with health problems that caused him to walk slowly and with difficulty. I used to escort him to visits and he stopped constantly, racked with chest pains.

He was a popular man, whose wisdom Mandela seemed to respect. They agreed that it was easier to negotiate and debate with each other as members of different organisations in prison, in contrast to their clashes in the outside world.

He had been president of the Transvaal Teachers' Association, and was first imprisoned in 1960 for campaigning against the pass laws. He served three prison sentences for his activism and was released in 1989, before dying a year later.

Another PAC supporter, Nontente Kamteni, was a special guy. He was just 22 when he was sent to the island for 20 years for sabotage. He had been shot in the hand by police when he tried to stop them arresting people in Queenstown, Cape Town, during a riot.

Kamteni was irrepressible. He was our tea-boy, all eyes and ears and friendly to everyone, staying in the communal cells and earning himself easy access to the reception office and the study office, bringing tea to the warders. He totally endeared himself and was able to knock on doors and just walk in. He was trusted with the warders' money to buy tea, coffee, and biscuits, and was meticulously careful with it.

Of course, we all suspected he was collecting information

for his comrades in B Section, but he was so personable that we all liked him. If he showed reluctance when I wanted some tea, I would offer to show him his letters early, on a Wednesday instead of a Saturday, as long as he just read them quickly in the office and left them there.

Once a year, we had a barbecue for all the warders. Kamteni was the only prisoner we invited. We shared the food with him and almost forgot he wasn't one of us. He would sidle up to us warders and chat in our language, even calling fellow prisoners kaffirs and making a show that he was against them. I certainly didn't fall for that, I don't know about the others. Nevertheless, we liked him a lot. He was always cheerful and smiling, and after all he was just a young guy locked up on the island for the best years of his life.

Ben Ramotse was a tragic case in the end. He had been an ANC activist who went on a sabotage operation on the very day that the armed wing, Umkhonto we Sizwe, was launched. He was with a comrade when the bomb they were carrying, intended to blow up the Bantu administration office in Soweto, detonated prematurely. His comrade was killed and Ramotse was injured.

Ramotse was smuggled out of the country for military training but was captured and sentenced to 15 years on Robben Island. He was entrusted as a cleaner in B Section and because he was so easygoing he was put in with the Swapo (South West Africa People's Organisation) guys from Namibia in another section, the only Xhosa to be accepted there.

Ramotse was released in 1985 but, as a former political prisoner and convicted terrorist, he couldn't find work anywhere. He wrote to Mandela asking if the ANC could give him funds to buy a taxi. Mandela sent messages out to Winnie and his lawyers, but the funds never came through.

A year after his release, Ramotse's wife wrote to Mandela to say that he had been desperate, unable to support his family, and had hanged himself. She found him in the garage at their home. She was bitter about it, and of course I read the letter before it reached Mandela and I was also shocked and upset. When I gave the letter to Mandela, he went very quiet. He had tried his best to help, but things weren't always possible.

There were tragedies, crises and unwanted news of all kinds that arrived in the prisoners' letters. It was hard to pass them on when you knew the men were already struggling just to get through their day.

One man who never struggled, who refused to struggle, was the incredible Herman Adimba Toivo Ja Toivo. He was the leader of Swapo, fighting for independence for Namibia.

Ja Toivo had been sentenced to 20 years on Robben Island but believed he was being held illegally in a foreign country. Swapo refused to accept that Namibia was part of South Africa. As a result, he would take nothing from the government. He ate the food, only in order to avoid starvation and death. But otherwise he refused to receive or send any letters, accept visits, or study. He had no privileges the whole time he was on the island, and he remained in D Group while Mandela and others attained A Group status, so they could study and have more letters and visits and spend more money at the prison tuck shop. He was the strongest – you could say the most stubborn – man you could ever meet.

During the incident when the warders hosed the prisoners down outside and beat them in their cells, several prisoners were badly beaten. Ja Toivo was the only prisoner who hit back, knocking a warder to the floor with one blow. He was beaten in return and forced to clean up his own blood-spattered cell, before being put in isolation as a punishment with no food or exercise. Kathrada has since described that day as 'the worst day in my memory.'

He was trained in guerrilla warfare and would march military-style up and down the courtyard for exercise, clicking his heels as he executed a turn. He would do this for an hour, then stand to attention. His background was in the railway police and he believed in total discipline, but he would not accept it from the South African authorities. He mostly refused to talk to the warders and it was not until years after his release that I realised he was fluent in Afrikaans.

While he was on the island, his 90-year-old mother, who was blind, came over on the ferry. She had insisted on a visit, and he had refused to accept it; he loved his mother, but he would not play by the prison rules.

The head of prison was worried that this old lady would return to the mainland and tell the media that she had been cruelly prevented from seeing her son. So he had her brought into his office and seated her in a chair behind the door. I was summoned and told to bring Ja Toivo to the head of prison's office.

I escorted him there and marched him through the door where his mother was half-hidden. The door closed behind him and the head of prison asked him: 'Why don't you want to see your own mother? She is here for you.'

Ja Toivo looked around and saw her. She was in the traditional dress of the Ovambo tribe, their people. He went over to her and knelt down and took her hand. He kissed her and they talked in their language. It was his first and only visitor on Robben Island.

They should have only spent 30 minutes together, but the

head of prison relented and gave them an hour. The room wasn't bugged, and in any case we didn't know their language.

For me, this was a painful, heartbreaking experience. But when I escorted Ja Toivo back to his cell he was excited, animated, for the first time. He even thanked me.

Yet his stubbornness continued. He was signed off for release in 1984, four years early. By then, he had been transferred to his native Namibia, but he refused to leave the prison. He didn't want any favours from anyone in authority. They had to march him forcibly outside the prison gates and dump him in the road. His Swapo supporters came and picked him up.

When his country won independence in March 1990, he became Minister of Mines and Energy and later, ironically, Minister of Prisons. He was unforgettable, a legend.

In 1998, I was at the ferry embarkation office in Cape Town and spotted him with Kathrada. Kathy asked him: 'Do you remember this man?' and I got a military handshake and a huge hug that lifted me off the ground.

In fact, Ja Toivo was on his way back to Robben Island to show his wife and family where he had been imprisoned. He had arranged a special visit and wanted them to see his cell in B Section and the limestone quarry where he had worked. It was upsetting for him but he returned several times, in an attempt to give himself some sort of closure, I imagine. I told him that I still worked there, in the gift shop of the visitors' centre that opened there after it closed as a prison in 1997. That place was upsetting for all of us, but also finally a vindication of everything they had done and been through. Ja Toivo was the living proof that the attempts to break him and his comrades had failed. Here he was, a huge exuberant character now feted in his own country.

Long afterwards, I was on holiday in Namibia and I'd

brought some books from the visitors' centre at Robben Island that one of his comrades wanted. It was Helao Shityuwete's autobiography, *Never Follow the Wolf*, and he wanted 100 copies that I had in the museum bookshop. Shityuwete had arranged a celebration dinner with all the Swapo veterans of Robben Island, in a restaurant in Windhoek. There were five former prisoners of mine, all greeting me and my wife. Happy to see us, overjoyed and making jokes. I found no bitterness or sadness about them; it was extraordinary.

And Ja Toivo was still in charge. Handed the menu by a waiter, he bellowed: 'I don't want that, I just want meat, bring us all meat!'

He asked me about Mandela and the others. They had been close, finding a way through the layers of political differences between their organisations.

Later, I was driving along a gravel road in Namibia and the police pulled me over for not wearing a seatbelt. The traffic cop was getting difficult and hostile towards me, so I called Ja Toivo. He had a brief chat with the cop, and then it was all smiles and we were on our way.

We've seen each other since, and it's always a great pleasure. What a man, what unbelievable times we shared. Definitely not always happy times, but real and lasting friendships came out of it.

CHAPTER 7

Everyone who ever lived on Robben Island – lepers, slaves, prisoners, and warders – longed to leave. It was tough and isolated on the island, and there was no vestige of family life or comfort. Warders like me had to sign on for a minimum of two years there, but every one of us applied for a transfer as soon as our time was up.

I had applied in 1981, and it took a year before my transfer came through. That suited me in many ways, as I was planning to get married on 13 March 1982 in Cape Town.

My fiancée Estelle and I had brought our wedding date forward because both her parents had died, and she and her brother could not take over the tenancy of the family house in Epping, as she was only 20 and her brother was even younger. The answer was for me to live with them as head of the household.

We had booked the church ceremony and reception and invited the guests, but at the last minute the priest said he couldn't marry a minor without her legal guardian's permission. For us this was a crisis. Estelle had no legal guardian. We quickly applied to the nearest court, at Goodwood, for special permission to marry, and the judge there was totally sympathetic but said it could take weeks to resolve.

He puzzled over the matter for a while with us, then picked up the red phone on the judge's bench and called Pretoria. He took some advice from the Ministry of Justice, then he told us our only way forward was if he formally adopted Estelle. Astonishing as that sounded from a man who had only just met us, he said he could do it that day. He found the forms, and the whole thing took just two hours.

By 11.00 that morning, we walked out of the court with a signed consent form, both of us still stunned by the judge's kindness and our good fortune. We never forgot him and we were sad one day, years later, to read in the newspapers that he had died.

The wedding went ahead as planned, and we had a lovely reception with friends and family. We drove off to a sunshine honeymoon in the coastal resort of Mossel Bay. I was 23 and now had a wife and her younger brother to live with and take care of.

While I'd been on leave, I'd been officially informed of my transfer from Robben Island to Pollsmoor Prison on the mainland in Tokai, a leafy, mainly white residential area of Cape Town. So, after the whirl of chaos around the wedding and setting up a new home as a married man, I found myself on the familiar ferry boat on my way to Robben Island to collect my belongings.

I was officially off duty, so I had no way to say goodbye to the men in B Section. I packed up my things, my uniform and my fishing rods, in the single warders' quarters, and happily turned my back for the last time on the pervasive fishy smell of my shared room.

I looked back at the bleak prison building as we drove down the rough track to the harbour. As I sat outside waiting for the ferry for the last time, I had the strangest mix of feelings. I was glad to be starting a new life, but I realised I was heart-sore to leave behind a group of men who had been almost like family to me. And I hadn't even had a chance to say goodbye.

There were some warders arriving with the ferry, so I asked them to be sure to give my greetings to Mandela and the old guys in B Section. I didn't really have the words to send a proper message. What was there to say? That I'm so happy to be leaving this godforsaken place, but I'm going to miss you? They wouldn't even pass on a sentimental message like that. So we set off across the water, and I got hold of myself and put my mind to what lay ahead – my first night shift at Pollsmoor. Estelle and I were living in the Cape Town suburb of Goodwood, so I was able to easily drive to the prison. It wasn't a prospect I was looking forward to. I knew its reputation. It housed the toughest gangsters in South Africa. The three main prison gangs – comprising about 600 men – were segregated on one floor to stop them recruiting new arrivals. These men were known as the numbers guys – the notorious 26s, the 27s, and the 28s, still a huge problem to this day.

They were mostly mixed-race guys from deeply deprived areas around Mitchells Plain where drug-taking, violent crime, and unemployment are still rife. Members would have their whole bodies, including their faces, tattooed to show their ranking in the gangs, so that even outside prison their status was clear.

Pollsmoor housed more than 3,000 prisoners, a mix of those awaiting trial, hardened re-offenders, and murderers serving life, including some in solitary confinement. It all took me back to my nightmare days of training at Kroonstad. The difference I saw on my arrival at Pollsmoor was that there were now coloured warders working with us whites. There was even a black African warder, although we were all separated for the daily inspection parades.

I dreaded the gangs and felt apprehensive about which

section I would be posted to. I hadn't been told which men I'd be looking after. But on the first night that I reported for duty I was taken by surprise.

I was told to draw a firearm because I was going out with a sergeant and ten others on a special mission. We were put in the back of two trucks, with a car escort, and told we'd be collecting prisoners. We had no idea where we were going.

As dusk fell, we drove through the suburbs and onto the motorway. I realised we were going towards Cape Town's waterfront, the shipyard where ferries came in from Robben Island. Today this is a tourists' mecca, known as the Victoria & Alfred Waterfront, a glamorous mix of shopping malls, cinemas, restaurants, and wine bars. Back then, it was a cheerless place with ships in dry dock for repairs and the busy comings and goings of a working port.

Clearly, we were picking up prisoners being brought over under cover of darkness. As some of the warders stood in a cordon, on guard in every direction, I was told to help unload stuff from the ferry.

And there they were – Mandela, Mlangeni, Sisulu, and Mhlaba – all walking towards me from the shadows, looking worried and mistrustful. They stared at me as they passed, and we said nothing.

They were loaded into a truck, while I rode in the vehicle behind them. It took 40 minutes to get back to Pollsmoor. My thoughts were spinning.

As the men were unloaded, they were surrounded by warders and I noticed they weren't wearing handcuffs or leg chains. There were so many security measures surrounding them, it just wasn't necessary. It was completely dark by now so the spotlights were on, and dog-handlers stood at the ready. All the warders chosen for this special delivery to Pollsmoor were white. The authorities didn't want coloureds or Africans to see these big guys from the ANC.

Each of them was carrying a cardboard box with his belongings. Now they half-greeted me, just a slight nod of the head and an anxious smile of trepidation.

We took them up to the top floor, the rooftop of the prison. They were marched into one big cell with a side door. There was a huge glass window with bars built into it. They couldn't see out, but warders patrolling the corridors could see in.

Inside, there were four beds made up with pillows, sheets, and blankets. For the first time for nearly 20 years, these men would not be sleeping on a cold concrete floor. In addition, there was no toilet bucket, and instead there was a separate shower and a flushing toilet.

We showed them in and then I went outside, closing the grille. As I went, I said quietly to Mlangeni: 'I've got married now, and I've been transferred here. Like you, this is my first night. If you need anything, you can knock on the window and I'll be there.'

My shift lasted until midnight, then a second shift took over, led by another warder who knew them. We worked out that this was a secret operation. The terrorists from Robben Island, the lifers, were not to be seen by any other prisoners. There would be no visitors, not even warders from other sections. They were to be kept totally isolated.

A solid steel door and a further grille opened on to the rooftop. That was to be their exercise yard. It was about five metres wide, with solid surrounding walls and a view of tree-clad mountains beyond. You could see the famous Elephant's Eye cave, a favourite hiking spot in the Table Mountain range.

As soon as Mandela had a chance, he asked me: 'Why have we been brought here? What is this about?'

I told him that we hadn't been informed, but that we warders had discussed it and thought we had worked it out. 'I think you're going home soon, you are closer to that now,' I said. That is what I truly believed, but I was quite wrong.

Within weeks, we began to realise that the imprisoned leaders of the ANC had been influencing and recruiting the younger guys on Robben Island, and the authorities wanted them to completely disappear. They were to be kept in isolation, never seen or heard by others. Their whole world from now on would be on the rooftop of Pollsmoor Prison.

Six months later, Kathrada arrived too. He had taken over Mandela's role as leader back on B Section and had begun encouraging other prisoners to study and to learn about the ANC. He came to join Mandela and the others in their strange new world. This was where the government planned to break the ANC spirit once and for all.

There was a new guy too. Patrick Maqubela, a lawyer in his thirties, turned up one day out of the blue. They hadn't wanted him to serve his sentence on Robben Island because he would be able to advise others about their rights and cause trouble.

Now there were five beds in the communal cell, and I could tell the old guys didn't like it. They were suspicious of Maqubela; they'd never heard of him. We were listening in to Mandela's legal consultations once again, and we heard him asking about Maqubela's background. They heard he'd been practising law in Pietermaritzburg and was an activist serving 20 years for terrorism.

Walter Sisulu, in his wisdom, took the guy under his wing, ordering cigarettes for him because he was a lower-grade prisoner and couldn't get them for himself, befriending him and probing for information.

Maqubela registered for studies, wanting to do a higher degree in law. He registered for five subjects, and Mandela was soon telling me: 'This young chap, he never studies properly, he'll never get enough work done to pass five subjects. He's spending all his time playing table tennis.'

But Maqubela passed his exams, and by now he was accepted as one of them. He was bright, and Mandela told me he felt sorry that this young man had to put up with living with them, old and grey as they were.

Maqubela himself found it hard to adjust to the prospect of many years inside. He told me: 'Mr Brand, 20 years is too long, I'll never survive it.' He was often down and depressed.

But I told him: 'No, 20 years will fly by if you copy Mandela's ways and fill your day with activity. He and his comrades have already nearly done 20 years, and look at them.'

Patrick Maqubela later became a judge in the Western Cape High Court. Sadly he was murdered by his wife in early 2013. By now, the days really were filled with activity. Once we were inside the section, no one could see us, not even the prison officers. The main steel door could only be opened from the inside, so no one could arrive and take us by surprise.

We had table tennis equipment, and an area marked out as a tennis court, an exercise bike, weights, and sports clothing, all donated by the International Red Cross. They also sent an entire set of the *Encyclopaedia Britannica*, a brilliant resource for prisoners doing studies. Today I have installed the encyclopaedias at the Robben Island Museum.

I began to actually look forward to my shift. It was hot up on the roof in summer, and we were all flying around playing competitive table-tennis and tennis.

I would take off my prison uniform jacket and play table tennis stripped to the waist. The prisoners wore white singlets. The keys to the section and the cell would be left somewhere nearby, as no one was going to escape. That would have meant running down several flights of stairs into the arms of guards with dogs and handguns. Besides, life was okay up there in the rooftop world I was sharing with a bunch of the country's most notorious terrorists.

Andrew Mlangeni was the king of the table-tennis tournaments, but sometimes I could beat him. He liked to give the warders a thrashing, but it was all done with good humour. Mlangeni liked to win; he used to goad us and call us beginners. He and the others became brilliant at spinning the ball. You would watch like a hawk as it came flying towards you then took off in a completely unexpected direction. Mandela was also very good – I liked to partner him when we played doubles. They used to want the pairs to be one prisoner, one warder. We all accommodated each other, and we had a lot of fun.

The tennis pitch itself was narrow, and the floor was made of concrete slabs. The prisoners had applied in writing for court markings, and some of the criminal prisoners had been sent up to paint the white lines.

The Red Cross obliged again with tennis racquets, poles, and a net. Mandela was an excellent player. Tall, slim and fit, he had long arms and would stand there, relaxed, at his end of the court just blocking the balls I served him. I would be haring around at the other end and he would just stand there, leaning over a little to just bat back the balls. It was maddening really, but great exercise.

If an officer arrived on the outside and had to be allowed in, there was a ready-made excuse for my sweaty appearance. I would just have time to put my jacket back on, do up the required three buttons, and get my cap on my head before unlocking the steel door. The sun beat mercilessly down on the white-painted walls, and soon the officer would be sweatingtoo.

On the day Mandela finally left Pollsmoor, he didn't want to leave the tennis racquets and the exercise bike behind. He knew they wouldn't go to other prisoners; the authorities would snaffle them up on sight. So he gave them to me, and I still have them at home. Extraordinary mementoes of extraordinary times.

But elsewhere in Pollsmoor some horrendously violent incidents were taking place, and occasionally they spilled into our rarefied world. I was standing with Mandela on the rooftop one day when there was a hell of a noise starting up nearby – blood-curdling screams and dogs barking. We could see something like 30 or more prisoners climbing up the grille towards the roof.

Mandela was very alarmed. 'Mr Brand, what's happening here? What's wrong with these men?'

I told him we should leave, and I quickly got him back inside the cell with the others and then reported to the head of prison that the ANC prisoners had witnessed an uprising. The next day, new solid steel doors were erected to block out all views from our section.

There were often small uprisings like these in the main section of the prison, and violence was commonplace. Occasionally, despite the warders' best efforts, one prisoner would be killed by another and in response there would be a 'carry-on': an intervention by armed warders when a murder had taken place among the gangs and no one would own up to it. The corpse would be removed from the cell, and twice as many warders as prisoners would crowd in there with dogs and batons. They were solid rubber batons called tonfas. Warders would aim at the prisoners' heads and bodies, trying to break bones.

It was the prison's brutal way of getting real information. The carry-on would be accompanied by much shouting and noise. I hated it, but I was familiar with this method of enforcing confession. The idea was to beat the truth out of all of them until the murderer was revealed. Otherwise, the whole cell-full would go to court and probably get life sentences.

A typical method of gang murder, which I once witnessed myself, was when one of the new recruits was ordered to kill and mutilate a chosen victim, slicing his chest open with a knife and removing his heart, so that he could eat it in front of the gang.

Another time at Pollsmoor, when I was helping with duties in the section where hardened criminals were kept, I had opened a cell door and found a severed head on the toilet bucket. Seven prisoners had carried out the murder, cutting up the body and flushing the mutilated parts away.

By contrast, my prisoners – the men considered the most dangerous in the world – were reading encyclopaedias, studying for their exams, and knocking a table-tennis ball about in the sunshine.

After several months, the political prisoners were told they were being transferred to the other side of the roof, because the authorities needed more space for punishment cells for prisoners to be put in solitary confinement.

By now attached to their space and their bearable life, the men were anxious when they heard about this. But they were all put in another big communal cell, and the daily routine continued.

Mandela was still studying and taking exams, but he was finding it painful to write. He was developing arthritis in his hands and they would become numb, especially during a three-hour exam. The doctor gave him medication and a prescription he could send to UNISA, requesting more time for exams. Eventually, the message came back that he was allowed an extra 20 minutes for each hour. I was the invigilator, so I made sure Mandela could stay when others had finished. Exam days could be complicated, with coloured prisoners having to write their exams separately from blacks. Trevor Manuel, a coloured man who was a celebrity prisoner as he was a leading member of the United Democratic Front, in Pollsmoor without charge or trial, was also keen to study. I would invigilate his exams in the mornings and Mandela's in the afternoons.

On Sundays, we had visits from a priest. Because Mandela was a Methodist, he had a church ceremony of his own in the visiting room. The Reverend Moore, from Stellenbosch, was a kind man who turned up in a suit to avoid any fuss. He would pick up the Bible and read a passage while they sat close to each other. He chose special passages that referred to good men who were punished for their beliefs. Then he gave a short sermon and they prayed together, Mandela lowering his head and closing his eyes.

The priest told Mandela news about his church and congregation, some of whom were being detained or were activist leaders in the community. I always had to interject at that point and warn him not to give names. So he sent their greetings to Mandela without naming them.

Reverend Moore told Mandela that the whole church congregation prayed for him regularly. Then he would give him

Holy Communion, after unpacking a small white cloth from his bag and setting his things on the table. The communion was a wafer and a sip of grape juice. Even if I had wanted to join in, it was not allowed. We were not supposed to share food or drink with prisoners, although there had certainly been times I had done so before.

Later, when Mandela was in isolation, the priest continued to visit, and I think it helped him. He was grateful for anything that gave him added strength.

Of course, even in these improved circumstances in Pollsmoor, Mandela was still busy writing demands and complaints to the head of prison. He even complained to Winnie. He told her he was not getting his Pantene hair oil any more. That was an important part of his personal preparation each day. He still put it on the shopping order to give me each month, but international sanctions meant that supplies had dried up.

Winnie, in fighting mood, complained to liberal politician Helen Suzman – a great supporter of the Rivonians and for 13 years the only member of South Africa's Parliament unequivocally opposed to apartheid. She took it up in Parliament, and I got orders from on high: find some Pantene hair oil for Mandela, wherever you have to go and whatever you have to do to get it. The order came right down from the Minister of Prison Services in Pretoria to the Commissioner of Prisons and down to the head of Pollsmoor. He called me into his office and told me to take a prison car to trawl around the pharmacies. 'Don't come back without it,' he said.

I usually bought 100ml bottles from the local Checkers supermarket, but those supplies had long gone. I drove over to the distribution warehouse in Cape Town, but they had sold out and did not expect to receive any more. The hair oil came from America, and that country was no longer trading with South Africa.

In the end, I went to about twenty pharmacies all over the city and outskirts, but I only found six bottles. I bought all of them, and Mandela was happy to pay for them. I wondered if it pleased him that we were running all over town for him.

Years later, on his 80th birthday, when he was president of the country, I got together with Kathrada and the other Rivonians to tease him about the hair oil one last time. We made up a gigantic card in the shape of a Pantene bottle and we all signed it. We were all invited to the presidential residence in Pretoria for his birthday party, so we took it with us and set it up on the veranda in front of the grand front entrance. I had three bottles of the hair oil packaged in a white box with a pretty ribbon and presented it to Mandela as a joint birthday present from all of us. Kathrada had hunted down the card and the hair oil from America. We brought Mandela outside and made a ceremony of it in front of the big card. He was very tickled, very happy that we had thought of something so personal that went all the way back to his prison memories.

I realised that nothing would ever take away what we had all been through together, and that it must have meant something because there we all were, still good friends and laughing together.

In Pollsmoor, the Pantene hair oil incident made Mandela aware that he had some small control over things. He sent in another written complaint to the head of prison, with a request. He said it was tedious for the prisoners to be looking at cement walls every day, with mountains far away in the background. They wanted some greenery of their own. He wanted to make a garden again.

The authorities would consider his requests and accommodate them if it was no trouble. They wanted the ANC leaders to just wilt and die up there, not to cause problems, so this was an easy way of keeping them quiet. Permission was duly granted, and the authorities sent up 15 forty-four-gallon drums cut in half, producing 30 big flower-pots, to be placed on the roof and wedged in with bricks. I worked with some of the criminal prisoners to bring up soil from the Pollsmoor prison gardens, although, of course, they had no idea who was going to be using these makeshift plant-pots. Mandela and Sisulu would patiently mix manure with the soil to start their vegetable plot.

Mandela grew tomatoes, onions, and aubergines. He tried to grow mealies – the maize cobs that made pap, the African staple diet – but it wasn't successful as a garden plant. He and I remembered fields of mealies that our parents planted when we were kids, and we compared the different methods of making rows, his country memories coming from the Eastern Cape and mine from the farm I grew up on in the Western Cape.

When insects attacked the crops, Mandela asked for a visit from the sergeant warder in charge of Pollsmoor's gardens. He came and sprayed against insects and diseases and warned us not to eat anything from the plot for a few weeks. I drilled some holes and fixed up netting to protect the plants.

Mandela was a good gardener. He would send shiny purple aubergines down to the kitchen to be baked with meat and made into stew. He persuaded the prison gardener to give him spinach bedding plants, and they were very successful. After this, he would often send a bunch of spinach down to the kitchen too, and they would put it with the meat and aubergines. We had a great feast on those days. The pot of food would arrive, and they invited us warders to help ourselves first. They would then take theirs into their cell.

In Pollsmoor, I used to tease Mandela about the way he chewed his chicken bones after a meal, to get the last little bit of taste out of them. There would be nothing left afterwards. I told him: 'You'll never be able to keep a dog, because you're eating all the bones.'

The prisoners had tables for eating and studying in the cell, and chairs and a steel cabinet each for their things. They ate together around a big table, and there was always a huge pot of tea. I would be invited to help myself to a cup, but it was too sweet for me; they loved a lot of sugar in their tea.

Mandela and the others had their own special diets. He ate steamed fish or chicken most days, unless he had organised the spinach and aubergine stew. However, he was being seen regularly by a medical officer, and it was decided that he should try to lower his cholesterol. The Red Cross was monitoring medical reports, so Pollsmoor was doing it by the book. Despite this, sometimes Mandela would smell other appetising food, like the soya mince given to other prisoners, and ask for that. I had to keep it secret that I was smuggling food that wasn't on his special diet, otherwise the medical team would intervene.

Mandela also made his own cottage cheese. I think it was something from his childhood. He would put fresh milk in the cupboard and wait until it was sour and watery. Then he took the thick pieces off and ate it on bread with Aromat, a salty seasoning. He drank the water and said it was good for his health.

No other section of the prison knew what was being sent up to us, so, after all the years of semi-starvation on Robben Island, there was suddenly too much food. We put the leftovers to one side to give to the criminal prisoners who were delivering and collecting food pots. They could eat it later in the kitchen. Sometimes Mandela complained. His chicken was grilled instead of steamed, or it was all too salty. I called up the prisoner who cooked the food, the guy who did all the special diets. His name was Louw, a coloured man, whom Mandela liked and for whom he would sometimes order cigarettes or tobacco. Louw was a repeat offender who was in for continual break-ins and robberies. He was released one day but he had no family to go to, so he broke into a house near the prison so he could come back.

I heard years later that an old warder took pity on him when he was next released, and brought him to live with his family. In return, he did jobs around the house and garden and cooked the food. But his kindly benefactors all died in a tragic drowning accident, and once again Louw was homeless. He carried out more break-ins and went back to prison. When the food pots were empty, one of the prisoners would tell us and we summoned guys from the kitchen to fetch them. One day, I threw away a sandwich left over from the lunch-box my wife had made for me. It was wholewheat, something Mandela had never seen before. He ate it and enjoyed it.

I told him what the grains were, and he was intrigued. The next day, he wanted wholewheat bread. But the head of prison said he couldn't just order as if it was a restaurant, he would have to apply in writing.

By then, it was part of my job to go shopping for the special prisoners in my care. On Robben Island, they had written lists of things they wanted from the tuck shop, and I would take the money from the float that we kept in the reception office where all withdrawals were meticulously recorded.

Now I was actually doing their shopping. I would take my

motorbike and go to the local Checkers supermarket once a month and check the price of everything on their list. This was important, as they were still only allowed to spend R25 a month. Then we reviewed their orders together, and I drew out their money and took a prison van back to Checkers in the Blue Route mall to collect the shopping. I had to use a different supermarket basket for each of them so that I could pay for their things separately and come back with the receipts for them to sign.

I bought coffee for Kathrada and Sisulu, and they made some for me and offered me Ouma rusks with it. These were biscuits Mandela loved too. He always wanted the muesli rusks. He bought Sensodyne toothpaste, and all of them wanted Oral-B toothbrushes.

Now Mandela was asking for five loaves of wholewheat bread each month, and neither of us had any idea what that would cost. I found myself walking up and down the supermarket aisle, making a note of all the grocery prices.

The next problem was how we should keep the bread fresh, as it had to last Mandela the whole month. So I began taking it home to put in my freezer. Every second day, I would bring him a quarter of a loaf, already sliced. When I went on leave it was a problem, but then he just had to wait for my return.

I also took Mandela's letters out to post on a daily basis. The other warders saw me on my motorbike and sneered. 'You're doing too much running around for these kaffirs,' they said. 'We've got 500 prisoners on our section to count and dish up for and clean up after every day. You've only got six of them, and they've got you running off to do their shopping.'

They were quite bitter, jealous of our VIP prisoners. They began asking if they could see them, see what was so special about these old guys in the High Command. But I wouldn't let anyone sneak in. We had a good relationship, a good routine with no big problems going on and no violence. I didn't want to allow anything that might upset that.

There was just once that Mandela had to break up a screaming match between the warrant officer warder Terreblanche and Andrew Mlangeni, but it didn't get physical. They were standing in the doorway of the cell, shouting and swearing. Mandela came along and took Mlangeni away, and I saw them talking quietly in a corner. Mandela apologised to Terreblanche afterwards, but he refused to talk to Mlangeni for a long time after that.

I asked Mandela if it was all okay. He said: 'We are politicians, not criminals. We should never argue with the warders. We should debate, not scream and fight. If there is anything wrong, we should sort it out between ourselves, not involve the warders.'

Mlangeni could be argumentative, though. He was in charge of table-tennis balls and other equipment. If someone damaged the balls, he wouldn't let them have any more. Mandela had to put his foot down to get some for our next game. Small battles, but Mandela would assert himself and re-establish leadership every time.

When the authorities at last allowed them a radio, Mlangeni decided he would have it for himself. He took it away and pleading from the others was making no difference. Mandela stepped in. 'This is important for all of us,' he said quietly. 'We all need to hear the news and find out what is happening in the country. And we all need each other. Now give me the radio, and let's agree to put it somewhere so we can all listen.' Mlangeni handed it over.

It was a small, sulky incident, but I think that sort of thing was inevitable in the artificially close community they were living in. Always it was Mandela who defused the situation. He was not going to allow petty behaviour to undo the greater good for which they were working.

We had become an unlikely family up there, isolated from other prisoners and officers. We even watched movies together, which they chose and paid for. I fetched two films a week for them in town – they were no longer being censored, so we had a much bigger choice. Mlangeni liked to be in charge of the projector, just as he was in charge of the sports equipment.

But, when it came to it, they knew I was really the one in charge. I liked to go home early on a Friday, so I would lock them up before time. Mlangeni and Kathrada called me Mr Lock-Up, grumbling that they had lost half an hour.

Occasionally, there was so much going on – chess games and dominoes or cards, and table-tennis and tennis – that Mandela craved some peace and quiet to get on with his studies. I agreed to lock him in an empty office on his own when he wanted to get away from the others. But one day I left him for a long time, and he was angry when I returned. He had needed to urinate and had to use the window. He demanded a bucket of water to clean it up. Later he apologised to me, but it was clear he didn't take humiliation kindly.

Often he would wrap himself in his cell blanket, fastened with the pin I got him from Robben Island, and sit in a corner of the roof courtyard with his books. He used prison mats to keep his feet warm and sat there even in the wind and cold.

CHAPTER 8

Life was undoubtedly much sweeter for all of us now that we had made a virtual social club out of our rooftop hideaway at Pollsmoor. Mandela and his comrades at last had plentiful food and healthy activities to fill their days. All of them were getting more visits and letters so their outlook was less bleak, and we were isolated from the violence and gang problems that racked the rest of the prison – indeed, our comings and goings remained a total secret to everyone else. For me, guarding them had become such a calm and rewarding ritual that I welcomed every shift.

But there were terrible and ominous storms rumbling all around us in the outside world, where hundreds of thousands of oppressed black people were increasingly defying the apartheid laws.

We had an FM radio, which the ANC leaders could now listen to uncensored. In 1982, a few months after they arrived at Pollsmoor, the prisoners heard, and grieved over, news of a mass killing of 42 of their Umkhonto we Sizwe commandos, along with women and children, in neighbouring Lesotho, and of the bombing of South Africa's Koeberg nuclear power station in retaliation.

That same year, Mandela heard that his house had been raided by police and all the family's books destroyed. A few months later, a massive ANC car bomb at South Africa's military headquarters in Pretoria killed 19 people and injured more than 200. The military wing's acts of sabotage, widely touted as intending to destroy only government installations, were now causing casualties.

By now my wife and I were living in a staff house at Pollsmoor Prison, and we had our first child, a boy we called Riaan. We were increasingly aware of the danger around us so I bought myself a firearm, a .38 Special, to carry at all times when we were away from home. Occasionally, I had to escort the government bus that took children to and from schools in case it came under fire.

I knew our country was burning. I longed to take my family and move back to the platteland, the countryside, to find some safety and peace. It was obvious that South Africa could be heading for civil war.

By 1983, the authorities were targeting the many political organisations affiliated to the United Democratic Front – a coalition of non-racial anti-apartheid organisations, sharing Mandela's dreams, which had been launched that year. Their members were arriving by the hundred at Pollsmoor, and the nearby Victor Verster Prison was also overcrowded. I saw many of my former Robben Island prisoners coming back, having been re-arrested.

One day after my work shift, I was driving across Cape Town to visit my parents. My wife and I had little Riaan with us, and we got stuck in heavy traffic near the University of Cape Town. It was terrifying: thousands of students were protesting in the road and were in a pitched battle with the police. While they chanted and threw stones, the police responded with water cannons and rubber bullets. It was clear that now, before undertaking any journey, I had to think about the exact route and the possible dangers.

Sanctions against South Africa meant that we couldn't travel abroad, even if we had been able to afford it. No one wanted us. Many African countries that sympathised with the ANC refused visas to South African whites, and our vision of Europe was that it was a part of the world that hated us. We had become pariahs. I could see where it was all heading. I was thinking that a change must come, that there should be justice and a decent life for everyone of all colours. Mandela was the man to do it, to lead us all to a peaceful solution. It seemed bizarre that I was spending most of my days quietly with him and his comrades, and the rest of my time plunged into terrifying danger and chaos.

Prison warders were of course major targets of black anger. My colleagues whose homes were outside Pollsmoor told me about using blast tape on all the windows of their houses to protect against hand grenades or bomb attacks.

It was a chaotic time, when everyone – both white and black – was living in a danger zone with no visible way out. By now, the government was sending police and troops into every township where protests and demonstrations were taking place, firing teargas and live bullets. The death toll on all sides was mounting.

Mandela and his fellow prisoners felt powerless. Leaders of a great movement that had justice on its side, supported by international organisations the world over, and they were unable to carry out their life's work – to lead.

I saw them increasingly worried, huddled together to discuss strategies and encouragement they might be able to pass on through briefings with their lawyers, their only channel to the outside. Unlike Robben Island, in Pollsmoor, there were no prisoners arriving and leaving whom they could use to smuggle out messages or instructions.

This, we knew by now, was why they had been moved. The apartheid government had successfully cut off the head of the troublesome ANC. Now they were just growing older, totally under the control of the government, impotent.

But other news was also coming through. That same year, 1983, the prestigious University of London made Mandela a life member of its students' union. Local authorities in England were naming streets and parks after him. Glasgow gave him the Freedom of the City. He was given honorary citizenship of Rome and of Olympia, in Greece. That autumn, the British Labour Party invited him to be the key speaker at its annual party conference, a fantasy of course, but one that held a message: decent-minded people in the West were campaigning for his release. He was far from forgotten.

The ANC had successfully promoted Mandela's name as the hero of its party, the man at the centre of its hope for a fair, non-racial South Africa where all could live in peace. His name was on banners and posters and public buildings in the whole of the free world.

Release Mandela committees were forming everywhere. Protestors had been holding a constant vigil for several years outside the South African embassy in London's Trafalgar Square. Mandela was presented, in his absence, with the Bruno Kreisky award for merit in the field of human rights, in Vienna, Austria. UNESCO awarded him the prestigious Simon Bolivar International Prize, jointly with King Juan Carlos of Spain. And in New York City the square in front of the South African mission was renamed Nelson and Winnie Mandela Plaza.

But the stated purpose of his life, as well as of Sisulu,

Kathrada, Mhlaba, Mlangeni, and Motsoaledi – and Mbeki and others still on Robben Island – was to take the struggle all the way to victory. Instead they were there with me, playing table-tennis. Mandela was nevertheless pressing on with his Afrikaans language studies, and I often insisted on speaking to him only in that tongue. In return, he taught me some Xhosa. I would say '*ukutya kusetafileni*' when the food was on the table. And '*ukutya kuyaba*', the food is ready. I announced their daily medication as '*amayaze*', and one of the other sergeants would greet them, like me, with '*molo*'.

We played jokes too. It was partly the boredom, partly an increasing sense that we were all in this together and it was okay to have some gentle fun. For example, when the prisoners were locked up, we warders could look through the one-way window and see if they were using the toilet. We could flush it from the outside, so we thought that was very comical. When they protested, we said, 'No, sorry this is an automatic device, nothing to do with us.'

In the prison office, I was getting parcels addressed to Mandela from all over the world, many containing medicine and pills that people knew he could not get in prison. Some of them had Latin or French names so I asked Ebrahim Rasool, a multilingual ANC activist who had been detained without charge, to help me translate them. We found all sorts of unsuitable things – for example, some pills that were the precursors to Viagra, to enhance sexual performance. There was no way I would give that to men locked up and deprived of any contact with women. Of course, some of the warders were happy to relieve me of them.

Ebrahim, who later became South Africa's ambassador to Washington, has joked with me about it many times since. I still visit his elderly mother in Cape Town and talk about old times. Their family was among thousands devastated by the Group Areas Act, which literally bulldozed homes in the city's District Six to make it a whites-only area.

Ebrahim remembers with pain the day in 1972, when he was 10 years old, when he came home from school to find all the family's furniture on the pavement and his father desperately looking for a way to get it to another place because the house was about to be demolished. He has written of how 'my parents' sadness and the loss of community has stayed with me throughout my life'.

In Pollsmoor, visits were still the most important events in the prisoners' lives. There had been none allowed in the first month, and that was a cause of huge anxiety. Now the prison had devised a secret route to the visiting booths where we could take them without others seeing them.

The booths had bigger glass panels than on Robben Island, so that prisoners and visitors could see each other from head to foot. Two visitors were now allowed, for forty minutes. Winnie was no longer under house arrest, and she could get to Pollsmoor more easily.

By 1983, the regulations had softened slightly and prisoners were allowed contact visits, though only with their first-degree family members, which meant their wives or children or parents. Kathrada had a problem, because he had a brother but no other first-degree family. We fixed it so that his friends could apply as first-degree and they too could have contact visits with him. We had a tricky time over his nephew Cassiem's wedding. Kathrada's extended family, with its deeply held Indian bonds and its respect and love for him, desperately wanted to make him part of the occasion. But there was no way 60 people could possibly come for a visit. So I fixed it that the bride and bridegroom, resplendent in their wedding clothes, could sit in the visiting room with him and the rest had to walk through quickly, just stopping briefly to greet a delighted Kathrada. The entire wedding party drifted past him like a beautiful fashion show, with him as guest of honour.

On another occasion Kathrada's lawyer, Ramesh Vassen, had his little daughter with him, and she would not remain in the car while her father visited Kathy on a legal matter. The warders in charge relented and allowed Priys to come in with her father. Throughout what was supposed to be a legal visit, Kathrada was completely overwhelmed, and he kept talking to the child and even stroking her hair. It was his first real contact with a child for over 20 years.

There was a special treat for Mandela too, once these contact visits were allowed. On 12 May 1984, I was told to escort him down from the roof section for a visit with Winnie but he had to come to a room next to the office, not to the usual visiting booths.

I had no idea what was happening; I just waited with him in there while another warder went to fetch Winnie. He had told her what to expect as he delivered her to the room, but Mandela and I were to be taken by surprise.

Suddenly, Winnie was walking through the door and putting her arms around him. Mandela, usually so correct and controlled, was completely overwhelmed. He hugged and kissed her and was nervous and jittery in a way I had never seen before.

It was his first official contact visit since he had been imprisoned. Once, on Robben Island, a warder had allowed Mandela to kiss her briefly, but other than that this was the first time he was able to hold his wife in his arms for 21 years. They sat down, still holding hands, and they were happy and laughing, not sure how to handle this unexpected situation.

It was extremely emotional. For me it was like watching a couple on their first date. Winnie looked beautiful, all dressed up. Mandela was thrown completely off balance. He had his notebook and pencil as usual, but he didn't know what to do with them. He tried to get the conversation under control, but he was totally lovelorn. He just wanted to look into her eyes.

I felt like an intruder. I knew I shouldn't be a witness to this love affair happening in front of my eyes. I didn't know where to look or what to do. It felt indecent.

I had to let them know there was just five minutes left. Mandela immediately asked for a double visit: 80 minutes. He didn't want to let her go, even if it meant forfeiting a future visit. Of course, the room was bugged as usual, but I don't think the security police benefited from a single mention of any politics that day.

Afterwards, Winnie told the media excitedly that she had at last been able to hug her husband. Journalists were always waiting when she had a visit; they were there when she arrived and there when she came out, hungry for news of Mandela.

Meanwhile, I was escorting him back to the section. His friends looked up and saw his eyes sparkling. They thought perhaps he had brought something special, maybe a pot of jam, which would be a cause for celebration. Instead, he told them his amazing news.

Next time Winnie came, Mandela asked me if he could take her some chocolate. I used to buy him Cadbury's milk chocolate slabs in the supermarket with his money, and it would be eked out square by square. I said he could give some to her, and that became a little habit of theirs, something to share at last.

But Winnie unfortunately decided she could visit any time she felt like it, and there was always a willing media audience tagging along with her, hanging on to her every word and listening to her complaints when it didn't work out. Many times I was called to the front gate by the guard in the security kiosk. Winnie would be there, all dressed up and wanting a visit.

If it was a weekday, there was no leeway at all. I could not let her in. Visits were only allowed at weekends. She would tell me: 'I've got very important urgent news. I can't come tomorrow, I have to be in Joburg. I need to see him now.'

I would tell her firmly that it was impossible, and there would be shouting and screaming: 'I want to see my husband!' Then she would go back outside to the media, gesticulating at the prison: 'You see these people are refusing my rights!'

I used to tell her: 'Ma'am, I would love to help you, but these are instructions from the top.' Even if she came at weekends, sometimes Mandela's quota for the month would already be full and there would be no way I could let Winnie in. At that time, Mandela was allowed up to five visits a month, but a maximum of thirty for the year. Lawyers had to have special permission to come, although their consultations were not deducted from the quota. They had to say what their agenda was, whether it was a family matter or perhaps a court order. Their applications were sometimes turned down.

Despite this, all of the prisoners were enjoying slight relaxations of the rules compared to the restrictions on Robben Island. Walter Sisulu wanted to give his visitors tea, so he applied to buy a kettle and some cups, and that was approved. But the noise of the kettle interfered with our bugs, so we used to boil the water before his visits. He kept powdered milk, tea, and coffee, and he would always make an extra cup for the warder monitoring the visit. Sometimes I made the tea while he talked to his visitor.

I was in charge of sending off the tape-recordings to the security police after all visits. They came a couple of times a week, and I was meant to hand over all the recordings. But I had my own way of joining in this softening of the rules. I let a friend of Kathrada's visit, the daughter of prominent anti-apartheid activist Fatima Meer. Yasmin Shehnaz Meer was a lawyer – later a judge – married to a white advocate. That visit was very useful to Kathrada, and I had booked her in as his niece, so it all looked straightforward. I never sent off the recordings of their conversations. By then I was keeping quite a lot of secrets, forming some personal judgements that made perfect sense to me then and still do today.

For example, the head of prison ordered me to be wired up with a recording device so they could put Mandela's strength of mind to the test. I had a tiny microphone attached to a button on my prison jacket with a wire leading inside to a battery in my pocket. I was to try to undermine him by suggesting that Winnie was having affairs with other men. They knew that was his most vulnerable emotion, his love and adoration of his wife. I was given the question to ask: 'Mandela, how would you feel if you heard that Winnie was seeing someone else while you're in here unable to do anything about it, if she was sleeping with other men?'

I had to somehow let him know I was bugged. Aside from other considerations, I was afraid he would chat about playing table-tennis and we'd both be in trouble. When I approached Mandela, I showed him the microphone and also touched my ear to signal others were listening. I didn't want him to miss the clue and get this wrong. He stayed perfectly calm. 'Mr Brand, I would have to accept that. She is a beautiful woman, and she has needs. I love her enough to accept anything she does.'

Afterwards, I decided it was time to share another secret with him. We had an understanding, we trusted each other. And I had been keeping a secret for a considerable time. For four months, I had had three special prisoners on a section of the rooftop screened off from Mandela and the other Rivonians.

These men were considered public enemies. They were activists who had caused so much trouble that they were being 'disappeared'. They had never been charged or tried, or sentenced. They had just been removed from society and were being held at Pollsmoor without their lawyers, their families, or their colleagues or political associates knowing whether they were dead or alive.

Their leader was Matthew Goniwe, a teacher in his early thirties, made from the same mould as Mandela. He was educated, intelligent, and well mannered, a man of iron will and an unshakeable sense of justice. I liked and admired him.

Goniwe was kept in a single cell in his own clothes – two tracksuits that he had brought with him – and he was allowed no privileges at all. No money to buy food, no study, no books. He was given a Bible and allowed one visit a week, from a judge whose job was to report on his prison conditions. I was not allowed to speak his name or tell other prisoners or warders that he was there. Goniwe and his two comrades were not allowed to communicate with each other either, but they emptied the water from the toilet bowls and spoke to each other through the pipes. Goniwe had been a brilliant teacher in the Eastern Cape, leading protests about school conditions for black children and fellow teachers. He had a huge following, so the intelligence services picked him up one day from a meeting and spirited him away to the other side of the country, to my rooftop domain.

He was allowed one hour's exercise per day, and he did yoga. He could stand still the whole time in a chosen position. He would pick through the meagre food rations and discard anything stodgy. He was totally disciplined.

I told him confidentially that he was being kept just yards away from his revolutionary leaders, his heroes. One day, I managed to keep the solid security gate between their sections open a fraction so that he could greet Mandela, Sisulu, Mlangeni, Kathrada and Mhlaba. He was like a child running into its parents' arms. They all greeted one another and exchanged a few moments' worth of information.

We made a pact never to mention the incident again. The friendship and cooperation I already enjoyed with my group became even stronger. Kathrada was especially sorry for Goniwe. He managed to get his lawyer to send a message to Goniwe's family to tell them that he was alive and safe in Pollsmoor.

Some six months after the men had been detained, a decision was made to release them on 10 October 1984, and it was my job to get Goniwe out of Pollsmoor and onto a train at nearby Retreat. Goniwe was worried that he didn't know his way around, and he was anxious as he got into the prison van. As we drove along, an unmarked police car pulled us over and the prisoners were ordered out. The police, who had seniority over us, said they would escort them to the train. A week or two later, I heard how all three had returned to their political activities in the Eastern Cape and had been intercepted after an evening meeting.

In June 1985, their burned and mutilated corpses were found next to their burning car on a remote country road. I felt so sorry that such a well-educated and well-meaning man, a good man with good intentions, had to die like that.

Soon afterwards, Sisulu went into Woodstock hospital near Cape Town for a prostate operation. He was originally convinced that they anaesthetised him for a checkup, but actually they carried out the operation, and he had to stay in hospital for a further week.

I took turns with another warder to guard him, and senior warders came in regularly to check us. After 6 p.m. one day, my fellow warder du Toit left me with Sisulu so he could go home quickly. He lived just 15 minutes' drive from there.

He had arranged with the nurses, who were very sympathetic, that he could fetch a portable TV. Of course they thought it was for us, but we had it in the room with Sisulu, and that was the first time any of the Rivonians saw a television, as the state-run South African Broadcasting Corporation had not existed in our country before they were incarcerated.

The TV was black and white and the programmes mostly in Afrikaans. Soon Sisulu was sitting up in bed watching the news in English and was tremendously excited about that. On the Saturday there was a rugby match, and we all watched it together. We knew we wouldn't be caught, because all the other officers would be watching it elsewhere. When we escorted Sisulu back to Pollsmoor, we told him to keep quiet about it. Those guys were all good at keeping secrets.

Years later, when he was free, I met Sisulu and he hugged me in greeting. His wife was standing by, furious, and pointed out contemptuously that I had been his captor, his oppressor.

'No, you're wrong,' he told her. 'He is our man, he was always our man.'

In our rooftop days, I had started buying their chocolate and biscuits, and sometimes fruitcake for them in the supermarket, and one day I shared a piece of cake with Mandela and found it very dry. At home, my wife had started cooking with a microwave oven for the first time, and she had made a really delicious fruitcake. So I offered to bring some into the section. All of them loved it – it became my wife's famous cake – so I agreed to make a plan so they could buy some regularly. They had to buy it because they had to produce a receipt for everything that came into the prison from outside.

I put a paltry price on it and began bringing in the 2kg cakes, booking them in as 500g because that was the maximum allowed for foodstuffs. All the ANC leaders wanted to buy it and share it. Mandela especially had a very sweet tooth.

I brought my wife's cake in regularly, and it took on an important significance between us. Perhaps it represented a sharing of a tiny part of family life. Even after they were all released, Estelle still cooked it for them, and I later heard Kathrada telling friends proudly that he received two of her fruitcakes every year – one at Christmas and one on his birthday.

Mandela had also experienced health problems while he was in Pollsmoor. In February 1983, about a year after he arrived, I had to escort Mandela to Woodstock hospital because he had a worrying growth on the back of his head, and he had a painful ingrowing toenail. The doctors decided to do both minor operations at the same time. I left my firearm outside and went into the operating theatre, all scrubbed up in a white surgical gown, mask and hat, standing next to the surgeons while they worked.

There was a list of names on a blackboard on the wall. Mandela was down as One Black Special. He really objected to that. He said: 'What is this name? Is it supposed to be me?' We knew it was, but I told him: 'No, man, it isn't you. It's another guy, we don't know who.' Then he was put under, and the doctors set up a screen so neither of them would be distracted. I watched as the skin was pulled away from his skull and the growth cut out expertly. It was put in a bucket and sent away for tests.

Mandela was wheeled out to the recovery room, and I was at his side when he came round. By then, I suppose I had been with him for many important moments in his life, and actually, when I think about it, I realise that they were important for both of us.

Back at Pollsmoor, he began to have problems with his prostate gland, noticing blood in his urine and experiencing pain. So I escorted him to Woodstock hospital again in September 1984. This time the name on the list was David Motsamayi, the alias he used when he was working underground, pretending to be the gardener at Liliesleaf Farm.

Mandela, for all his illness, was not having that. He demanded to see the hospital authorities and asked them: 'Who is that? That is not me. I am Nelson Mandela, that is my name.' They agreed to change the name, but of course they didn't.

They had no intention of using his real name and alerting everyone in the hospital that they had a world-famous revolutionary in there.

He had further exploratory procedures and was very sleepy and confused when he recovered. Another warder had thought it was funny to exploit his confusion and tell him he had had to be sedated and hidden away because some people had been threatening to kill him, calling him a kaffir.

When Mandela was conscious, he remembered this and was upset. I told him, 'No, you just had a disturbing dream, you're quite safe.' I had to find a urine bottle for him and help him, he was so weak. He was very grateful for small kindnesses like that, and unused to it from a white man I suppose.

It was around this time that he secretly wrote to my wife. He smuggled a letter out with another warder on a folded piece of paper tucked in between the Cadbury's wrapper and the silver foil of the milk chocolate slab. I knew nothing about it until the day Mandela was released.

I still have the letter, a treasured possession. It is written on prison notepaper and reads:

Madam,

Your husband is a very talented man with a heart of gold. He is always in a good mood and helpful. But he lacks determination, and consequently neglects his own interests and future, as well as those of his wife and children.

On countless occasions I have tried to persuade him to study, but all my attempts have failed completely. I must now request your help. Perhaps you will succeed in getting him to do what other responsible young people across the world do – promote their interests and future.

Estelle didn't tell me about the letter, but she began to press me to take up degree courses. I reasoned with her that I already had to study criminal law to ensure promotion in the prison service, and I had a full-time job and a busy family with a baby son, so I had no extra time. In exasperation one day, I told her: 'You're beginning to sound just like Mandela. He never stops nagging me about studying.'

His letter to her is written in flawless Afrikaans. Sworn to secrecy so as to avoid trouble for both Mandela and myself, Estelle had hidden it and waited seven years before she showed me.

Mandela would often offer an act of kindness out of the blue. I once told him about an accident I'd had on my 125cc Suzuki motorbike. I'd been driving through a coloured township to buy spare parts for my car and found the road littered with burned tyres and broken traffic lights after a protest.

A pickup truck drove straight out of a side street and into me, knocking me off the bike and into the road, where a crowd quickly gathered. It was a bad situation, and I only got out of there by insisting the truck driver take me to the nearest police station, where I'd be safe. Once there, bizarrely, I saw a former prisoner of mine from Pollsmoor who was there scrubbing the floors, and he helped me take off my helmet and attended to my injuries.

I had cracked ribs, severe bruising, and a gash that needed stitches in my foot. Although the truck driver had admitted being at fault, I was now getting demands to pay for damage to his vehicle. I showed his letter to Mandela, hoping his legal mind could help. The bill was R420, a small fortune at that time. He immediately wrote a stern letter setting out the circumstances, demanding the claim be dropped and insisting I was to be paid compensation. Of course, I had to take the letter home to have it typed. If anyone saw Mandela's handwriting, it would have been serious for both of us. I tore up the original and flushed it down the toilet.

I sent off my typed copy by registered post as he advised, and quickly won the case. Mandela, terrorist and revolutionary, had solved a minor civil case for a non-paying client, his prison warder.

Soon, I was able to carry out some kindness of a different kind for him. In 1985 his prostate problems returned, and it was decided he needed another operation. There was a consultation with him about which hospital he should go to. Various private clinics were suggested, primarily because of security concerns, but he insisted he trusted the surgeons at Woodstock. He wanted to return there. He busied himself preparing for another trip from the prison, giving Kathrada strict instructions about watering and weeding the plants in his garden, as he was concerned about their upkeep while he was away.

Once again, I was with him throughout the operation. I was happy to do that job when other warders were not keen. I had been brought up on a farm and had seen plenty of 'operations' – I'd done some myself on frogs to use them as bait for fishing, and I'd helped to slaughter pigs and chickens. I wasn't afraid of seeing blood and actually I was very interested, fascinated even.

But I was also anxious about Mandela. He was nearly 70, and this prostate gland problem seemed to be becoming chronic.

As he was coming round afterwards, I reassured him. 'It's all right, it's all been done and it was very quick. You're going to be fine. You are safe here with me, you can sleep now.' I watched him gratefully sink into a deep sleep.

Earlier in 1985, Mandela had been made another offer of freedom in return for renouncing violence. President P. W. Botha had declared to Parliament that he would free all political prisoners on that condition and claimed: 'It is therefore not the government which stands in the way of Mr Mandela's freedom. It is he himself.'

Mandela had written a powerful statement of refusal saying only free men could negotiate, that prisoners could not enter into contracts. He ended: 'I cannot and will not give any undertaking at a time when I and you, the people, are not free. Your freedom and mine cannot be separated.'

Winnie was still under house arrest and unable to read her husband's statement to the public. So it fell to their daughter Zindzi, 24 years old, to face a packed football stadium at Orlando, in Soweto, and bravely read out her father's speech. She did it proudly in a loud, clear voice, and the response was deafening. Mandela's entire family, and his people, were more definite than ever that they would not cave in to the apartheid government.

The other political prisoners under my care refused too. They had heard that offer before, back in 1967, and refused it then as well.

Botha was furious. He had made this offer on public radio and was now having to bluster about the refusal. I was instructed to get myself wired up with a bugging device again to record Mandela and ask him why he hadn't accepted.

The tiny microphone was hidden under my jacket, and other warders were listening in from the office. I approached Mandela, sitting alone in his usual place on a concrete step in the courtyard, sheltering under the roof and reading. Once again, I put my finger silently to my lips and showed him the microphone attached to my shirt. I greeted him, and he got it straight away. He answered in a relaxed way, calling me 'Sergeant Brand' and talking about his garden. He said the spinach was doing very well.

I asked if he had any complaints he wanted me to take to the office. Then I said, as instructed: 'Mandela, why don't you agree to the president's offer?'

He told me then that he would never agree to being released

unless all of the political prisoners were released. I walked back to the office; I had done my job. That night on television, P. W. Botha said he would never give in to Mandela. The old enemy lines were still drawn.

But Mandela totally understood when Denis Goldberg, the only white trialist at Rivonia, took the offer of release. They had all been given a month to respond to Botha's offer, and I had heard that all the political prisoners on Robben Island declined it, save for five of them who had not been involved in the violent struggle.

Goldberg was different. As the only white Rivonian, he had spent 22 miserable years in isolation in Pretoria Prison, where he had no comrades with whom to share the suffering.

I talked to Mandela about it while we were tending the vegetable garden together. 'He couldn't be with us, he's had a much harder time,' he said. 'He may have had better rations, but to keep someone in solitary will kill him sooner than starving him if he is among his own people. And Denis has no family in South Africa. He needs to go to them.'

The government was coming under increasing pressure to recognise the need for justice and freedom for Mandela, his comrades, and his people. Oliver Tambo, leading the ANC in exile from Zambia, sent out a call for the people to 'Render South Africa Ungovernable'. In response there were mass strikes, stayaways, and subsequent police brutality. The sight of uniformed police brandishing batons and felling men, women, and children was utterly shocking to fair-minded people all over the world.

By July 1985, the government had declared another State of Emergency. The rand fell drastically, as banks and international companies pulled out of South Africa. It had become a business and political outcast, a country with natural riches where no one wanted to invest.

Mandela, meanwhile, was going back to hospital again. There were worries about prostate cancer and, put bluntly, the last thing the government wanted was for him to be an elderly martyr of the revolution who died in their care.

This time, he went to Volks hospital in central Cape Town. A white nurse tending Mandela told her that her husband had been the medical officer on Robben Island. Mandela remembered him as a good man, he was very fair like that. Unlike the previous occasion, I was not present in the operating theatre but instead was on guard outside. Security was tighter than ever. Even the cleaners had to have special clearance to be near Mandela.

Winnie was allowed to visit before the operation, and I escorted her in. But I wasn't prepared for the next visitor – it was Kobie Coetsee, the Minister of Justice. Mandela maintained his composure, although he must have been astounded. Coetsee behaved as if he was visiting a friend, and Mandela behaved in the same way. Outside the room, I was very aware of the momentous event, however normal it was being made to look. Maybe the government was beginning to come round towards the ANC. Could that be possible?

I heard that Winnie had seen Coetsee when they were on the same plane from Joburg to Cape Town. She had boldly gone up to him – the very same minister who had signed her banning order – and demanded better treatment of her ailing husband locked up in ~~jail~~ prison. It has been said that she influenced him into visiting Mandela, but no one really knows. Coetsee had surely worked out for himself by then that he had the power to help steer his country away from civil war if he made some conciliatory moves.

Mandela was in hospital for eight days, and he certainly had plenty to think about. But, typically, he asked me to buy chocolates for all of the staff, and he wrote individual notes of thanks to each nurse. I delivered them on the day he left.

Coetsee's visit wasn't the only surprise for Mandela on this trip. The escort party taking Mandela back to Pollsmoor was joined out of the blue by the prison commander, Brigadier Munro. It was the brigadier who told Mandela that he was going to new quarters. He was given a cell on the ground floor of the prison wing, with three rooms and a separate toilet. He would be there on his own, in total isolation.

I already knew that Mandela wasn't going back to his friends. While he was recovering in hospital, I had been preparing the new cells. We brought his bed down from the rooftop and his steel cabinet containing his clothes, books, and sports equipment. I was told that as he was recovering from his operation he needed to be closer to the hospital section, though I sensed the truth wasn't that simple. Inevitably, the National Intelligence guys had sent a team in to put sophisticated bugs everywhere. On Mandela's return, I saw Brigadier Munro's car arriving with an unmarked police car escort. There were no sirens, nothing. Mandela got out wearing his prison clothes and was brought to the new section. I welcomed him back from hospital and showed him around. He looked and seemed to accept everything, but he was highly suspicious of this move and, although his new home was spacious, it was also low-lit and smelled of damp.

Two days later, he got his own television. At the same time, his comrades upstairs were told they could also have a television if they paid for it. Mandela's was free, a present from the government.

I was told that a warder would be on permanent day shift, locked in with him. By then I had been promoted to warrant officer, and I was running the office that supervised all the terrorist prisoners and detainees. I would still be seeing Mandela every day, at least twice a day. But I think we both realised our table-tennis days on the rooftop were over.

CHAPTER 9

For the first time in 21 years, Mandela found himself completely alone.

He missed the companionship of others, he missed his all-important garden, and he missed the sunny aspect of the rooftop from where he had been able to at least see the mountains and the sky.

I was still visiting him twice daily and was in overall charge of his life in prison, but the one man who could have made a difference – the warder assigned to spend all day with him, stationed in the passageway between cells – refused to communicate with him at all.

He was a veteran warder who was once in the police force, and he spoke only Afrikaans. He ignored all of Mandela's efforts to talk to him in his own language. He turned down invitations to share coffee or tea, and he would not even take the newspaper Mandela offered, preferring instead to get his own, the very same newspaper, but untouched by a prisoner. He wanted nothing from any prisoner and would spend his whole shift just observing Mandela and reading the Bible. Mandela complained to me that the sergeant would not even watch television with him in the cell.

However, this situation did not last long. One day, the warder went for a sinus operation in hospital and developed a blood clot while he was in the recovery ward. His wife was shocked to find him dead there.

Mandela was upset, too. But his replacement warder was something of an old friend – a man who had known him on Robben Island and who would at least pass the time of day with him. They used to chat in Afrikaans.

At this time, I was also thinking I might leave the prison service. But I discussed my situation with Mandela, and he encouraged me to stay. 'Mr Brand,' he said, 'we don't want to lose good people like you inside. You are good with how you communicate with the people outside; the way you make sure our letters are posted; the way you consult us about our visits.' These were small things I was doing, just treating him with some dignity. But when Mandela said he did not want to lose me, I stayed.

I had permission to take Mandela into a quiet courtyard in the section for some exercise. There was no tennis or table-tennis there, but he could walk around for an hour. Other prisoners from the criminal section could see him from their cells on the second floor. They were uneducated people who only knew that this was some sort of VIP getting special treatment, and they didn't like it.

They were jealous. Mandela used to wear the sombrero-style hat made out of cardboard by his friend Japhta Masemola, a cherished possession, and the prisoners shouted at him: 'Hey, Amigo!' and pelted him with the dried peach pips left over from their food pots.

They were aggressive. No 'Amandla!' or slogans of political support. They were completely ignorant of Mandela's status or politics. All they knew was that he had been given huge premises of his own and that I was doing his shopping. It was ironic that thousands of these prisoners were the very people whose freedom Mandela lived and breathed for. Now they were attacking him.

Mandela would try to clear up the peach pips in the courtyard, ignoring their shouts. He swiftly worked out that they wanted to engage with him, to get him to plead for special privileges for them and get them tobacco and food.

One day, I entered his cell to talk to him and saw a rope dangling near the window, tied to a parcel. Mandela gestured to me that I should look at it. He had clearly received these unsolicited parcels before and was weary of the messages in them. Inside the parcel, I found pleas from the criminal prisoners offering to smuggle messages out for him when they went to court hearings in return for him buying them tobacco, sugar, jam, or Marmite.

'This is from the top section,' he said. 'You need to report this.'

The next day, louvred shutters were fitted to the cell windows upstairs, and Mandela felt sorry they had to do that. Now those prisoners would have no sunshine either.

He knew that Walter Sisulu and his other comrades had also been moved and were now in a section of the female prison, far from him. He seemed calm when I gave him the news, although it meant the end of the rooftop life for them too, and also that his garden had dried up and collapsed, which made him sad. I offered to try to set up a new garden for him, but that dark cell didn't really lend itself to growing anything. There was little natural light and an unhealthy, dank atmosphere.

However, Mandela knew something else was going on: All this must be happening for a reason, and he seemed to be at the centre of it. He was open to all possibilities, as long as he and the others were not just written off and left to grow old and useless.

He never discussed political possibilities with me. He just seemed totally preoccupied with trying to stay one step ahead of what might be happening in the outside world. Preparing himself perhaps for a golden chance to finally take part in a momentous change in the country, something he had longed for all his life.

In many ways, he was under siege – from the prisoners surrounding him, from Winnie bringing family problems, from apartheid manipulators who were playing mind games with him, and from the National Intelligence guys who bugged and recorded every one of his words and actions.

When he found a little heap of white solder filings on the floor of his cell one day, he looked at me and asked what it was, knowing full well that some extra bugging devices must have been fitted. He was becoming weary.

I always respected his privacy and did not probe. Mandela was deep in thought during those days, and kept all hopes and fears to himself. But he wanted to talk to Sisulu, his mentor and the one man who might be able to help him make sense of all these changes taking place.

Mandela put in a written application to see Sisulu. It took two months to be approved, and during that time some enormously significant events came about and had to be dealt with by him alone.

After Mandela had returned from hospital, he had decided to approach the government to initiate talks. Soon, a meeting was set up. One Saturday night, after lockup time, I was told that I would be taking Mandela out of the prison and driving him to the home of Kobie Coetsee, the Minister of Justice.

We had to leave Pollsmoor by 9 a.m. the next day. I went to the store to find a prison release suit to fit him. These were very functional grey suits, a cheap cut that could at least be smartened up with a white shirt. I hastily chose three, guessing at the size. Two of them turned out to be too short in the arms, but the third was more or less all right.

The warder working with me, Captain Swart, couldn't find a tie, so he had to rush to his staff quarters in the prison and fetch one. All he could find was a bright red tie, which didn't really please Mandela at all. 'So you are forcing me to go to the minister's house dressed like a Communist!' he said, but he was smiling.

We were amazed to see how expertly he knotted his tie. It reminded us that he had practised as a lawyer, before his arrest all those years ago, and was used to dressing smartly for court appearances.

Swart tidied up his collar for him, and we looked at him with approval. He was in a quiet, thoughtful mood. He must have been trying to work out how his meeting was going to go. He hadn't told the rest of the ANC High Command about it, nor sent a message to Oliver Tambo, who was leading the ANC in exile in Zambia. Mandela has since written that sometimes a leader has to make lone decisions for the whole flock, just believing in himself and finding strength in his own judgement. But it was an extraordinary outing for him. It was a beautiful Sunday morning, and the sun shone as we bundled him out of the fire escape at the back of the prison and into a car. No one could see us except the guard in the observation post, and he had been alerted.

I opened the rear passenger door of the white Ford Cortina, an unmarked government car, and Mandela sat in the middle of the back seat, leaning forward throughout the journey like a small child, to peer at everything between me and Swart seated in the front. Another unmarked police car followed us for the 15-kilometre journey. All the time, Mandela was asking where we were and saying how green and lovely it all looked.

We drove him into the Bishopscourt area, past embassy residences and grand government-owned villas with huge gardens. I showed him the house where Bishop Desmond Tutu lived, the tireless activist who rallied the masses against the apartheid government. Mandela was fascinated. 'That's good,' he murmured, as I told him about Tutu.

At the end of the road was a security gate surrounding a government complex where Kobie Coetsee lived. Pik Botha, the country's notoriously hardline Minister for Foreign Affairs, was one of his neighbours. Several police officers were waiting for us, all on high alert and talking into their hand-held radios. A smartly dressed white man met us at the gate. He signaled for me and Swart to stay in the car and escorted Mandela inside. We waited there from 10 a.m. until about 1 p.m. We were thinking that maybe negotiations for reconciliation had started, or that Mandela was being questioned about the recent big uprisings. It occurred to us that, ironically, Minister Coetsee was actually our overall boss, but that we were forbidden to even enter the gates of his residence, while our prisoner was inside with him, having drinks.

One of the household staff brought some cold drinks out for us and told us that Coetsee had offered Mandela refreshment. Mandela had told him: 'I'll have whatever you are having, sir,' and had been given a large whisky on the rocks. Now we were thinking that Coetsee was trying to loosen him up and probe him for information. But we knew Mandela would never fall for that. It was exciting even to be on the fringes of this very special occasion, the country's Public Enemy Number One being entertained by the minister in charge of prisons.

Finally Mandela emerged, looking quite relaxed and very dignified. He didn't say much, but I got the impression that they hadn't discussed deep politics. It was more of an icebreaker, a getting-to-know-you session.

I was longing to know what was going on, but you had to respect Mandela's privacy when he went quiet. He was giving off this air of intense thoughtfulness and didn't want it to be interrupted, so we drove him back to the prison mostly in silence.

As soon as we returned him to his cell, he applied again to see Walter Sisulu. He badly needed to talk things over.

He also took the suit off straight away and folded it up nicely, before putting it back in its zip-up cover. I took it back to the office and kept it there for him to use again, along with the red tie. I had a feeling this outing was just the beginning.

In all his prison years, Mandela had done his own washing. But now, in isolation, he had no facilities. We sent one of the criminal prisoners in to collect the shirt. He brought it back the next day, washed and ironed, and Mandela thanked him with some chocolate and cigarettes. After that, he would add items to his monthly shopping order, wanting to show his appreciation for a fellow prisoner doing tasks for him.

That prisoner had a sad story. After he was released from Pollsmoor, he set up a small business selling fruit and vegetables door-to-door. But he had a partner who one day attacked and robbed the farmer supplying the vegetables. The partner disappeared and was never seen again, leaving the ex-prisoner to face a murder charge. He was given a long sentence and was moved from prison to prison.

I last heard of him in Worcester jail, where he had joined an evangelist church movement and started a band with other prisoners, singing hymns. I tried to help him with a letter supporting his application for parole. He still had Mandela's prison clothes and has promised to pass them on to the Nelson Mandela Foundation through me. Soon after Mandela's first outing, I was being told to get him prepared for another, this time just a drive around. The commanding officer said I should fetch him straight away and told me that he would be going out in his prison uniform, with no need for the smart suit this time. The CO himself drove his white Mercedes, fetching Mandela again at the fire-escape exit from his cell.

I told Mandela: 'Sorry, I have no idea where we are going.' He went to the toilet before agreeing to leave, and wanted to take a notebook with him. We told him he wouldn't be needing that. During the journey, he sat perched in the middle of the back seat again, anxious not to miss a thing.

We drove a short distance, about 200 metres, out of Pollsmoor and turned into a farm gate. We were in Steenberg, a smart private farm. Today it is also an exclusive golf course, but at the time they were just growing grapes there. The CO said he could get out and stretch his legs, walk for a while, and pick some grapes.

Mandela was very cautious. He said: 'Surely the farmer will shoot me if he sees me picking his grapes?'

He was told it was okay, that the farmer was a friend of the prison authorities. Anyhow no one appeared from the farm, so Mandela walked slowly up the lines, occasionally picking a small bunch of grapes, while we watched.

They were the Cape's famous hanepoot grapes grown for the table, not for wine-making. There were red and white, and Mandela was choosing to pick the ripest ones. We told him not to eat them until they were washed, because they might have chemicals sprayed on them. We had a plastic bag with us, so that he could take grapes back to the prison. Mandela was so impressed with the setting. He looked up at the mountains and breathed in the fresh air.

Back at the car he said thanks, he had really enjoyed a few minutes of freedom. He couldn't believe the huge number of ripe, healthy-looking grapes, and we explained that it was a plentiful crop ready to be harvested soon. I opened the rear passenger door for him, and we drove back to Pollsmoor.

These outings were so secret, and the top raft of government officials were so cautious, that Mandela's millions of supporters in the country were left in ignorance of them. The angry mood of the masses was totally contradicting the overtures being made to Mandela.

The previous year, in August 1985, there had been a huge protest march to Pollsmoor Prison to demand Mandela's release. Police violence was so intense that 31 protestors were killed in the resulting running battles. At the Truth and Reconciliation Commission where this was discussed years later, it was reported that 'nobody was spared from the violence of the police. Children, women and old people were all beaten and those who took part in the march had to run for their lives.' The violence continued after the protests, with the townships in the Western Cape remaining in upheaval until the end of the year. In 1986, when the State of Emergency was extended for the third time, there were so many random arrests and detentions of political activists that the prisons overflowed and disused warehouses were commandeered to take in detainees.

All this while Mandela was picking grapes.

Meanwhile Mandela finally got permission to see Sisulu, and they were to meet for an hour in the visiting booth. It was a contact visit, and I was present throughout.

It seemed that Mandela had decided to keep his own counsel about the meeting with Coetsee and the extraordinary outings. He must have wrestled with this over a long period, and maybe sensed that his comrades would not approve.

Of course I was still seeing Sisulu, Kathrada, and the others regularly, and when they saw me without my prison uniform occasionally, they wanted to know what was going on. I told them I was taking Mandela out. I did not want to play any of them against each other. It was better to just tell the truth, although not with any detailed information. I simply informed them that Mandela was being allowed to make some private visits.

At Mandela's meeting with Sisulu, the two men talked about their mutual friends, their health, and their recent visits and family news. Sisulu had a lot of news to tell about his own family. His wife and adult children were all closely involved in the struggle and were renowned activists in their own right. The two prisoners shared coffee and chatted. Sisulu was so happy to see his old friend, and Mandela told him for the first time about his prostate operation. They were being bugged and recorded, but we didn't interrupt their conversation to stop him telling Sisulu this, because they were both in prison and wouldn't be taking any inside information away with them.

Sisulu pressed Mandela to complain to his lawyers about being put in isolation. But Mandela must have decided by now that the isolation was giving him a chance to think things through and to strike out in a new direction. He told Sisulu he didn't want to complain, it would only cause more trouble.

He also carefully sounded out Sisulu about approaching the government to offer talks. Sisulu, ever loyal, said he would support Mandela in whatever he decided to do.

It was strange for me to be supervising two prisoners having a visit. Everything was rather strange at that time. The Rivonians by then were getting all the newspapers every day, and Kathrada was marking all the articles that were important for Mandela to see. He hoarded dozens of them until he could get them to Mandela. They were all as hungry for news as ever. I was finding it easy to slip messages between Mandela and Kathrada inside the newspaper cuttings I took back and forth. I thought of it as my small contribution towards peace in our country.

Sisulu and his cellmates asked me all the time about outings or appointments involving Mandela. I could see they were getting suspicious, worried even, that Mandela was making decisions without consultation.

Meanwhile I got another phone call, this time when I was off duty at home, telling me to prepare Mandela to leave early the next morning for another visit to Coetsee. I had to collect Mandela's suit, shirt, and tie and get them to him right away. By then I was a warrant officer, so I had the authority to go to the cells after lockup.

My wife was out at a social function, and I was taking care of our small son Riaan, who was just 18 months old. So I took little Riaan with me, toddling along at my side. The warder on night shift let me in and there we were in front of Mandela, who was delighted to see a small child. He wanted to pick him up and talk to him, but Riaan was a bit overwhelmed, a bit afraid of this stranger. He clung on to me and wouldn't go to Mandela.

So Mandela got on his knees to find some sweets in a drawer in his cabinet. Riaan watched him all the time and then hesitantly took the sweets. After that, he was very happy to see Mandela or Sisulu and the guys who kept sweets for him. They had a regular supply of treats these days because by now they could see their own families and young children, and so they would put extra orders on their shopping lists for them.

I drove a prison-issue white Ford Cortina with Captain Swart next to me when we took Mandela to Coetsee for this second visit. He was inside for about an hour and a half. We asked the National Intelligence plainclothes guys there what was going on, but as usual they were tight-lipped and uncommunicative.

Soon after that, the head of prison came to Mandela's cell and told him he could have a stroll around the part of the prison where pet animals were kept. There were black and white rabbits, Angoras with long coats, some chickens running around, and even a young steenbuck, a small deer. There was also an aviary with birds and a dove-loft. Prisoners ready for release were encouraged to try to rehabilitate in readiness for the outside world, and this was part of the process. They could sit in the sun in the pet zoo courtyard, and relax or read a book. Some prison officers trained homing pigeons, and there was a time when prisoners were allowed to take part in that and let the birds free, sending them to their families in the city and watching for them to come back. Then we found pigeons dying on their return. A close inspection showed they had Mandrax pills and tubes of cannabis stuck under their wings – a crafty ruse to bring drugs into jail. We hadn't foreseen that. The homing pigeon idea came to an abrupt end.

Mandela's favourites were the fish pond and the aviary, although he said he didn't like to see live creatures imprisoned like he was.

Despite his improved conditions, he still made regular complaints. He was getting fed up with the way food was served to him in his cells. He didn't want to eat his main meal at lunchtime. He had got into the habit of sleeping for an hour in the early afternoon, so he wanted to eat light and save the food for the evening. By then, it would be cold and unappetising.

I bought him some rice from the supermarket, and he used to put it in his coffee flask with boiling water from the prison urn and cook it that way. We didn't cook rice in the kitchens; the staple was always porridge made from mealie-meal. I told him that a hot-plate would be a great idea for him. I had to explain to him what that was and how it worked, and how much it would cost.

He decided he wanted one, and in June 1988 he applied for it in writing. He was told the regulations forbade it. He applied to a higher authority and was turned down again. Then he wrote to the Commissioner of Prisons at head office in Pretoria, who also refused.

Mandela was exasperated and asked my advice. I told him the head of prison was due back from leave and didn't know anything about the hot-plate requests. He was an obsessive rugby fan, and maybe Mandela could feign an interest in the game, get friendly with him, and try again for a hot-plate.

The head of prison duly came on a routine visit to Mandela to check on conditions and ask about any complaints. Mandela had done his homework and started talking about the national rugby team, the Springboks, and their most recent match. The two men chatted, and Mandela said it was a shame he couldn't watch rugby on his television, but it would mean eating cold food. He was advised to send it back to the kitchen to be heated, but Mandela said he had tried that and never had the food returned.

He said he had heard there was such a thing as a hot-plate that could heat up food. The head of prison agreed that was the answer, and that Mandela should put in a request immediately to his office.

The hot-plate arrived within days, Mandela signed for it, and that was that. When I told Kathrada and the others about it they wanted hot-plates too, and they were delighted when their requests were approved.

There were questions the next time the Commissioner of Prisons arrived and found Mandela warming up milk for a hot drink, but I just told him it was all approved and nothing to do with me.

There were some close calls over Kathrada's cooking, too. He had given his lawyer money to bring in some meat illicitly from the butcher, and the Commissioner walked in while he was cooking up a biryani with fresh beef. Nothing was said, though Kathrada said he was numb with anxiety during the visit. He had broken the rules; the lawyer had broken the rules. He feared he might lose privileges, but there were no reprisals. Things were changing for all of the ANC guys.

CHAPTER 10

As I was now a warrant officer, I had some seniority in the prison. My home was opposite the female section where the remaining ANC men were in their communal cells, and I was able to sometimes bring over meat and vegetables and cook up a potjiekos, a real Afrikaans stew cooked slowly in a big cast iron pot.

We would make a fire with charcoal and I would fix the pot on it, stirring occasionally and enjoying the aroma, as I had done all my life. I brought rice with me to cook with boiling water from the prison urn. They enjoyed it very much, and we kept a nice helping on one side for me to take to Mandela.

Meanwhile the unexpected outings continued, and soon he and I were informed about another trip outside the walls of Pollsmoor. Mandela was to stay in prison clothes again, as we were not going far. This time, the commanding officer drove his blue Audi to the back exit for Mandela. We drove around the prison – a huge area with courtyards and gardens, staff quarters, and a big dam. We parked up on the sand road and Mandela was told he could take a walk around the dam. Some teenagers were standing at the far end with fishing rods. They had no idea who this man now approaching them was. He greeted them and chatted to them about fishing. The next minute, they were letting him use the rod and showing him how to attach bait.

There were four or five of them, the children of other warders. Mandela spent about half an hour with them while we watched from a distance. When he came back, he said they only caught one fish, too small to eat – the boys were going to feed it to the cat. He didn't say if he had told them who he was. He was worried about them being close to the deep water and said it was dangerous. The CO told him not to worry, they were good swimmers. But Mandela insisted there should be an adult with them.

He was very interested to see the large prison vegetable gardens and chatted with the CO, who was also quite knowledgeable. They talked about growing potatoes and pumpkins. Mandela was impressed that the Pollsmoor gardens produced enough vegetables to send to other prisons.

Some time later, I got instructions to prepare for a lunch in one of the officers' smart houses for Mandela and an important group of visitors. He was to be the guest of honour at a meeting of the Eminent Persons Group set up by the British Commonwealth and headed by General Olusegun Obasanjo of Nigeria.

Obasanjo had recently retired as president of Nigeria and had guided the country from military to civilian rule. It had been agreed that he might help to bring the warring sides in South Africa together.

I arranged for some nice food to be cooked in the officers' mess and delivered to the dining room, where ten people would be seated. On the morning of the lunch, Mandela looked incredibly smart in a pinstripe suit, which had been delivered the previous day by the head of Pollsmoor. He had organised a tailor to make a bespoke suit that fitted him beautifully, and he was also given a shirt, tie, shoes, socks, and underwear. All of the members of the Eminent Persons Group were in business suits. Mandela looked perfectly at home among them. When the head of prison saw him dressed, he told him: 'Mandela, you don't look like a prisoner any more. You look like a prime minister.' The Commissioner of Prisons was there with Minister Kobie Coetsee and Mandela approached them, openly putting a plea to them to consider further talks between the ANC and the government. However, those two didn't stay long. They refused his invitation to join him for lunch. Extraordinary to think that one of their prisoners was formally inviting them to dine with him in one of their staff houses. Mandela pulled it off perfectly and said he was sorry they were leaving. He had nothing to hide, he told them; they were welcome to join in. By contrast, he had been greeted with enthusiasm and hugs from his fellow black Africans. Of course, the entire house was bugged and I was stationed outside the dining room to observe.

Mandela saw me and insisted I join them at the table. He sat next to Obasanjo and dominated the conversation throughout, with everyone listening quietly and attentively to everything he said. He explained what the ANC was and what it stood for. He explained why the organisation had felt compelled to answer violence with violence and set up Umkhonto we Sizwe.

As they left, Obasanjo shook my hand and said I would be welcome in Nigeria any time I wanted to visit. That was a very unlikely idea and unfortunately never happened.

The Eminent Persons Group had intended to return and promised to encourage talks between the ANC and the government. But they retreated after South African troops attacked ANC bases in Botswana, Zambia, and Zimbabwe. I guess they felt their mission now had no chance of success.

During the period of these outings, visits, and meetings,

Winnie was visiting Pollsmoor regularly. I was always in the room with them, and I realised that Mandela had clearly decided not to confide in her about the delicate talks, just as he was not confiding in Sisulu and the others.

She complained bitterly about him being put in isolation; she was very upset about it and wanted to take further action and even go to the newspapers. But Mandela told her firmly:

'Darling, if you fight it, everything will get worse. Can't you see they are trying to break me down? We must show the enemy they cannot achieve that. I will deal with it like a man, I will cope.'

All their visits were by now contact visits, and he could make her tea and touch her. But there was a lot of turmoil around Winnie. One day she turned up at the prison gates without an appointment, her arm around a woman friend who was in floods of tears. Mandela was told he would be allowed this unexpected visit from his wife, but there would be no contact. They would have to meet in the booths with a glass panel between them.

He was furious, one of the only times I saw him lose his temper. He absolutely refused to accept the visit. He felt he had spent many years slowly gaining privileges, and he did not want to go backwards, back behind the impersonal glass panel. I could do nothing to persuade him and, meantime, Winnie and her friend were making a tremendous fuss. I got him to talk it over with the head of prison, who was exasperated. He said: 'Mandela, just go to the visiting booth and tell your wife yourself that you don't want to see her. We won't take it from your quota of visits. You are the only one who can calm her down.'

Mandela was shouting, angry and upset. But when I took him to the booth he looked through the window and saw the wife of his clan cousin, Sabata Dalindyebo, tribal king

171

of Mandela's people. She was sobbing hysterically. Mandela agreed to the visit, and was soon asking for an extra 40 minutes, a double visit.

It turned out that this was important family business. Dalindyebo, a principled and proud man, had refused to support the idea of the Transkei as a homeland under the racial division of the apartheid government. He had come into conflict with the paramount chief, Kaiser Matanzima, who had him arrested in 1979 for 'injury to the dignity of the president of the Transkei'. To Mandela's eternal shame and chagrin, Matanzima, his own nephew, and once a man he had looked up to, had collaborated with the government and agreed to the Transkei becoming a homeland, which meant total segregation for black people in that area.

Mandela had refused visits from him, rightly assuming that Matanzima wanted to use the family ties for political advancement. He was on a mission to persuade Mandela to accept release from prison and to go to live in the Transkei.

Dalindyebo himself had called homelands 'pigsties and dummy institutions'. He was forced into exile in Zambia. His wife was coming to tell Mandela that he had died at the age of 57. She had his body brought back to the Transkei, where she planned to bury him. But the army was sent to surround her hotel and imprison her there while Matanzima's men took his body from the funeral parlour and buried him in a commoner's grave at the riverside.

In tribal terms, this was a serious injustice that only Mandela, son of a chieftain himself, might be able to put right. He tried to soothe his cousin's widow. He would somehow make contact with clan elders and give Dalindyebo his rightful burial in the chieftains' graveyard.

It took until 1989 for Dalindyebo's body to be exhumed.

Then he was reburied as king of the Thembu people under ANC colours.

Mandela, preoccupied as he was with great matters of state and the glimmer of hope that momentous changes were coming, was continually burdened in this way with pressing family matters. Locked up in prison with limited control over affairs outside, he had to use all of his inner strength to work through these problems with a clear head.

One day, I was shocked to see how angry he became when his daily newspaper disappeared. It seemed like a sudden outpouring of all his inner anger and frustration. The warder on night duty had taken it from the grille on his cell window while Mandela was asleep and forgotten to replace it. In the morning, Mandela looked for his newspaper and was really angry that it was missing. He made a huge fuss, demanding to see the night-duty warder. When he confronted him, I thought for a moment that Mandela was going to hit him, he was so worked up and upset.

He remained like that, completely out of sorts, for the rest of the day. I tried to talk to him and explain that there was no malice in what had happened. The person who took the newspaper returned it the next day; it was just a slip-up.

Mandela was very on edge at that time. He had no friends with him with whom he could play sports or talk in Xhosa, his own language. He had no sense of humour at all at that time, and small things were upsetting him. Of course, there were serious matters of great importance on his mind, and his tension just sometimes all spilled out over a small thing.

At heart he was still a family man, just as I was. He grieved over the problems that Winnie told him about. Their daughter Zindzi was not studying well at university, and Winnie herself was constantly watched and harassed by security police. Mandela felt, quite rightly, that she wasn't safe, and he felt ashamed, emasculated, that he couldn't help her. She was his wife; he should be able to take care of her. Instead, she had to continually trek back and forth to the prison.

Every time he saw her, he would take a notebook full of instructions for her, and when they next had a visit he would check with her that she had carried out his wishes. Often, she had forgotten or had been unable to achieve a meeting with someone or gain a decision from someone else. Mandela was quite hard on her then, telling her firmly that she must also bring a notebook and write everything down. 'Darling, you are meeting a lot of people and getting distracted, and I need you to remember everything we are discussing. Please note it all down and do what I ask.' She was his main instrument to keep his name and his ideals alive in the country.

For his part, he was dealing with many family problems. In April 1987, his daughter-in-law Rennie came to see him. She was divorcing Mandela's younger son Makgatho and wanted to leave the country. She asked Mandela to help settle her son Mandla at boarding school.

Mandela agreed to take control of Mandla's education and arranged it through his lawyers. He was fond of his daughter-in-law and sympathetic about her marriage problems. He took his responsibilities as ultimate head of the family very seriously, despite all the restrictions on him.

One night there was an incident where I imposed another problem on him, simply because I knew he was the right person to deal with it. I had been brought in late at night to supervise the lockup of newly arrived prisoners. There were crowds of them, all juveniles and new remands. Some of them were teenagers, but there was also one very small coloured boy. I judged he was about eight years old.

I went over to him and looked at his ticket. They all had prison tickets in their pockets, stating their ID and their offence. This child's offence was murder.

I couldn't put him in with the bigger boys, as he was too small and too vulnerable. So I locked him in a single cell and spent a few minutes trying to find out what he had really done. He came from Manenberg, a dangerous, gangster-ridden slum area of Cape Town.

He told me his family was sandwiched in between rival gangsters' territories. He had been abducted and held at gunpoint. He was told to go to a gang leader's home and shoot him. They gave him a handgun and said if he didn't kill the guy his parents would be shot dead. The child went to the house and shot the gangster in the chest at point-blank range.

Now he was in prison for murder.

I knew about Manenberg, and I knew about gangs. This boy, thin and frightened, was almost certainly telling the truth. But how could I get him out of here and into some safe place? Instinctively, I knew Mandela was the right person to turn to. He would have the compassion and perhaps the influence to find a way.

In the morning, I unlocked the boy's cell and told him to walk with me through the prison corridors. He was barefoot, in short trousers and a grubby T-shirt. I brought him to Mandela in his isolation cell and said: 'Show the uncle your ticket.' We talked in Afrikaans, where the term uncle is a sign of respect for an older man.

Mandela, who had been sitting in his chair reading, put his head in his hands.

'This child is innocent,' he said. He thought about it for

several minutes, then went to his cabinet and took out some sweets for the boy.

'Mr Brand, please call my lawyer Dullah Omar and tell him to come today to sort this out. This place is not for children. If he stays here, he'll turn into a gangster himself. Nothing good can happen to him here.'

I phoned Omar and he came straight away. The boy was back in his single cell, still crying, but at least I was able to tell him that we were doing something for him. All the warders felt sorry for him. He was a young boy with no gang initiation, no tattoos or police record. I had seen many youngsters in prison, already turning into criminals, but I had never seen one this young. He was just a child from a poor but decent home.

That evening, Omar returned with some social workers to take him to a foster home. He promised Mandela and me that he would personally deal with the murder charge and the court proceedings. Later, he told us the court ruled that the child should not return to Manenberg. He was to be taken good care of by foster parents, and his parents could have regular contact with him until they were able to move to a better area. Every time Omar visited after that, Mandela would start by asking after the child.

Now that it was common knowledge that he was being held at Pollsmoor, Mandela was a cause of great curiosity to everyone in the prison. Other warders wanted a glimpse of him, and the criminal prisoners were clearly jealous. But any new political prisoners admitted to Pollsmoor were totally in awe. They were continuing the struggle in his absence but felt keenly that he was still their leader, their inspiration.

In June 1987, I booked a group of student activists known as the Wynberg Seven into Pollsmoor to serve their year's sentence. They were five men and two girls who were to be kept separate from others to prevent them recruiting. They had been sentenced for public violence during the school protests and boycotts. I had cleared a section especially for them, right next to where Mandela was held, and they often saw him sitting in the courtyard alone reading a book with a guard nearby.

My job was to ensure they had study material so they could complete their exams. I became friendly with one of them, Igshaan Amlay, and I got into the habit of giving Mandela's newspapers to him once the older man had finished with them, which was strictly against the rules. I had to make sure I collected them before the shift changed the next morning. I would also visit Amlay in his cell in the evenings and collect notes he wanted me to drop off at his parents' house in Wynberg. His parents would give me sweets, chocolate, money, and messages for me to take back to him.

Amlay's father, who has since died, was the engineer who made the metal burglar bars I have at my home. When Igshaan visits me these days, we often talk about those times at Pollsmoor. Today he is a successful businessman and social activist, currently bidding to bring the Grand Prix to Cape Town.

One Monday morning, he and the other students were going for medical checkups, and I said I'd try to make sure they had a chance to meet Mandela. It was a very brief encounter but meant everything to those young people. At that time, the world had not set eyes on Mandela for more than 20 years.

I knew it was important for him, too, to have some personal contact with leaders from the outside. He didn't want the world to forget him and what he stood for. He was always gratified to hear that many thousands of people were making sacrifices to continue the ANC fight against apartheid.

When Mandela had checkups, the appointment always had to be held very discreetly. He would be the last patient to be booked in, so there could be no contact with the public. The specialist's clinic on the fifth floor of a modern office block near the foreshore in Cape Town would already be closed when we got there. We had a special arrangement with the doctor for him to stay late to see Mandela.

The doctor would spend an hour and a half with him, checking blood pressure and doing cardiac and breathing tests. I would stay in the examination room with Mandela while the other warders waited outside. There was a view of the harbour from a big picture window, all lit up with the twinkling lights of anchored ships.

One time when we left the clinic, we started towards Pollsmoor along Beach Road, a different direction to the way we had come. We were in a convoy with a police escort. It was about 8 p.m. and quite dark when I drew the minibus into a gravel parking place next to the ocean. The other warders wanted a smoke break. I told Mandela we could get out and walk down to the sea. He looked across to Robben Island and said: 'What is that place out there?' I told him it was his old prison.

He was completely taken aback. 'No, it can't be,' he said. 'It looks like a big ship moored out there, or maybe a small town.' The island was dark at night. The street lights were switched off, and there was just the single beam from its lighthouse blinking on and off.

He wouldn't believe me. All you could see of Robben Island was its looming black shape. Mandela was certain the water he could see was a river, but I told him to listen to the waves. I then took him across a few rocks strewn with bambous, the huge strands of seaweed he spent years working with, and told him to dip his hand in the water. 'You see it's salty, it's the Atlantic,' I said.

We stood there for about five minutes. Mandela was overawed by the sound and smell of the ocean and the huge sky. He stood there staring around him and up at the stars. 'I've never been out this late before,' he said.

We both had memories of those terrible times on the island, too awful to even want to share. We walked back to the car in silence. It had been a strange few moments.

South Africa, my country, was by now virtually in flames. After the State of Emergency had been extended in 1986, giving even more powers to the police and army, the situation became increasingly out of control. Now we had curfews all over again. No non-whites were allowed on the streets without express permission to be there. Thousands were being detained and 'disappeared'. Every township in the country had a contingent of armed troops standing by. Yet, with all this going on, the press was banned from reporting any political unrest.

Oliver Tambo's call to make the country ungovernable was working well. The economy was on the point of collapse, and the free world was shocked and outraged at the violent scenes they were watching on TV footage smuggled out of the country.

I knew Mandela was writing regularly to the Commissioner of Prisons and to Minister Coetsee but not receiving replies. Meanwhile, he celebrated his 70th birthday in 1988 with a lunch in the visitors' centre. His dear friends Sisulu, Kathrada, Mhlaba, Mlangeni, and Motsoaledi were invited, and it was like old times. They laughed and joked and enjoyed the food. Knives and forks were provided for the first time, which amused them, and there was even dessert.

The government had banned all public gatherings to mark Mandela's 70th birthday and arrested dozens of people who tried to defy it. But not everyone would be cowed.

Just before Mandela's 70th birthday, the renowned Marxist Italian film director Bernardo Bertolucci had decided to send him an exclusive copy of his epic work *The Last Emperor*. He had somehow heard that Mandela wanted to watch it, but that Pollsmoor's projector could only show 16mm films. He got together with the British director Richard Attenborough and the Italian government, and wanted to make a big gesture to go with it. Thus, for Mandela's birthday, he sent a delegation to Pollsmoor with a lawyer to present the reformatted film to him. Of course, they were refused entry and kept outside the gates in full view of a fascinated media.

Dullah Omar, who often acted for Mandela and other political prisoners, was with them, and I advised him to take the movie to a shop called Cine Place in the Woodstock suburb, which was where I hired all the prisoners' films from. I could let the manager know about it, and Omar should be there at 10 a.m. to carry out this secret operation. That was the only way *The Last Emperor* was getting to Mandela.

But there was to be no secrecy. I had been taking a trade unionist prisoner, Oscar Mpetha, to his daily physio session at Groote Schuur hospital and planned to take a detour on the way back to Pollsmoor to quietly pick up the movie. By the time I got there, a huge crowd had gathered at the Cine Place, and Bertolucci's people wanted to make a big speech. I accepted the movie and promised to give it to Mandela. I had to get the manager to make out an invoice so that I could bring it into Pollsmoor, and we finally got the job done.

In the end, Mandela watched his special copy of *The Last Emperor* on the same day as tens of thousands of his supporters were attending a Free Mandela birthday tribute concert in London's Wembley Stadium. South Africa's own Miriam

Makeba and Hugh Masekela performed on a star billing that included Dire Straits, George Michael, Whitney Houston, Stevie Wonder, and the Bee Gees. An estimated one billion people watched it live on TV in over sixty countries.

We were sent a short version of the concert afterwards, and I watched it first with the other warders, ready to cut out unsuitable sections. But we left it whole and let Mandela and the others see just how popular they were all over the world. Later we were sent the complete ten hours of the concert on half a dozen cassettes, but we were forbidden to give it to Mandela. Somehow, though, Ahmed Kathrada managed to get hold of it so they could view it.

But all this was a world away from Mandela's day-to-day situation at Pollsmoor. Despite his increasing small freedoms, he was still heavily institutionalised after so many years behind bars.

A few months passed and Mandela wanted to visit his friends over in their new section of the prison, so I got permission to take him in a car. I was told by the head of prison that Mandela must get into the car on his own. I still don't know to this day if that was a cruel joke or an act of kindness, perhaps preparing Mandela for life on the outside.

Of course, he stood at the rear passenger door of the Ford Cortina and was unable to work out how to use the handle. He had never seen a lift-up handle on a car door before. He shook his head and said: 'I've just been in prison for too long.'

After his visit, I got a call on the radio while I was driving him back to his cell. I was instructed to go to my home, a married quarters flat in the prison compound, and wait for an important phone call on the landline. I parked up and left Mandela in the car, both of us slightly concerned. I told my wife she should perhaps go and say hello to him while I was on the phone.

The call was to tell me to take Mandela to Coetsee's house that evening. While I was receiving my instructions, my wife took our son Riaan outside with her and had a short conversation with Mandela through the car window.

After this next visit to Coetsee, Mandela seemed optimistic about a solid proposal coming from the government. There was obviously a huge flurry of activity going on. He didn't know the half of it, but he was happy to go along with the mind games. He was nothing if not persistent. I was posting his letters, and I could see how regularly he was lobbying government officials. Mandela was now a cause célèbre supported all over the world, yet he was still not allowed to talk to most of his fellow activists in the same prison. However, I knew how much it meant to the others just to be detained near him, and I started to help with a series of 'coincidences' where they could at least shake his hand and have a brief chat.

The trade unionist prisoner Oscar Mpetha was being a terrible nuisance around this time. He had had a leg amputated and needed to go to physio at hospital every day. He actually spent most of his prison sentence under armed guard in a hospital ward. He was supposed to be dressed and ready to go at 8.00 a.m., but without fail he was always still in bed when I went to fetch him.

I asked Mandela to please influence him, but they were not allowed to meet. So I made a dental appointment for Mandela at the same time as I was taking Mpetha out to hospital. It was early, before the criminal prisoners' cells were unlocked.

I told Oscar he should come out at exactly 8.45 a.m. and he could meet Mandela around the corner. He had been hoping to see Mandela for years, and now his eyes lit up. He would be ready on time, he promised.

In fact, Mpetha was up early, pressing me to set off. He had his artificial leg on, and he was dressed. When he saw Mandela, he abandoned his crutches and ran into his arms. Mandela could hardly hold him upright.

I had to fake alarm at the situation, so I was a few feet away shouting: 'Someone come and separate them! This shouldn't be happening.'

On the way to hospital, Mpetha leaned over and squeezed my arm. He was so emotional he could hardly speak his thanks; it meant so much to him. He hadn't seen Mandela since the 1950s. I saw him after his release from prison, and he was still talking about it. By then, he had had both legs amputated and was in a wheelchair. He had been a hero himself, a working-class docker who rose through trade union ranks to become president of the ANC in the Cape, and who was only released from prison shortly before Mandela. He lived just long enough to realise his dream of freedom for the black majority, and to see Mandela made president of South Africa. He died at his home in Gugulethu township six months after Mandela's inauguration.

I also arranged for the guys from the Ashley Forbes terrorism trial to meet Mandela, mainly so that he would tell them to calm down and accept prison life. Forbes was 24, the youngest commander of Umkhonto we Sizwe in the Western Cape. He'd trained in guerrilla warfare in Angola and then been picked up for terrorism offences. He was interrogated and tortured by notorious members of the apartheid apparatus – later named and shamed at the Truth and Reconciliation Commission – and sent to Pollsmoor to await trial.

He and his fellow defendants were singing protest songs and shouting and refusing to go to their cell. They were treated brutally by the guards in return but never backed down. One night, several of them were discovered cutting through the bars of their communal cell in an escape plan. The warders reported the disruption, and we were ordered to intervene with a 'carry-on'. I was the officer in charge, but I could not bring myself to take part in the swinging of rubber batons and the beatings. I couldn't stop the intervention, but at least I could stand aside.

Forbes was blamed for the incident and given 30 days in solitary, in a single cell in ankle-chains. He was charged with attempting escape and starting an affray, and he counter-charged with a claim of assault against the prison officers. In the end, there was a compromise. Both sides dropped the charges.

He and his fellow defendants deserved to meet Mandela, their hero and their leader. I waited till Mandela was walking in the exercise courtyard, and I brought Forbes and some others down, ostensibly to pick up tennis balls they had knocked over the wall, and to take empty food buckets to the kitchen. They shook hands and embraced, and came back inspired by just a few words from the great man. He was happy too to have met these young lions.

Forbes was later sentenced to 15 years on Robben Island, but he was released in 1991 when the last political prisoners left the island. The prison became a medium security institution for criminal prisoners for the next five years, until it closed its doors in 1996. Forbes was appointed senior estates manager when the island was declared a World Heritage Site in 1997, and he worked there for 10 years.

Trevor Manuel, a coloured political detainee who later became South Africa's finance minister, also managed to meet Kathrada and Mandela when I fixed up a dental appointment for him.

Meanwhile, meetings between Coetsee and Mandela and

other government officials had resumed and were seemingly increasing in importance. I knew also that he was determined to meet the apartheid government's president, P. W. Botha, so far without success. There seemed to be a deadlock, with each side demanding an end to the violence.

I was aware that Mandela was mentioning some of this to his comrades to test their judgement about it, and also writing to ANC leader Oliver Tambo in Zambia. But it was his own judgement he was relying on to make decisions, and this was causing tensions. I was regularly seeing Kathrada, Sisulu, and the others, and I sensed that they were anxious, suspicious even, about talks between Mandela and the government, from which they were excluded. Even one of Mandela's own activist lawyers, Priscilla Jana, whom I am still friendly with today, had suspicions about his secrecy.

This led to mistrust on both sides within Mandela's circle. Kathrada had been sending special food over to Mandela for Eid, the Muslim festival, and some curries and other dishes were stored in the cupboard in his cell for too long. He became sick with food poisoning and refused a visit from Priscilla and a fellow lawyer. They insisted on seeing him, so he went to the visit room where they confronted him about 'talking to the enemy'. Mandela rushed from the room, and I found him vomiting in the corridor. I helped him back to his cell, while the bugging device in the visiting room recorded Priscilla discussing the possibility that Mandela had run out on them because he didn't want to admit he was secretly 'selling them out' to the National Party.

They returned the next day and Mandela apologised. I saw what he was up against, this man now isolated in both body and soul, mistrusted even by his own comrades, but still brave enough to soldier on towards his brilliant version of the truth.

CHAPTER 11

Mandela's health was an increasing worry. A strong, fit man for the whole time I had known him, he now seemed to be growing older and weaker in front of my eyes.

The weight of his many responsibilities was a heavy burden. He had agreed to meet regularly with government representatives, but they were playing a hard game with him. Their continual demand was for him to order the end of the ANC's armed struggle. Mandela did not even need to refer to Oliver Tambo or his other comrades to refuse this outright, even though it deadlocked the possibility of further negotiation.

The apartheid government was under siege internationally to release Mandela and abolish its racist regime; it needed to do business with the ANC. But they were putting forward impossible demands. They wanted an end to the ANC's military activities, a renouncement of Communism, and an end to the call for black majority rule. Mandela was intransigent on all three issues.

They seemed to believe they could wear him down, these officials with their privileged lives and their freedom, coming in numbers to offer tempting possibilities to a 70-year-old man locked up in isolation and desperate for release.

They underestimated him. Mandela had not suffered 26

years of humiliation and deprivation just to cave in now. I knew he would rather carry the anguish of disappointment to his deathbed than ever sell out the ANC to a half-hearted compromise. He was allowed to meet several times with his comrades Sisulu and Kathrada and the others, and they were given permission to sit in the big house next to the officer's mess, the same setting where the Eminent Persons Group had met Mandela for lunch. Of course, the rooms were all bugged and they knew it.

Tea and sandwiches were served and it was such a new sensation that, despite the overwhelming subjects of government and nationhood they were discussing and the awesome decisions these great men were considering, Kathrada found time to wonder at the dainty food and the tea poured into china cups with saucers. He told me afterwards what an unexpected treat that was.

The ANC needed to seize the moment, while South Africa was in crisis. The apartheid government was clearly in disarray, and the common decency and humanity of the world was supporting their cause. Mandela had emerged as a world figure, a giant of a man who could almost singlehandedly lead the way to reconciliation and a bloodless transition to a free and fair life for the benefit of all, black and white.

But I saw his health failing, a dry cough racking his lungs and causing sleepless nights and fever. I brought the medical officer and a government doctor to his bedside. They gave him cough mixture. Of course there was no improvement, and it was clear Mandela's respiratory problems needed further investigation. It was decided to get him to hospital for expert observation and more tests.

On 12 August 1988, I got him to a car outside his cell and we drove to Tygerberg hospital in unmarked vehicles. Three rooms had been cordoned off, and warders patrolled the corridors. Presumably they were there to fend off intruders or the media; they could not possibly have thought Mandela might make a run for it.

Mandela was gasping for breath, and he was wheeled straight to the theatre. Fluid was drained from his lungs, and back in the ward I watched him become thinner and weaker over the next six weeks. He was not eating, and he was himself in an anxious state about his health. He told me he had never had 'flu or persistent colds or coughs, and he could not understand what was wrong with him.

I was bringing him his newspapers and letters every day and taking my turn with the warders guarding him. Meanwhile, the doctors were doing endless tests. One morning, I was with Mandela in his room. He was sitting up in bed in his green and white striped prison pyjamas, with his study books. A doctor came in and told him he had tuberculosis, a dreadful disease. He said there would be more treatment and that it meant a further long period in hospital.

My heart sank, and as I looked at Mandela I saw him keeping himself under control. He thanked the doctor for telling him the truth in such a straightforward way, and said he was prepared to go through any treatment necessary.

Tuberculosis is rife in South Africa, and the bacteria flourishes in crowded places like prisons and hostels. It can survive in damp, dusty, and dark conditions for a long period, especially if ventilation is poor. With Mandela's immune system at a low ebb from stress and previous hospital procedures, he was a prime candidate. Nevertheless, the depressing news was a huge blow to both of us.

It was decided that staying in Tygerberg, a state hospital, was too risky in terms of security – there were too many people going in and out. Too many black people was what they really meant: people who might see and actually recognise Mandela and spread the word. The last thing they wanted was for him to be sprung out of hospital and back into the community.

The head of Pollsmoor decided we should send Mandela over to Constantiaberg Medi-Clinic, a private hospital. Towards the end of August we put him in a wheelchair, still in his pyjamas, and took him to the ground floor in the goods lift. At the back of the hospital, we quickly got him into a car. The one hospital security guard who helped us did so well that he was offered a job at Pollsmoor.

At Constantiaberg, a whole ward had been screened off. There were five warders on each shift, and I was ordered to make Mandela at home there. I brought all his things from his cell at Pollsmoor – the steel cabinet, books, and clothes all piled into a prison pickup truck – and set up home for him. He was the first black patient ever to be admitted to this hospital.

Four nurses had been selected to take care of him. They and their family and friends had all been checked out by the security police for their political views. These young women seemed fearful of nursing Mandela at first, but he shook hands with each of them on introduction, taking both of their hands in his, and within days they were smuggling in special treats for him and enjoying his good humour and easy manner.

Like me, they had been charmed into breaking the rules for him. They were bringing him cake and chocolate mousse and even pizza for him to try for the first time. This was all strictly against regulations – the warders were supposed to taste and test all the food going in to Mandela.

Minister Coetsee made personal visits to the hospital, keeping up the all-important contact that could, in an ideal world, lead to peace in the country. Mandela was advised by the prison officers that he should buy himself some smart clothes for his talks with government representatives. He had a few thousand rand in his prison account and authorised me to go with the head of prison to choose trousers, shirts, shoes, and a jacket. For some reason, the head of prison chose the most expensive men's clothing store in the area, in an exclusive white shopping street in Wynberg suburb. I wondered if Mandela was being given a lesson in how expensive life was on the outside. I never discovered if this was deliberately cold-hearted or a helpful gesture.

I had to hide a smile when I saw Mandela send at least half of it back. A pair of shoes from that shop cost R800, which would be £184 – expensive even by today's standards. The head of prison warned him that was what everyday items cost outside of prison. It wasn't true.

Some of the clothes needed altering so we brought in a warder called Visagie, who worked in Pollsmoor's tailoring department, to do some measuring. He was a coloured guy, which took the hospital staff aback. The head of prison told the nurse to bring food for me and Visagie while he worked and, although I could see her falter, she didn't refuse. Things were changing and the whites had better get used to it; that's what I saw at that moment.

Mandela made great friends with his nurses. He told me how they wanted to take him to their staff Christmas party downstairs in early December, but of course that was impossible. So they brought some turkey and trimmings up to his ward and had their own little celebration with him there. The Christmas crackers had to be opened up, taken apart, and put together again by the security-conscious warders, but that went off all right. Mandela, in great spirits, had his party.

Minister Coetsee continued to visit, and of course all their conversations were bugged. He was rushing back and forth to carry messages to the other interested parties.

The nurses told me afterwards how Mandela would point all around the ceiling to let them know where the bugs were. He told them once how 'the bees are buzzing, lots of activity in the hive today', getting them to shake their heads and wonder what on earth he was talking about.

Mandela had dug in his heels over the government's demands, but he wanted the dialogue to continue too, so a high-stakes game was taking place. Back on the ward in his striped prison pyjamas after these meetings, he made many notes, at the same time taking his medicine and following doctor's orders to regain his health and keep moving forward.

One evening in early December, some three months after Mandela's arrival at the hospital, the head of prison appeared in Mandela's ward and told him he should get ready to leave. Mandela was to dress in his new clothes – slacks, a shirt, and a dark-coloured casual jacket – and put his hospital dressing-gown on top.

It was getting dark, and I used the confusion of a shift change to get him out. He and I walked down the fire-escape steps together and went outside, where I had arranged for the security alarm to be turned off. Like Mandela, I had no idea where we were going.

I was told to drive at high speed and to follow an unmarked police car. There were five vehicles in our convoy. None of us, police or warders, was wearing a uniform. I was thinking this must be very significant. We were driving away from Pollsmoor, and it was all being done under cover of darkness.

I thought maybe Mandela was actually going to be released. A year earlier, Mandela had put it to government representatives that his fellow political prisoners should be released. He was glad and thankful to be told that Govan Mbeki was to be brought over from Robben Island with four others and they would be freed. The four other prisoners were serving life sentences for activism, and they had accepted President P.W. Botha's offer of release in return for renouncing violence. Mbeki hadn't, but it was still decided that he should be released.

Mandela had had the pleasure of telling Mbeki himself that he was leaving prison. The official reason was his age – he was eight years older than Mandela – and his ability to quell uprisings in the Eastern Cape. The two met in a contact visit in Pollsmoor, then Mbeki was flown out that night and met by lawyers in Port Elizabeth. He was still to play a highly significant role in further negotiations.

But Mandela himself was far from a release date.

Warily, he looked around him as we drove through suburbs and out into the countryside.

Eventually, we drove down a dirt track towards farmland and in through the gates of Victor Verster Prison in Paarl, a rural town an hour from the city of Cape Town. Mandela was sitting in the middle of the back seat as usual, peering forward. All the warders at the gate saluted as we drove by.

We parked up by a newly built white-painted wall with observation posts nearby. Behind it was a cream-coloured bungalow with a pretty stoep with three archways. There was a tiled roof, a well-tended garden, and a swimming pool.

Beyond the high wall was farmland, where the low-security

prisoners worked. There were pigs and chickens and fields of vegetables, so pleasing for Mandela to see after all these years. It was in the middle of nowhere, but there was countryside and fresh air, something he had longed for.

He was very cool, very dignified about the whole thing. He just walked from the car into the house, noting the staff quarters outside where his warders would be on 24-hour standby, listening in to the bugs undoubtedly planted everywhere on the premises. The security police were stationed in a large metal container unit with one next to it for National Intelligence. The head of Pollsmoor Prison was moved in to be in overall charge of the setup, and a cook warder would spend daylight hours with him.

Mandela took it all in, strolling from room to room. He was going to be living alone in a house with a big main bedroom and a big kitchen. 'It's beautiful,' he murmured. 'But why is there a television in the kitchen?'

'It's a microwave,' he was told, and he listened in genuine wonderment while its functions were explained to him. He liked the look of the pool but thought it was dangerous, a place where children could drown. He had always told Winnie they would never have a pool at their home. He was obsessed with safety and freedom for children, animals, everyone.

In the sitting room, someone turned on the television and he saw a news bulletin announcing that he had been moved to Victor Verster. He couldn't believe that they already knew that. I stood in the big bedroom with him and opened the wardrobe door. He looked inside, amazed. Then I opened another door and there was the en suite bathroom. Amazing, he found everything amazing.

I told him I had to say goodbye, but I was coming back. He shook my hand. All he had with him was the portable radio that never left his side, and a small overnight bag. He told me: 'Please drive safely and don't forget to bring my things. My books, my exercise clothes, and my photo album.'

He was told he could ring a bell and call anyone at any time of night. There were no prison bars, but there were many people around – warders, security police, government spies.

For the first time for many years, he was looking at comfortable furniture in mellow colours, with carpets on the floor and pictures on the walls. I left him in the sitting room, just standing there. He looked tired; after all, he had just left hospital. But he also looked content, as if he might settle in all right.

He told me he wouldn't use the big bedroom. He wanted to move into a smaller one. When I looked back, he was still standing in the sitting room and every light in the house and garden, even on the stoep, was blazing. I heard he left the lights on all night, even in the bedroom. It was all he was used to after 26 years in prison.

CHAPTER 12

Mandela told me the next day that he had taken a walk around the garden and liked everything except the razor wire. There were pretty flower beds, but his gardening days were over. He didn't need to grow vegetables any more; he had his very own chef and the food was good.

He was so taken with the design of the house that he made a rough drawing of it and, years later, he built a replica of it in the village of Qunu where he spent his childhood. His daughter Zindzi rationalised that his affection for the house at Victor Verster was prompted by the fact that it was the first place he had lived in for 26 years that was anything like a normal home. The brick-faced bungalow in Qunu with its tiled roof and front stoep beautified by three arches is a home he loved, and he wanted it to be his last resting-place.

Mandela was no swimmer, but when it was very hot – sometimes the temperature would climb to 35 degrees centigrade – he enjoyed just standing in the cold water in the pool. One of the warder's sons offered to teach him to swim but, although Mandela tried, he had no real enthusiasm for it.

Of course, the warders on night duty also loved to get in the pool. But they were discovered by some officers and forbidden to use it again. That upset Mandela. He told me he had heard them splashing around at night and had enjoyed watching through the window, seeing people having fun.

He made good friends with his chef, warder Jack Swart, who has since told of how he reminded Mandela that they had met before, on Robben Island. Swart was the driver who used to take Mandela and the others on outdoor work parties, driving so fast and so hard along the island tracks that Mandela once knocked on his window and told him angrily to stop hurtling over all the bumps and potholes. 'We're not sacks of mealies!' he had protested.

In fact, Swart had been told by Robben Island's senior officers to cause maximum discomfort for the prisoners, so he had just been doing his job, much as he appeared to regret it later.

Mandela was slightly unamused to be told this same guy would now be his constant companion, but he lightened the mood by saying, 'Well, I hope you're a better cook than you are a driver.'

They found a way to get on well, and soon Mandela was insisting on helping with the washing-up and making the sorghum beer that Swart brewed up so expertly from the wheat grain he brought from his friend's farm, fermented with brown sugar, raisins, and yeast. Mandela used to joke with his many visitors that they were only coming to see him because of the beer and the food.

That first day, I returned to Constantiaberg hospital to collect his belongings and I heard how the guards had stayed outside his room all night, not knowing he had gone. When the nurses arrived for their shift, they realised Mandela had been moved and were upset that they hadn't said goodbye. But he had instructed me to buy boxes of assorted chocolates for them and small cards so he could write to them individually. He gave me all the nurses' names, and I delivered them. I got the feeling each of those nurses would treasure his words for life.

I also collected the television from his cell and brought it to Victor Verster for him. He said I should give his iron and his coffee flask to the criminal prisoners. And there were cigarettes, chocolates, and a note of thanks for Louw, the cook in the prison kitchen.

When I returned, I went through the solid steel side door into Mandela's garden and he was already coming out of the house to greet me, happy to see a familiar face but also pleased to have assessed his new surroundings and found them comfortable. He was wearing a dark-coloured tracksuit, a white t-shirt, and trainers. The International Red Cross had been sending money for him and other prisoners to spend on exercise clothing. I never saw him in a prison uniform again. We brought in about ten cardboard boxes full of study books, sports equipment, newspaper clippings – all dated and indexed – along with Mandela's desk calendars for every year he had been imprisoned, and his clothing. He asked us to stack them in the sitting room. He wanted to sort things out on his own. He was making himself at home. He had already acquired a bodyboard to help with swimming. I was invited to take the encyclopaedias.

At 11 a.m., Mandela asked Swart to bring us cold drinks. He was by now quite the gentleman of the house, settled into his role. He showed me around the pool area and the garden and was very happy with a big tree at the centre where he could sit in the shade to read.

I had brought letters with me and told him I'd bring them regularly. He sent warm greetings back to the 'old guys' in Pollsmoor and said he hoped to see them soon.

Raymond Mhlaba was particularly angry and upset that

Mandela had been taken to another location. He said he and the other Rivonians believed the authorities planned to kill him. They put in daily written demands to see him at Victor Verster. Meanwhile, I heard that Winnie had been his first visitor and they had talked over many family problems. Of course, I could find out everything they talked about because the house was bugged all over.

As I left, my fellow warders showed me the operations room full of tape recorders and switches for various bugs. There was sophisticated sound equipment everywhere, more technology than in Pollsmoor – even the furniture was bugged. The chair legs were hollow and fitted with recording devices operating from batteries. The trees in the garden and all the flower beds were bugged. Mandela could not have gardened there even if he had wanted to. The walls literally had ears, but he was aware of it so it was virtually counter-productive. He wasn't going to openly discuss ANC tactics.

When visits started with Sisulu, Kathrada, and the others, he would sometimes walk them to the toilet cubicle, the only place where he couldn't be overheard, for a quick exchange of news and views.

Sisulu wrote to a friend at that time saying that Mandela seemed fit and well, but lonely. He only had the warders to talk to. Mandela's neighbours were the ever-vigilant security police, sweating in their metal container of an office. Next to them were the National Intelligence guys. Close by was a braai area where Mandela could entertain visitors with a meal of cooked beef and sausages. All that area was bugged too.

It took Mandela six months to get approval for a visit from Sisulu. When the day came, I drove him in a government car with no escort. He was in the back, wearing his prison uniform. I was supposed to take a different route from Pollsmoor to Victor Verster Prison each time so as to avoid any media attention, and it was a pleasure to be driving through the countryside at Somerset West and Stellenbosch, with a dramatic mountain range behind us.

Sisulu was very excited, noting the farmland and the crops with everything looking green and alive. As we drove past the turn-off to Strand, I pointed out that Eddie Daniels, a popular fellow prisoner on Robben Island, lived there. He was glad to hear that and so interested in everything, wanting to know about the winelands, which he'd never seen before. Like Mandela, he came from the bustling township of Soweto in Johannesburg, the big city. He had seen nothing of the beautiful Western Cape. Even on rare visits to the doctor or the dentist on the mainland, Sisulu and the others had been in the back of prison trucks, unable to see anything around them.

We drove through the gates at Victor Verster, and Mandela was at the steel door waiting for him. They hugged and were happy and somehow relieved to see each other. All the old friendship was still there; they still needed each other very much.

Mandela was longing to show Sisulu around the place, and he was duly fascinated by the idea of an en suite bathroom: such luxury. Of course they played with the microwave in the kitchen together, Mandela mightily amused by his new party trick, putting a plastic beaker of water in for 60 seconds and then producing it boiling hot.

They spent about an hour and a half together alone indoors, while Swart organised tea and snacks. Everything they said was listened in to by the swarms of spies stationed outside in their sweltering operations room.

Mandela described how he was seeing a medical officer every

day, and a doctor twice a week. They were taking his blood pressure and checking his pills. Someone definitely wanted to make sure he survived. He was still doing sit-ups and press-ups regularly and now had a new exercise bike in one of the spare rooms. I felt he was beginning to look better, back to his usual healthy, handsome, and dignified self.

Sisulu was glad that Mandela had recovered fully from his periods in hospital. On the way back to Pollsmoor, he told me: 'It was good to see him in a light mood again, and fit and healthy. He deserves some luxury in his life after all this time.' I got the feeling that Sisulu was going to keep to himself some of the matters he and Mandela had discussed.

On the journey back, we stopped at a little shop and bought some cold drinks. Sisulu asked for a Diet Coke. There were coloured children playing around the car, but they didn't take any notice of us in our warders' uniforms and him in prison clothes. We had driven slowly for the whole trip, all of us glad to be out of the daily routine for a few hours, and we got back to Pollsmoor just in time for lockup.

The commanding officer was waiting for us. He told Sisulu he was being moved into Mandela's old cell, that miserable damp place. Now it was his turn to be alone. Sisulu accepted it calmly but, when I fetched his belongings from the communal cell, Kathrada was terribly upset.

'Sisulu is old, he shouldn't be alone,' he said. 'Who is going to take care of him? It's my job to look after him. Who is going to do that when he's in isolation?'

Kathrada was kindness itself, and he had been close to the whole Sisulu family even before he was imprisoned. He had become like a son to Sisulu, helping him to the shower and continually checking on his health and diet.

The regime had its reasons for isolating Mandela and Sisulu, the main conduits to Oliver Tambo in exile. It was too late to break them – that was evident – but they could limit their influence on others.

In July 1989, I was told that Sisulu, Mlangeni, Kathrada, Mhlaba, and Oscar Mpetha could go to Mandela for a four-hour visit to include lunch. They were allowed to wear their own clothes, and to them it was a sure sign that all Mandela's efforts to get them released were surely going in the right direction. For me, I was not so sure. It could just be a security measure so that their journey and their visit could be low-key.

There was tremendous excitement: an outing and a reunion to look forward to. Mpetha was at hospital for physio again, so he would be joining the rest of us en route.

I drove the others in a prison minibus with another officer sitting next to me. We left Pollsmoor at 8.30 a.m. and parked up on a grassy patch near the river at Maitland, waiting for Mpetha to join us. When his vehicle arrived, we set off in convoy towards Victor Verster.

Mandela came out of the steel door, impatient to see them. It was very touching to watch them, and for Mpetha it was a moment he had wanted for years. I had sneaked him that brief encounter with Mandela in the corridor at Pollsmoor, but now was the first time he was meeting the other Rivonians. Their friendship went back all the way to the 1950s.

Mhlaba was doing his usual big, noisy laugh; they were all in great high spirits. All the old guard of the ANC High Command, two of them now living in isolation but not one of them a broken relic of the revolution, as the government had intended.

In his book *Conversations With Myself*, Mandela wrote about these comrades, saying: 'I wish I could tell you more about the courageous band of colleagues with whom I suffer humiliation daily and who nevertheless deport themselves with dignity and determination. I wish I could relate their conversations and banter, their readiness to help in any personal problem suffered by their fellow prisoners so that you could judge for yourself the calibre of the men whose lives are being sacrificed on the fiendish altar of colour hatred.'

I walked behind them as they went into the house. They had to be shown every room, and the microwave party trick. They were having a wonderful time.

I left them talking in the sitting room and went outside. Swart was offering to bring drinks and they all had tea. About an hour later, they moved to the dining room and had a proper lunch served to them with place-settings and knives and forks. I had a big smile to myself at their delight.

Swart served Mandela some white wine and Mlangeni wanted beer. Kathrada, a Muslim who didn't take alcohol, had a fizzy apple drink. Sisulu asked for the same but didn't realise there was no alcohol in it. So he was very funny afterwards, acting as if he was slightly drunk. The whole thing was just in his head, and we teased him about it endlessly.

Kathrada had hidden a book in his bag. It was Mandela's second prison biography, written by his close friend and fellow activist Fatima Meer, called *Higher Than Hope*. Copies had been sent to Pollsmoor in the post, and the censors had agreed that the prisoners could have it. But still Kathrada could not be sure what restrictions there were on Mandela. He asked Mandela to autograph the book, and in fact they all signed it and then wrapped it in brown prison paper and gave it to me for safekeeping.

Fatima Meer and her husband Ismail had been loyal friends

who took many risks to hide Mandela during his underground years when the police were searching for him. They witnessed the development of his relationship with Winnie and supported and cared for her for many years while he was in prison. Fatima and her husband always believed that Mandela would be released one day and lead South Africa. They had watched him through his first, often reckless, years as a revolutionary, and they shared his unshakeable faith in the future.

Even while I was with him every day and doubtful that this ageing man could ever walk free and have the energy needed to change the country, he was writing to Ismail Meer about their shared hopes and plans. One of those letters, written from Robben Island, was later published. In it, Mandela reminisced about their early days, arguing their different politics – Ismail was a member of the Communist Party and Mandela was going in another direction then – and he described how

a litany of dreams and expectations kept me going throughout those lean years. Some of them have been realised while the fulfilment of others eludes us to this day. Nevertheless few people will deny that the harvest has merely been delayed, far from destroyed. It is on there, our rich and well-watered fields, even though the actual task of gathering it has proved far more testing than we ever thought.

It was astonishing that the authorities had allowed Mandela and his comrades to have the book. Mandela had agreed that Fatima could write the authorised story of his prison years, as he did not want to display the 'vanity' of writing his own autobiography. He later relented, in the knowledge that his

Long Walk to Freedom was not a personal vanity at all but a journey he took for all South Africans. The lunch they were all enjoying that day was a celebration of *Higher Than Hope* and a very important reunion to underscore their belief that they could still change the world.

They were drinking wine for the first time in years, a semi-sweet wine that Mandela had started to enjoy. Mlangeni and Mhlaba loosened up and were quite noisy. The next day, Mlangeni complained of a bad headache, though I think even he thought it had been worth it. All of them had been in high spirits on the way back. We delivered Mpetha back to hospital with a police escort, and I took the rest of the party home to Pollsmoor.

A month later, Wilton Mkwayi, their great friend and the self-appointed cook of crayfish and abalone during grim times out working on Robben Island beach, was transferred to Pollsmoor because he needed hospital treatment for a back problem. There was more rejoicing in the communal cell when I brought him to the Rivonians, and now he was able to go with them on occasional visits to Mandela.

Mandela had found a way to communicate with Oliver Tambo in Zambia through his lawyers, reporting on progress with his offer of talks and negotiations with the apartheid government. Tambo had advised caution, and others in the ANC were completely against any reconciliation. But Mandela was charting his own course, the course he believed would result in less pain, less bloodshed.

Sisulu went on one-to-one visits to Mandela and, as they knew all their conversations were being overheard and recorded, they made conciliatory verbal gestures and talked of their intention to be reasonable with the regime, all strong hints that talks should continue and be speeded up, even if they were only talks about talks.

I heard about several visits from Coetsee, the Minister of Justice, who was actually now bringing bottles of wine with him, and I was at the house once when the Commissioner of Prisons was talking to Mandela.

I could see him becoming more straightforward with his demands. His priority was to get veteran political prisoners released. He refused to negotiate further until that was resolved.

One Saturday morning, an outing was organised for him to drive up the scenic west coast away from the Cape to the tiny fishing resort of Paternoster. Several warders came, with me driving a white Mercedes and a police escort behind us.

We had heard there was a 'red tide' up the coast. This was a fascinating phenomenon when tons of plankton and other algae had over-germinated due to freak weather conditions and an upwelling in the ocean. When this happened, the sea was red and purple, brown and orange. And literally tons of crayfish became stranded on the beach and rocks, having moved to shallow water to get more oxygen.

As the tide went out, the crayfish were left there, suffering from lack of water and a blazing sun. The government arranged helicopters carrying cargo nets to airlift them back into the sea miles up the coast to keep them alive. The fishing industry was vital to that area's economy. However, the local people, many of them subsistence fishermen, came in hordes to collect the valuable crayfish to sell or eat before the helicopter could collect them. It was an exciting event, a spectacle we all wanted to see.

It took us two hours to get there, and when we arrived we could see crowds of white people, holidaymakers and vendors selling the crayfish. We found a small restaurant at the beach and decided on a table. I suppose we were an unusual group, four big white guys with a black man, though none of us were wearing prison clothes. Nobody stared. Nobody seemed to notice us as we drank coffee. We walked down the beach and watched people bringing in boats. We drove back through the coloured fishermen's living area where kids were playing around the old whitewashed cottages. We had tinted windows fitted so no one could see in. We drove slowly through the area so Mandela could have a good look. And that was the last time I was with him outside prison until his release.

During this time, he told me he was feeling that some of the warders and their cohorts in the security police and National Intelligence were not sufficiently respectful towards him. He put in a complaint that they were calling him Nelson, and these were men much younger than him, all this occurring at a time when he was at his most assertive, his most dignified, needing to make his status obvious to those in meetings with him.

Orders came in from on high that we must call him Mr Mandela from now on. He had successfully played a game of his own in the face of all the mind games imposed on him.

It was different for me. I would always be 'Mr Brand' to him, or 'Warrant Officer Brand' if I was in uniform. He would shake my hand and greet me warmly, saying: 'How are you today, my friend? How are things at Pollsmoor? I hope your family is well.' For more than ten years, I had called him Mandela, so I couldn't change that overnight, and he did not mind at all.

It was only when I met him regularly as president that I started calling him Mr Mandela, and then I was upbraided by others for not calling him Mr President. Actually, it didn't matter what we called each other; we had a warm and special relationship, which was nothing to do with names or titles and everything to do with what we had been through together.

For all those years, going back to my first meeting with the Rivonians, I had been thinking that these people didn't belong in there, in those terrible places. The punishment the government had given them was wrong. They were old, polite, friendly, and disciplined men. They were high-minded idealists who believed with all their hearts that their suffering was worthwhile.

Their great supporter, the anti-apartheid campaigner Helen Suzman, visited them several times and was impressed with their resilience. She said: 'They were strong and united, and they were organised, and they were informed.'

If they were on the outside, they could help to control the violence that was constantly bubbling under the surface of our country, erupting at any time.

When Mandela was first put into isolation, I was thinking and hoping that would be a first step towards freedom for him. He had the power to stop the bloodshed, and there was a lot of blood flowing. Maybe black and white and coloured could live in harmony with his guidance. And he could be free. He was a good man – that was clear to me from the start.

I thought about all this a great deal and, even today, I wish I had done more for him and his comrades. The rules were so strict, but I tried to make life a little easier. Perhaps, though, I could have been more lenient during visits, and not followed the rules so rigidly when censoring their letters.

I loved my country and I was steeped in the Afrikaans culture, so I had very mixed feelings about how South Africa might turn out. My parents were always definite that there should never have been apartheid, no Hendrik Verwoerd bringing his cruel fascist notions over from Holland and Germany.

When the Truth and Reconciliation Commission was set up by Mandela after he became president to hear testimony from people who had suffered during the apartheid years, many ordinary white people were genuinely shocked. They had been living in a police state with no knowledge of the oppression that led to black protests or riots or demands. It was impossible for them to have black or coloured friends or associates as that was banned by law, and the news was heavily censored. They didn't know about the torture and deaths. They only knew about terrorist attacks by the ANC.

I knew more. I had been living with a great deal of extra knowledge. I felt ashamed of my government.

I remembered a warder working with me on Robben Island. One day, he had given a lift to a coloured lady in the pouring rain after she had visited a prisoner. He let her sit in the back of his pickup truck, still exposed to the weather but at least reaching shelter more quickly. It was against the law, the Immorality Act, for him as an unaccompanied man to be in the same vehicle as a coloured woman. He was fined and left the prison service soon afterwards. That small act of human kindness had cost him his career. It could not possibly be right for that to happen.

I thought back to my childhood on the farm, when my father would stop his vehicle when he saw people of any colour walking the rough tracks, and offer them a lift. People of all skin tones could be seen on the village streets together. But in the cities where the police were ever watchful, there was total segregation.

I recently met a coloured lady in her eighties who remembered our days on the farm. Her husband worked with my father. She remembered all of my family and our friends with fondness and talked of those happier days when we didn't realise the turmoil in the cities and the suburbs.

She reminded me of a time when my father's truck had a puncture and we were stranded by the roadside. A black African man stopped to help, lending us a spare tyre and saying we could return it the next day. That was in 1974, when such interaction would have been literally impossible away from the farmlands.

All this went through my mind as I watched the extraordinary events going on in front of me at Pollsmoor and Victor Verster, the increasing official visits, the phone calls to and from Zambia, the courtesy with which government representatives were treating Mandela.

A new regular visitor was Niel Barnard, the head of National Intelligence, who was a close adviser to President P. W. Botha. He had in fact been meeting with Mandela secretly since 1988. Mandela had asked many times to meet with Botha but had been refused. Barnard was there as his eyes and ears, reporting back with the help of tapes recording every meeting.

Mandela had written to Botha proposing that they meet to discuss conditions for negotiations, as the prospect of real negotiations was completely deadlocked. He was determined that an immovable precondition would be the release of his fellow long-term prisoners. In early July 1989, Mandela was taken secretly to the Tuynhuys (the Townhouse – the Cape Town office of the South African presidency) for his first meeting with Botha.

I heard later, with some astonishment, that the head of prison had thought Mandela's tie was done up badly and re-knotted it himself. When they arrived at Botha's office, Niel Barnard was similarly unimpressed by his shoelaces and knelt down to tie them properly. What moments to have captured for history. I just wish I had been there to see for myself.

Over the years, there had been many occasions when I could have taken photographs of Mandela and the rest of the Rivonians. They would have liked it and encouraged it. But there wasn't a photographic processor in the whole country who would risk developing it and, if they did, we would all have ended up in prison. That was the strength of the fear we lived with. It's a great shame.

I was not involved in the trip to the grand Tuynhuys office; other warders took Mandela. But it is common knowledge now that Botha was staggered by his familiarity with every aspect of the Afrikaner nation and its history. Their meeting was tentative but cordial, though Botha continued to angrily disagree that there was any similarity between black South Africans' fight for their rights and the Afrikaners' battles for recognition in their 1914 uprising.

There would be further meetings, and the ANC in exile in England and Zambia were also having roundtable talks with governments that had influence in South Africa. George Bizos, Mandela's lawyer who had represented him at the Rivonia trial, made a trip to Zambia to take detailed information from Mandela to Oliver Tambo.

On Mandela's birthday two weeks later – a day so cold you could see snow on the top of the mountains – he celebrated with almost his whole family, the first time he had ever had his wife and children in one place together for 26 years. He told me how much it hurt to realise what he had been missing.

When his daughter Zindzi later described that day, she said she was trying to work out what the government was hoping to achieve. By now, the government had given permission for certain members of Mandela's family to stay overnight at his house in Victor Verster. Zindzi felt that the family was being encouraged to perhaps move in there with her father, to reduce his martyrdom status, to 'compromise the Mandela legend'. She was almost certainly right.

Neither she nor her mother Winnie ever agreed to spend one night there. Winnie said it was a nice house with a nice garden, but it was still a prison, and she would never ever make it her home.

Outside in the rest of the country, the trade union movement had joined up with the former UDF, the United Democratic Front (now known as the MDM, or the Mass Democratic Movement), to forge ahead with a major defiance campaign in sympathy with the ANC. In the prisons, there were hunger strikes and a state of near-anarchy, which forced the government to release about a thousand political detainees.

In August, P. W. Botha suffered a serious stroke and resigned as State President. On 20 September 1989, F.W. de Klerk was sworn in and announced that his government would talk to any group that wanted peace. If it was a signal to Mandela, he quickly recognised it and immediately wrote to de Klerk renewing his offers to talk.

Soon afterwards, I was told I could take Mlangeni, Mhlaba, Sisulu, and Kathrada to visit Mandela at Victor Verster again, and once again they could wear their own clothes. A tailor's assistant had been into Pollsmoor to expertly measure them, and I made sure he had Oscar Mpetha's measurements too. Fine suits were made for everyone, and I took Oscar's to him in hospital. I also found there was a suit for me too, a very nice fit.

The new clothes had already had their first outing, and there is a great photograph of all the prisoners together with

Mandela – Oscar still in his hospital dressing-gown that day – in the garden at Victor Verster, looking very spruce.

Now, on what turned out to be another special day, the guys were very happy to be climbing into the minibus with me. We decided to make a braai that day for four of us warders from Pollsmoor, two or three of our colleagues at Victor Verster, and the prisoners. Poor Oscar was stuck in hospital again so couldn't join in the fun.

Mlangeni had recently had a terrible setback. His twin sister had died and, despite his written application pleading to go to her funeral, he had been turned down due to 'security reasons'. The police were terrified that the sight of one of the Rivonian heroes in public would trigger crowd hysteria.

We were sorry for Mlangeni for this piece of cruelty. Unsurprisingly, he had taken it very badly. But now there was a party that might cheer him up a little. We had sausages and lamb chops and beer, with an agreement that we could spend five hours there, before leaving at 6 p.m. It was quite relaxing in the sunshine, and someone in the prison service took a group photograph of Mandela and his friends sitting under his favourite tree.

It must have been Mandela's idea. It turned out that he knew something we didn't. His friends were going home: He had won that battle for them.

I planned to take the prisoners back to Pollsmoor, but I got a message saying we couldn't leave. There were hundreds of people outside the gates. So I took them all over to the officers' mess, leaving Mandela at his house.

Mandela told them then: 'Chaps, this is goodbye.' But they wouldn't believe him. They said that they would believe it when they saw it. I organised some food and drink for them in the mess. They asked if they could have steak, and a television was brought in for them to watch. We turned it on just as it was being announced loud and clear that Mhlaba, Mlangeni, Kathrada, and Sisulu were being released. They were taken totally by surprise. They were all ecstatic, all incredulous.

The officers found some champagne, and the steak was served. Suddenly it was a celebration, and even some of my hardline colleagues looked happy and relieved for these old-timers who had been so suddenly set free. The least problematic and most-liked prisoners in South Africa were going home at last.

Everyone was enjoying the moment. The champagne still flowed, with Kathrada and Sisulu sticking to their apple drink. There were no mobile phones in those days, so they couldn't call anyone with their marvellous news.

At about 9 p.m., I drove out through a back route to avoid all the media at the front gates. It was like a party in the minibus on the way to Pollsmoor, with everyone talking at once and so excited. They said they didn't mind staying one more night; they would leave in the morning. They asked me, though, if their cell doors could stay unlocked. Despite everything, I couldn't agree to that, so we locked them up as usual.

But it turned out that the prisoners had to stay a further few days, while transport and other arrangements were sorted out for them. Eventually, one evening, I was told to get ready by 5 a.m. to take Mlangeni, Mhlaba, Kathrada, Sisulu, Motsoaledi, and Mkwayi to the airport.

Motsoaledi had been brought over from Robben Island two days previously, and Mkwayi had returned from hospital where his back problems had been treated. The two of them had missed out on the release party in the officers' mess, but they were still ecstatic to be going home.

First they all had to go to Johannesburg prison for their official release. All their belongings were sent separately. Kathrada secretly gave me a cardboard box he wanted me to keep safe for him at my home, which contained all his prison clothes, his mementoes.

A minibus waited to take them all to the airport. They all wore their new suits and looked great. It was still dark when we left the prison. We drove on to the tarmac at Cape Town airport, and they walked up into the plane and right down to the back seats. The other passengers would have had no idea who they were. They looked like businessmen.

It was all done in a big rush, with warders on the steps shouting: 'Come on, come on, get on the plane!'

I didn't have a chance to say a proper goodbye, but I shook each of them by the hand and we promised to stay in touch, a promise we all kept, and which still means a lot to me.

None of them had slept the previous night. They had been too excited and too busy packing. When I got back to Pollsmoor, Mhlaba's lawyer turned up to see him, bringing a suit. I said I would take it to him, but he could not have an impromptu visit. I was under strict orders not to tell anyone the guys had already gone.

I took the suit and poured myself a coffee and relaxed for 15 minutes. Then I came back and said the trousers were too long but the prison tailor could fix them. Of course, I knew Mhlaba was already in Johannesburg. We sent the suit up there for him, but I've no idea if it fitted him.

The next day, 15 October 1989, they were officially released from Johannesburg. The head of prison announced to them that an official fax had come through with instructions. Kathrada was mystified. He had no idea what a fax was and still could not get his head around it after several attempts at explanations. In the years after he was released, he enjoyed joking about it..

Mhlaba was flown out to Port Elizabeth in the Eastern Cape where he lived. The others were released at 5 a.m., shown live on television.

Later that morning, I was telephoned from the gates of Pollsmoor Prison. Sisulu's nephew, recently released himself from Robben Island, had come to visit and did not know about the release. 'You can't see him today,' I told him. He was angry and argumentative. He had the day's newspapers with him. I said: 'Well, if you actually read the newspapers, you'd see your uncle has already left here, he's been set free.'

He was so disappointed to have missed the magic moment of Sisulu's release. He went straight to the airport to catch up with him at the family home in Johannesburg.

Mandela's dearest friends and closest comrades were free, and all of them committed to continuing the struggle to defeat apartheid. However, their ANC was still banned by law, and they would have to go back underground. It was wonderful for them to be out, but there was still work to be done. They would have stayed in prison, or died, rather than abandon the cause that bound them together.

Mandela had achieved one important goal. But he was to remain at Victor Verster alone until all the other goals were met. It took another four months.

CHAPTER 13

Mandela had the great gift of magnanimity. His people were being beaten and arrested and detained without charge. Some of them were little more than children. His own wife and daughters were suffering.

Yet he was able to produce a smile and a warm handshake for the very people who were ordering this. Mandela was not offering forgiveness to P. W. Botha or his successor F. W. de Klerk. He was playing a long game in order to win the biggest prize of all – liberation for black South Africa.

And for all the charming and courteous letters he was sending to de Klerk, asking for further meetings and talks, he was adamant that the real negotiating could only begin once all political organisations had been unbanned and their people released from prison, the State of Emergency ended, and all government troops removed from the townships.

Two months after his comrades had been released came the first important step; Mandela was invited to meet de Klerk at the Tuynhuys, in the same office where he had first met Botha. Mandela came away from that meeting feeling for the first time that he was being listened to. He seemed to me to be more hopeful than ever.

When it came to his own release, he had told de Klerk that he would never agree to it until the ANC was unbanned. I felt that only Mandela was capable of that – a man desperate for freedom, with 26 years of imprisonment behind him, telling his captors what conditions they must meet before he consented to walk out of the gates. Mandela was soon writing to Oliver Tambo, telling him there was a new note of hope and that he felt de Klerk was really trying to work with them.

During his long wait for responses in this vital cat-and-mouse game with the government, Mandela was still regularly receiving visitors. Winnie and his daughters came, and in November 1989 I was able to bring someone special to him.

Ashley Forbes, the young ANC commander, was serving his prison sentence on Robben Island where he had taken over Mandela's mantle, recruiting other prisoners into the organisation and teaching them its goals. I was told he had permission to come over to the mainland for a day. I met him at the embarkation point and, as the ferry arrived, I saw he was not wearing handcuffs or leg chains. Why would he want to escape when he was going to see Mandela, his leader and his hero?

Forbes was happy to see me and greeted me like an old friend. He told me what an honour it was to be going to Victor Verster to see Mandela. After their meeting, I took him back to the ferry. He was in a state of high excitement, and he couldn't wait to tell his fellow prisoners on the island that Mandela had promised he would not walk free until they were out.

I was working with a lot of political detainees in Pollsmoor by now, and many of them had been diagnosed with HIV/AIDS and were being kept separately. All of them were aware that Mandela was fighting for them and anxious for news from me every time I returned from seeing him at Victor Verster.

Eventually, some six weeks after the president's meeting with Mandela, de Klerk shook the nation by standing up in Parliament on 2 February 1990 and announcing that the ANC, the Pan African Congress, the Communist Party, and 31 other organisations were no longer banned. He said political prisoners were to be freed and that the death penalty was suspended. The State of Emergency was to be partly lifted. Mandela would be released.

De Klerk had stopped short of ordering his troops out of the townships, and the State of Emergency was still partly operating. But it was a huge step forward.

Mandela was too cautious to be elated, and I was hearing that he paced the passageway in his house at night, unable to sleep. He was totally preoccupied with the need to push the government further and to get himself free in order to work openly with his ANC comrades outside prison without the continual eavesdropping.

His bungalow at Victor Verster is today something of a shrine to Mandela. A bronze statue of him stands at the gate of the prison, and the house itself has been left as it was when he lived there. The grey carpet in the passageway is worn thin by his night-time pacing.

As with Sisulu and the others, Mandela wasn't allowed to leave prison immediately, and we weren't told what date had been set for his release. But he asked to see me on 8 February, and I sensed it might be our last meeting in prison; I could always tell when Mandela had momentous news, even if he didn't spell it out. I asked him when he was going home, and he said it would be soon. I told him: 'Mandela, when you are free, you must come back to Pollsmoor and visit your people. They talk about you all the time. Don't forget them.'

It was just a joke really. Whoever heard of a long-term prisoner coming back to the place where he suffered? Mandela would surprise me, but I didn't know that then.

Two days after our conversation, Mandela had a further meeting with de Klerk at the Tuynhuys. It was an evening appointment and, as the whole world now knows, de Klerk grandly announced to Mandela that he would be released the next day.

Mandela astonished him by refusing. He wanted a further two weeks at Victor Verster so that his family and the ANC could be prepared.

De Klerk was completely taken aback, angry even. He told Mandela of the plan to fly him to Johannesburg and escort him on to the balcony of the Union Buildings, the seat of government. Clearly, he wanted to use Mandela to win over the masses. It would be a great personal victory for him.

No, Mandela told him, that is not how it is going to happen. 'I want to walk out of the gates of Victor Verster,' he said. 'I want to be able to thank those who looked after me there, and I want to greet the people of Cape Town, which has been my home for nearly 30 years. I will make my way back to Johannesburg when I want to, not when the government wants me to. When I am free, I will look after myself.'

Mandela was going to get what he wanted, but he made a compromise to enable de Klerk to save face. He would walk out of the gates of Victor Verster but, bowing to the lesser demand, he agreed to do it the next day.

I felt so proud when I heard about that. Yes! Mandela was the bigger man. At 71, he could still be a great leader. He cared more for his people and his country than he ever cared about himself and his own needs.

He needed to write a speech to deliver to his people. While he worked on that, his belongings were packed up for him.

They made a strange sight. After 27 years in prison, he had accumulated 22 assorted boxes, a trunk, four baskets, an urn, a footstool, a cardboard hat, two large umbrellas, a set of exercise weights, an exercise bicycle, a giant birthday card, and a body-board that he used for swimming.

There was no doubt in my mind about his most prized possession – the sombrero hat put together and painted white by Japhta Masemola when they were on Robben Island together. Now his imminent release had been announced, there was panic and turmoil inside Victor Verster. Mandela himself stayed calm and made telephone calls to Winnie and Sisulu, and then some comrades from the ANC arrived for talks late into the night. He went to bed in the early hours but the prison authorities stayed awake, terrified of the potential disorder and sabotage that might accompany his release. There was inside information that Mandela could be shot as he walked out of the gates, and that it could be done by enemies within. The extraordinary decision was made to disarm the warders on guard that day. Some of the police officers were also disarmed.

I had requested leave. I knew it would be a madhouse. I had already seen swarms of police and crowds of media and the public. There were hundreds of thousands of people in the streets. I didn't want to be part of the chaos, and I was scared for Mandela – scared he would be attacked or even trampled in the hysterical rush to greet him.

There was an absolute scrum at the house with people coming and going, and Winnie had to get to Cape Town from Johannesburg, so of course she was going to be late. The chef had left boxes of food ready for breakfast, as he'd been told there would be many people arriving early, and now all the food and drinks, every last drop and crumb, was being devoured, while phone calls were made to locate Winnie. All the time there were police helicopters hovering over the house, whipping up clouds of dust so that no one could see anything or make themselves heard.

They say Mandela was meanwhile quietly reading over his speech and preparing himself calmly for the moment to come. It was 4.00 p.m. by the time he finally got to walk out of prison with Winnie.

This day was going to go down in history. I just longed to see him walk out of prison, safe and free. So I stayed at home and watched it all on television. My heart was in my mouth the whole time. Would these overenthusiastic well-wishers run him over by mistake or trample him, wanting to touch him? Would he be able to get safely to the car waiting for him?

Eventually, Mandela walked out, tall and proud, holding Winnie's hand, both of them giving the power salute. They shouted, 'Amandla!' and the crowd went wild.

His car disappeared from the radar at some point, as his driver realised they were in danger from crowds pressing themselves against the vehicle and slowing it to a stop. He took a detour right around the city and admitted to Mandela that he was lost as they circled the university area and Rondebosch suburb and finally made their way back towards the city centre.

I watched the television in a state of raw anxiety, until I finally saw his car inching towards the centre of Cape Town and the Grand Parade. The mayor had invited him to walk out on the balcony of City Hall to address the people.

Again I was worried. Would he make a speech in Xhosa that would speak to all his black supporters but exclude others? I knew the Western Cape. In terms of the white population, it was an Afrikaans stronghold.

I watched Mandela looking straight ahead. I had never seen

him so strong. He raised his fist in the power salute, and the people went mad.

Then he started speaking in English before switching to Afrikaans, greeting them all. Mandela was pulling off one of his greatest moments to perfection. I thought to myself how he could have started in Xhosa and to hell with the others, but that was not his style. He knew exactly what he was doing. After starting in English, he then spoke to the people of the Western Cape in Afrikaans, then in Xhosa, his own language, and finally back in English again.

In my heart I felt so proud. I could hardly speak, and there were tears in my eyes. Here was my prisoner, and I knew he was soon to be my leader.

Mandela and Winnie spent that night at the home of their fellow activist, and another great man, Archbishop Desmond Tutu, at his home in Bishopscourt. The next day, I had a phone call from their lawyer, Dullah Omar, to say that Mandela sent his greetings. He had had a great first night of freedom, and he was very tired. He had hardly slept. But he wanted to make sure that I knew I was in his thoughts. He had insisted Omar should call me.

That was so like Mandela. He had the adulation of the whole world in front of him that day. There wasn't a head of state anywhere who wasn't making plans to come and see him. Yet I was in his thoughts. It was touching and humbling, and was to be followed by many such moments in the years to come.

CHAPTER 14

It took Mandela 27 years to get out of prison, and just three weeks to come back.

It happened on my day off. I was at home in my staff quarters in Pollsmoor Prison and noticed a convoy of police cars, with their sirens on and blue lights flashing, drive past. I thought it was a government official arriving for talks with the head of prison, a routine matter.

But I heard later that Mandela, a free man, had chosen to come back to see us. He went to the officers' mess – by then, I suppose he could go anywhere he liked – and asked for me. I had been on night shift and was resting at home, although my fellow warders were convinced I was out fishing somewhere and told Mandela they couldn't find me.

It was an extraordinary thing for him to do, and unique in my experience. We have former prisoners who come back to visit their friends or relatives still inside, but I never heard of one wanting to see his captors.

I thought that maybe he was missing us, the warders closest to him. We represented the enemy over all those years, but at the same time we had been like his mother and father, feeding him and taking care of him and setting the boundaries, even putting him to bed if you imagine the nightly lockup as a form of safety and security.

It's not unknown for those held hostage to form a bond with their captors, but Mandela was taking it to an extreme. I liked that idea. I was so sorry I had missed him that day, and when I thought about it I realised that I missed all the old ANC guys who had now gone. I was, of course, happy that they were finally free, but the fact was that I missed all their faces and our routine; it felt like my family had broken up. I was hoping that Mandela would look after all of the others in the outside world. I knew he would definitely still be their leader, their inspiration. He was the one with influence and power, and his release was being celebrated all over the world. I followed all the news closely on television and in the newspapers.

Then I missed a phone call from him. My son Riaan, aged six, answered the phone and apparently chatted to him. Mandela asked to speak to my wife, but she was also out of the house at the time. The coloured lady who was looking after Riaan that day was overwhelmed by the idea of speaking to Mandela and wouldn't talk to him. I felt bad that he was trying to make contact and I kept missing him.

He had wanted to ask me about twelve of my political prisoners who had gone on hunger strike, demanding to be released like the Rivonians. Mandela had been negotiating with the government and had achieved an agreement by which ANC and other political prisoners could be freed if they had a home and family to go to, and the prospect of employment and stability.

I was working hard on this, making contact with local employers so that these guys could go out on parole. They would still be under some sort of supervision, but at least out of Pollsmoor.

Mandela knew about the hunger strike and the increasing

unrest. He next turned up in the administration office at Pollsmoor, where I was on duty in my officer's uniform. It was the same room where Raymond Mhlaba had got married on that special day when Mandela and Sisulu put on borrowed suits to be his witnesses and wore buttonholes and toasted him in sparkling grape juice.

This time, Mandela was in a smart jacket with collar and tie. Everyone wanted to hug him, it was chaotic. He saw me and came over to shake my hand. We had a good look at each other, and he asked me about my family. He was very fond of my son Riaan, and he wanted to know about our new baby Heinrich, who was just two.

I knew some of his bodyguards, and we chatted while Mandela addressed the political prisoners for about an hour. He shook hands with each of them and told them they would be released soon and that he wanted them to bear with him while he pressed their case with the government. It struck me then that, although he was free, he had no official position in the country, and like all blacks he was still unable even to vote. His only power was his own history and his charisma.

He had an aura of authority, just as he had all those years inside, and he calmed the hothead prisoners. They agreed to end their hunger strike and have confidence that their release was forthcoming. On his way out, Mandela said quietly to me: 'Mr Brand, one of these days your prison will be completely empty.' He had this way of making provocative comments with a hint of humour, so that you could not take offence. It just got you thinking: 'Is he being sarcastic? Is that an attack, or what?' And in many ways I wished that he was right. I wished the prison was completely empty. My job had taken me back to managing the savage behaviour of the criminal gangs, although at least I was in a position of authority in the office most of the time, rather than dealing directly with the murderous guys who were still coming in daily in their hundreds.

A month after Mandela's release, the remaining 343 political prisoners on Robben Island had started a hunger strike, in a fury at being left in jail while their leaders were out and being feted. They were being released in small groups at a time, many sent home or taken to hospital, and the remaining 48 were brought over to Pollsmoor to be rehabilitated. They were the tough guys, still on hunger strike. Mandela came to talk to them. This time he had Chris Hani with him, a young, charismatic people's hero who was leader of the Communist Party and chief of staff of Umkhonto we Sizwe.

Hani had joined the ANC Youth League at the age of 15 to protest at the Bantu education system. He was soon regarded as a young lion able to influence thousands of students, and was targeted by the security services for arrest and detention until he moved to neighbouring Lesotho.

Hani appeared to be in the same mould as Mandela and was widely expected to follow him into a powerful role in a new South Africa. He had returned to be at Mandela's side and promote the party with him. It was for that very reason that later, in 1993, he was assassinated in a right-wing political plot. The pro-apartheid Conservative Party MP Clive Derby-Lewis paid an immigrant Polish agitator to shoot Hani in the head and back outside his home, and both men are still in prison serving life sentences.

When I met him, Hani, then a rising star, had teamed up with Mandela to garner support among black people for continuing peaceful negotiations at a time when many would have preferred to overthrow the government in a violent coup.

When he was murdered, Mandela made an extraordinary speech, calling for unity and calm, while emphasising the need to continue the fight for the democracy Hani had fought for all his life. 'Our whole nation now teeters on the brink of disaster,' he said. '...The cold-blooded murder of Chris Hani has sent shock waves throughout the country and the world. Our grief and anger is tearing us apart.' He recognised that the people's reactions to this murder would be a watershed moment for South Africa – whether we would stand together or descend further into violence and bloodshed.

Mandela had spent many years of his life as part of the complex fight against apartheid and now, in the immediate aftermath of his release, at the age of 71, he needed all his wisdom and strength to bring together the many factions that could uplift or destroy South Africa. He could not be sure of which result, but he was fighting for all he was worth.

He came to Pollsmoor twice with Chris Hani to show his moral and practical support for the prisoners who believed they had been left behind. It would be another year before they were all finally released.

Among them was a big strong guy, Thulani Mabaso, who had served eight years on Robben Island. He was a heavyweight from Umkhonto we Sizwe who had infiltrated South Africa's Defence Force and planted limpet mines in the National Intelligence building in Johannesburg at the height of the 1980s uprisings. After arrest, he was beaten and tortured at the security police's notorious headquarters in John Vorster Square. On the tenth floor – a location that was synonymous with terror during the worst apartheid years – he was hung from a window while his tormentors threatened to drop him and claim suicide. Many detainees died that way.

Mabaso was a natural leader, and I came to depend on him to mediate with a troublesome group of the political prisoners who were demanding daily phone calls and extra visits and refusing to go into their cells. I offered to help them with the calls and visits if we could keep matters calm inside the prison. Between us, Mabaso and I achieved some peace. We became good friends, and I was able both to let visitors bring in extra food, and to personally pass on phone messages.

When he was leaving Pollsmoor, Mabaso asked for my phone number. We weren't allowed to keep up contact with prisoners, but I wanted to help him find work, and it made sense to stay in touch. Soon afterwards, I had a call from a friend of his inviting me to his home for supper with him and his family, along with his friend Mabaso. My wife and I had a really enjoyable evening, and it was good to talk to someone full of hope for the future and with no bitterness about the past.

That was the first time I was ever invited to have dinner with an ex-prisoner. Mabaso was a family man who lived out of town, and he was still arranging to get home at the time, so he was staying with his friend in Cape Town for his first night of freedom. He just wanted to share the occasion with me. It felt good. He was so happy to be on his way back to his wife and children.

I didn't see Mabaso for many years after that. But soon after I started work on Robben Island again – no longer as a prison warder but instead running the curio shop, now that the island was a World Heritage Site – I saw him on Jetty 1, our old embarkation point. He had just been interviewed for a job, and later it was announced that he had been appointed the manager of conducted tours of the prison. So we began seeing each other daily, in a different life to the one we shared at Pollsmoor.

When Mabaso had a special tour for VIPs, he asked me to come and talk to them. They loved to hear about the old prison days when Mandela was there. Many people arrange their own expensive private visit to Robben Island, arriving by speedboat or helicopter, and they want to talk to us guys who were there, who really know the history of the prison and its famous inmates.

After Mabaso was released from Pollsmoor, I stayed for a further four years. They were tumultuous times, and I have very unhappy memories of violence and brutality among the gang members who knew nothing but torturing or butchering each other for money or drugs. There were grudge wars and killings in the sections, and at the same time turmoil in our world outside.

I read of Mandela going on triumphal tours to Zimbabwe, Algeria, and the new independent Namibia. I imagined him and my former prisoner Ja Toivo, the Swapo leader, relating a host of memories they shared from Robben Island. How I would have liked to be there.

In April 1990, Mandela went on to London, where I saw on television that a crowd of 75,000 went wild to see him at Wembley Stadium, the place where rock stars had played for his 70th birthday while he was still locked up with us.

It was an extraordinary time. Back home, many whites were totally fearful of bloodshed in the country, that there might be a backlash against them by millions of blacks. And government forces were hard at work trying to divide and rule different factions among the black tribes by funding them and providing arms, doing anything they could to derail a peace process that could dismantle apartheid.

Even in Mandela's own party, there was distrust and discord.

He was an old man, his domestic life had failed to return to any kind of normality, and he was picking up the reins of an unpredictable guerrilla movement, which was reluctant to give up the armed struggle.

I heard how Mandela turned down an invitation to meet British prime minister Margaret Thatcher, who had never been an ally of the ANC. He was desperate to persuade the world to keep up sanctions against de Klerk's government, needing the economic leverage to push negotiations forward. He knew this course of action did not have Thatcher's sympathy.

However, supporters of the anti-apartheid movement in Europe and America gave him a tumultuous welcome on his tour to meet world leaders. Many political analysts and seasoned journalists were writing of their surprise that Mandela was not an egotistical leader who enjoyed the celebrity. He spoke always of himself as part of the ANC, the collective that could bring much-needed peace to South Africa. Although he returned to his home village of Qunu to be greeted as a tribal chieftain, his birthright, he did not want adulation for himself. Instead, he was deeply disturbed at the new level of poverty he was seeing there.

On a return visit to England, he agreed to finally meet with Margaret Thatcher and they had a long meeting in which she, predictably, continued to refuse to impose sanctions and he, equally predictably, made no promises that he would abandon the armed struggle and cosy up to the IFP's Zulu leader Mangosuthu Buthelezi, who she thought was 'a wonderful man'. She was intractable, but also charmed by Mandela. She described him as 'supremely courteous with a genuine nobility of bearing'.

That did not surprise me in any way. He was not the noisy, aggressive, or confrontational African leader many had expected. I knew that he led with courtesy and quietness, and by doing so he disarmed the de Klerks and the Thatchers. In any case, he was head and shoulders above them as a moral leader. I was optimistic that he might keep the world on his side, despite the blood still flowing in our townships.

But it was not going to be easy. The Zulu tribes in the Inkatha Freedom Party had been primed for war against the ANC through government agents wanting to foment trouble to ruin negotiations. At one time, more than 100 people a day were being killed. How could one man, even with the stature of Mandela, bring this overwhelming problem to an end?

I had my own reasons for optimism that the barriers could be overcome. In my life at that time, there was great personal pleasure in the continuation of friendships with Walter Sisulu, Ahmed Kathrada, and the other Rivonians. It was unusual, but I embraced it. I suppose I was the living proof that people from opposing sides could reconcile, pool their thoughts and wishes for their country, and form genuine friendships.

They probably thought I was their first convert, that fresh-faced 19-year-old who had entered the hell of their lives on Robben Island when they were already in their sixties. Through mutual hardships and the need for camaraderie, we had now completed a journey together.

Ironically, though, I was the last one of us still in prison every day, and the conditions there were terrible, even for a warder. We were experiencing regular uprisings in Pollsmoor due to criminals becoming resentful of the fact that they were not getting released under the amnesty for political inmates. I was locking up 800 new prisoners a night at one stage, with dozens of other warders on night shifts with me. We kept crowds of them shuffled together in the corridors, doling out food in swill buckets for them to eat standing up, while dog-handlers and armed guards searched 150 at a time. It was a conveyor belt of utter misery. It was rough when you just longed to be an ordinary family man, with your wife and two young sons at home wanting you to go biking and fishing with them, but you found yourself unable to put the horror of your last shift behind you.

I'd had several phone calls from Mandela and was glad of them. He was always solicitous, always asking about my family, still with that personal interest in my life, which always took me by surprise. At that time, he was literally the busiest man in the world and everybody wanted a part of him.

On a visit to Tanzania, more than half a million people mobbed him, and Winnie and Mandela lost each other in the confusion and chaos. The standing ovation, the singing and chanting went on for so long that Mandela had to leave the podium without making a speech.

By then, he was losing Winnie in a different, much sadder, way. I had always admired her and thought what great fortune it was that Mandela had a wife like her – so strong and powerful, and beautiful. His marriage to her seemed to mean almost everything to him during his prison years. He told her in letters, which I was at one point reading, how her love literally kept him alive.

But the newspapers were increasingly writing of their lack of a normal family life since his release, and there were strong suggestions of her infidelity, along with various other issues. Her vocal outrage against white oppressors and their brutality against the masses was putting her at centre-stage when Mandela himself was handling delicate negotiations behind closed doors.

In 1982, Winnie had gone on record with a South African journalist to point out that: 'Nelson is 63 now and I am like a young girl, still longing for the experience of married life.' Ten years later, he had finally come home to her, only for them to find that there could be no normal married life. Mandela was constantly touring Africa and Europe to garner support and raise funds, and when they were at home in Soweto there was a constant stream of people at his door and on his phone.

In October 1991, the media was writing of them not even speaking to each other for months, and on 13 April 1992 Mandela looked tired and lonely when he gave a press conference to tell the world that they were separating by mutual agreement. He painfully described how they had been unable to enjoy a normal life but also stated: 'My love for her remains undiminished. I embrace her with all the love and affection I have nursed for her inside and outside prison from the moment I first met her.' They divorced in 1996.

Whenever I saw Mandela or our mutual acquaintances during that period, we all remarked on his isolation and loneliness, a tragedy after the deprivations he had been through for years in prison.

His great friend Kathrada was calling me often and, of course, he wanted his prison mementoes back, the box of clothes he had left with me on the day of his release. We arranged for me to take them to his friend's clothes shop near Pollsmoor as it was convenient for me. But when I got there his friend said Kathy wanted to invite me to his house for dinner and to bring my wife and children.

When I arrived at Kathrada's house soon after, we had a long talk about all the warders, the latest news of Mandela, and the goings-on at Pollsmoor. Kathy had a home in Cape Town, but his main base was in Johannesburg. Throughout his prison years, he had told me of the flat that was being looked after by his family. He used to say: 'They're keeping everything exactly as it was when I left. I'll be able to walk through the door and find everything just as it was.'

I thought that was very unlikely after 27 years, but Kathy was right. His devoted family had cleaned and cared for his home over the years, and when he returned he did indeed walk through the door and find everything just as it was. He had written so much about it over the years that one day a stranger arrived with a VW Beetle, a car he had decided he wanted, and left it parked outside the door. He was a happy man, although he found the car a bit too small and ended up not driving it very often. For a short while, he drove me around Joburg again, although it was now dangerous and hair-raising. We laughed. He was the same Kathy but more relaxed and looking healthier and younger. He was pleased to see me and told me how he was working at the ANC headquarters, Shell House, in Joburg. We talked about old times in prison and he made jokes about me torturing him, telling his family I was the chief torturer. He told me about the other Rivonians, all busy with the continuing work of putting pressure on the government, keeping up the momentum and doing their utmost to bring together the warring factions in rival black communities.

I also talked to Sisulu several times by phone during this period and heard that his family was still campaigning for a united South Africa, supporting him in all his efforts to actually make the prison ordeal worthwhile.

If I'm honest, I had expected the Rivonians to forget me over the years, so I was very gratified to realise that they missed me and our time together as much as I missed them.

Meanwhile, I had started taking on some parole duties, working mostly at night-time to go into the townships to check on prisoners out on parole. I had to try to find them work and reassure potential employers that I would be monitoring them, that they would not demand such high wages as other workers, and that they would be living under strict conditions imposed by the prison. I placed several prisoners in jobs and kept up the necessary contact, but it was tough to be a white Afrikaner in prison uniform calling at township homes and workplaces after dark.

Everyone knew the gangs' turfs and the need to avoid them. But now I was by necessity plunged into that world. I knew from experience that one false move could literally be fatal. I had once been confronted by three gangsters who demanded the key to my vehicle, and I wasn't able to get to my revolver inside. It was a bad situation and my blood still runs cold when I think about it, but I got away safely and saw the same guys in prison a few weeks later on murder charges. That was the reality of my life at that time. There was no release from Pollsmoor for me. I was very weary of it all.

By 1994, South Africa was on the brink of its first democratic elections open to all. It was the most amazing time in our country. Every one of us was nurturing fears of one kind or another. My wife and I found ourselves in a queue of many thousands, snaking all the way round the polling station at Westlake, near Pollsmoor. It took us three hours to vote and it was the first time ever that white, black, coloured, and Asian South Africans could literally stand side by side to share a public event. That was incredible in itself, whatever the outcome.

I hoped and prayed that Mandela, the peacemaker, would come into Parliament. There was no way to know if he could be president; I just wanted to see him somewhere in the thick of it while we were all travelling into the unknown. By then he had offered up his whole life for his people's freedom and he was 74. He deserved this.

I suppose it was obvious who I was supporting. My workmates at Pollsmoor had already been calling me a kaffir-boetie (an Afrikaans insult as offensive as the American 'nigger-lover') for a long time. It really didn't matter to me. If the Rivonians could sacrifice the best years, the longest years, of their lives for their cause, how could a few cruel words hurt my feelings?

As we all know, Mandela triumphed in the polls. He was going to be our president.

Within days, unbelievably, he phoned me at Pollsmoor. He knew the prison was burning, with frequent uprisings. The place was like a time bomb, and he felt a responsibility and a need to defuse it. I told him: 'Mandela, everyone here wants to leave just like you did. We can't control them. All the warders are doing is beating them and keeping them in chains, it's hellish.' He told me he wanted to see me, he wanted to sort out Pollsmoor, but it was also time for me to leave there. He said: 'Call Kathy and talk to him about coming to meet me.'

I had been seeing a lot of Kathy, and he was busy in Parliament. He was certain to be playing an important role in the new government. He told me there could be an administrative job for me there. The very next day, I was phoned by a woman executive in Parliament to ask me to bring my CV and come to her office. I had no idea what a CV was, so I arrived with just my ID. She helped me put together a reasonably impressive list of my working experience. I was to start the next day, but we had both discounted the fact that Parliament was now in recess for three months.

I understood the chaos and the last-minute arrangements,

and I was grateful for the job offer and had already given in my notice to the prison service with feelings of great joy and relief. But now I needed to earn a salary for three months. I took a job with a private security firm collecting the takings from businesses in the townships. If I thought prison work was scary, this was something off the scale.

I was travelling to the shebeens, the noisy backstreet bars that were illegally operated during apartheid, selling scarily strong home-brewed beer to blacks. My job was to transport their takings safely away. I also collected from the supermarkets and we transported the cash in sealed containers, which inevitably were often found to contain drugs and were the live currency of the gangs.

I managed to survive, and was even offered promotion. But then Parliament started and I was happy to take up a job in the Constitutional Assembly. Nothing could be more important than the organisation set up to draft our new, all-inclusive laws, the most liberal in the world. I was employed as an administrative clerk and logistics manager.

The job meant a move away from Pollsmoor for the whole family, finally. I hired a truck and paid six of the trusty prisoners to help me load furniture and move it to my parents' home in Goodwood, a suburb of Cape Town. My mother, now widowed, had been living there alone since 1986 when my father died. She was glad to be joined by us, a lively young family.

The house was quite small, so I had to put some furniture in storage until I could afford to build an extension. Our boys went to the local school at Wynberg and were still close to their friends from the Pollsmoor staff quarters. My wife was working nearby in the government's Home Affairs department. I felt it was all working out well.

My sons were four years apart and quite different in personality. They sometimes fought but I noticed the younger one, Heinrich, would copy his brother's haircut and quietly admired him. Kathy liked my boys and remarked that Heinrich's birthday was the same as Einstein's – a good sign, he said.

I was kept busy with the daily paperwork for the drafting of the Constitution. One day, hurrying down the corridor in Parliament, I saw Mandela approaching with his formal retinue. He called out to me and I hurried towards him, pleased to see each other. He introduced all the politicians and civil servants and told them I was the man who did a great act of kindness for him at the worst time of his life. Then he went on to tell them about the time I put his baby granddaughter into his arms. Neither of us had mentioned it since the day it happened, more than ten years earlier.

Years after that, Winnie also found a way to thank me for what I'd done that day. She signed a copy of the book *Hunger for Freedom*, published by the Nelson Mandela Foundation, and she wrote in it: 'My dearest Brand! The wonderful memories we share are priceless! I remember how you refused to accept a gift from me because you were and still are so principled. Thanks for all the wonderful things you did for Madiba in prison. Only God can thank you! You are Amazing.' The gift she was referring to was, of course, the bribe she had offered me that I had refused. She signed it 'Winnie Mandela, 5 July 2008'.

I had another encounter with the Mandela magic when the Constitutional Assembly was nearing its deadline and held a major conference for a week at the coastal resort of Arniston, two hours' drive from Cape Town. I was ensuring all the documentation and support paperwork was in place and was driving to Arniston and back three times a day, delivering both the delegates and their boxes of papers.

At the end of the week, Mandela himself was due to arrive. In presidential style, he was to be helicoptered to a nearby military base and then driven to our conference centre. No one was allowed outside the building, and security was tight.

On the appointed day, Mandela walked in, elegant and statesmanlike in his pinstripe suit, every inch the president. There were about 60 people in the room, and nearly all of them instinctively rose to their feet. Only a small elitist group of hardline Afrikaners, those who still dreamed of a whites-only Volkstad state, remained seated in an alcove off the main meeting room.

Mandela worked his way expertly around the huge conference table, shaking everyone's hand and remembering their names. Even the experienced politicians were turning to mush under his smile.

But I was looking at the ten pro-apartheid guys in the alcove. Mandela walked over to them, his body language offering a welcoming gesture. He greeted them in fluent Afrikaans and held out his hand to each of them. They got to their feet as one, and I was able to breathe again. These were momentously significant moments. But why did I still feel personally responsible for him? That is the magic of Mandela, that's all I can say.

There was more tension to come for me. Mandela suddenly saw me and abandoned the all-important delegates. 'Oh, Mr Brand, you are here, that's very good. Let me introduce you to all these people.'

He made the introduction as if I was the most important person in the room. He told them all in great detail how I had cared for him on Robben Island, the things we got up to together, the table-tennis tournaments and the way we helped each other through intolerable times. I didn't enjoy all of the attention, but there was no stopping him. Mandela was saying I had been his boss, in charge of his whole life. Then he started asking about my family, still keeping the conference waiting. I felt so relieved when he finally let me get back to my desk to continue sorting out the documents.

He sat down and invited feedback about the new Constitution from officials like Cyril Ramaphosa – who himself went on to become president of South Africa in 2018. He then made an emphatic speech about the importance of our new, liberal, all-encompassing Constitution. It was fascinating to see this moment of history unfolding in front of me.

Afterwards I joined the other staff for lunch outside, and then all of us were told we must pose for an official photograph. It was funny to see that all the ladies wanted to be with Mandela; they arranged themselves next to him with a great deal of competition for the place closest to him. But he called me over, put his arm around my shoulders, and made me stand at his side.

I noticed many of the Constitutional Assembly staff treated me with extra respect after that. They seemed to think that if I was special to Mandela, then I must really be somebody. It made me smile actually. His influence was all you needed to get into everyone's best books. For example, one of the directors had never liked me because she had been imprisoned during the anti-apartheid struggle and she knew I had been a warder. But then she dented her car in an accident and I was on hand to help. This, combined with Mandela's personal endorsement, meant that I was suddenly her favourite person, regularly invited to tea in her office.

Similarly, one of the legal directors of the Constitutional

Assembly, Hassan Ebrahim, invited me into his office to join him and Cyril Ramaphosa for a whisky, and one Friday night I was driving him home when he insisted we stop somewhere for supper. I was getting a lot of favours and attention.

I had secretly enjoyed the idea that – until Mandela's big announcement – no one of any importance but the Rivonians and Ramaphosa had known I was a prison warder. Now they all knew.

But there were other reasons my past was useful to my new job. My immediate boss had been against the whole idea of employing me when I turned up on my first day. He was the service officer for Parliament, a former National Party stalwart who didn't trust the ANC. He came round to their way of thinking when he was treated properly with an employment contract and full rights, something he hadn't got from the Nats. But even before then I was able to reassure him. I told him I knew all the important guys, the people he was half-afraid of. They'd all been in prison with me.

He was rather old-fashioned and still wanted to do things the old way. When P. W. Botha was in the corridor, for example, everyone had been ordered to disappear, to go into any office, cloakroom, whatever was closest.

That's how he still wanted to run things. But Mandela was the exact opposite. He told everyone he wanted to see them and talk to them. They were not to run away when they saw him, they were to greet him and introduce themselves. He included the cleaners and the gardeners in this – he wanted to meet all of them and find out their names.

I was seeing quite a lot of Mandela at that time. We were constantly bumping into each other in the corridors of Parliament. One day, when the first draft of the Constitution was ready for signing, I was on my way to the executive office with some copies. It was the most important document you could have in your hands, and it was my job to deliver it.

But as I passed Mandela's office, where he had once met Botha during a trip from prison, he was standing in the doorway. He called me in, ignoring my protests about the urgent delivery. He made me sit down and tell him if I was enjoying the job. He kept saying: 'Oh, that's good, that's good.' Finally, he let me go with my precious pile of papers, but not before he autographed one of them for me.

So I was the first person to have the presidential seal on documents that were our country's new laws. How on earth had that happened? Somehow this prisoner, who was now president, and his warder found themselves in the grandest government office in Cape Town, when we both really belonged out in the veld, in the valleys and along the riverbanks.

One day, I heard that the big office that was now Mandela's had been renovated for him and a secret escape hatch had been found behind a cupboard. When you went through the cupboard, there was an escalator leading all the way underground to Cape Town's main railway station. A helicopter landing-pad had been installed on the roof of the building. Or I suppose a train might have been waiting. Botha, rightly paranoid, had needed an exit strategy – just in case.

Mandela gave orders for it to be sealed up. He hadn't spent most of his life in prison to start hatching escape plans at this stage.

CHAPTER 15

I already had my own personal copy of the new Constitution signed by the president, but the country had yet to formally adopt it. So I was happy to be invited to the Adoption Party in Fernwood, Constantia, at the end of 1996. My wife and I were among a huge crowd, comprising the top tier of the ANC and everyone from the Constitutional Assembly itself.

Mandela gave a speech in which he recalled the bravery behind the Freedom Charter drawn up in 1955 by activists who collected the demands of ordinary people across the country, which was now soundly echoed in the Constitution, which itself would soon be the law of the land. It was very heady stuff, and I was proud to be there. But I was brought down to earth when Priscilla Jana, one of his lawyers whom I had encountered previously, suddenly grabbed me and propelled me towards the podium.

'Tata, Tata,' she said, using the affectionate Xhosa word for Papa. 'Look who's here. That prison warder who fought with me in Robben Island.' She remembered the ugly scene when I had confiscated the chocolates she had brought for Mandela.

He stepped down from the podium, and soon we were all laughing. He had to repeat the story to Trevor Manuel and all the top guys. I protested that Mandela had got his chocolates in the end, and we enjoyed the joke. It was a moment of happy reunion. A circle was closing – we had all been around the block over the years in our different ways, and now we were together again, talking like old friends.

For me, the final adoption of the Constitution meant the end of my job in Parliament and, although Cyril Ramaphosa had given me some extra months, I needed work elsewhere. Kathy was helping more than anyone to find me another position, but it was hard to know where to go. There were opportunities in the prison service in Johannesburg or Durban, but that was a bleak prospect.

Kathy's next phone call closed the circle completely. He offered me a job on Robben Island, where he was chairman of the Museum Council. The island was a prison no more: it was a place of endless fascination to international tourists, historians, political activists, and anyone with an interest in South Africa's turbulent past. I would be back on duty in that place that had haunted me for so much of my life.

I would be stationed at the new exhibition centre on the mainland, on Jetty 1, the old embarkation point that I knew so well. The island had been declared a National Museum, and three years later UNESCO gave it World Heritage status. Robben Island was now one of the most important symbols of racial recognition in the world.

As I walked down the familiar path at the harbour's edge, I began to meet some of my ex-prisoners. They were coming for interviews as tour guides. Who better to tell tourists the gritty detail of those long years in prison? It was good to be welcomed warmly by them. I felt more glad than ever that I had been as humane as possible in my treatment of them.

It was October 1997, a full 15 years since I last turned my back on Robben Island. And now we were climbing on to the ferry, the old *Susan Kruger* boat I had travelled on so many times with prisoners, on our way for orientation at Robben Island in its new guise.

The island looked green and fresh; I was pleasantly surprised. And there were ex-prisoners of mine everywhere I looked. One of them was training as a tour guide and, although no one had a tenth of my knowledge about the place, I was content to sit there quietly and just take it all in.

We took an old government bus for a trip right round the island, all 11 kilometres where I once jogged every evening out of sheer boredom and desperation. We stopped at the lepers' graveyard and the warders' quarters. We looked at all the old shipwrecks, broken down more than ever through the harsh weather. There was the wreckage of a big yacht that hadn't been there during my sojourn.

I was experiencing very mixed feelings. A sort of excitement and nostalgia, and sadness I couldn't quite define. I certainly didn't want to go back to those days in B Section, but there was a familiarity about everything that was playing with my emotions.

When we got off at the main prison, I let everyone go ahead and look at Mandela's cell and the courtyard. I went off on my own to see the old Censor's Office, that monument to snooping and prying where I had learned every secret of my prisoners' hearts and souls and often reduced them to shreds.

Everywhere was empty and full of dust. My footsteps echoed, and the place seemed full of ghosts. I looked through a window to the courtyard and across the catwalk where you could once spy on the inmates.

I rejoined the group and found there was a reconstruction of Mandela's cell. Everything was quite faithful to the original, but of course he wasn't there, so it didn't work for me. We went into the exercise yard and we all laughed at some graffiti – a well-drawn caricature of a man holding bags of swag with dollar signs painted on them and the defiant message 'Happy Days Are Here Again'.

I told them all that was new. The place had been vandalised. My prisoners, I said, were never common criminals and robbers. They were victims, with ideals. Look at them today, I said, resisting the urge to preach any further. I couldn't take credit for anything that had happened to Mandela and the other Rivonians. All I did for them was to manage to bend the rules a little.

I found Mandela's garden and saw it was completely overgrown with some grapevines, not pruned or cut, but somehow finding their way through the undergrowth. The trellis and netting was broken. In his time, Mandela had kept everything clean and cared for. After he and his comrades left, the prison housed common criminals for some years, and they had left the whole place dirty and unkempt.

I looked out to sea and thought about my fishing days. I recognised some of the warders' old boats in the backyards of empty staff houses. Some broken-down cars were rusting there too. The old electricity power station that had kept me awake every night had been moved nearer to the prison, much too late to rescue my years of sleeplessness. The village shop where warders bought basic goods was there too, but now it was empty. I could have told many tales about all the places we were visiting, but I kept quiet.

I was tasked with starting a curio shop on the island, with a partner shop on the mainland. We sold t-shirts with Mandela's picture on them and heritage site logos, alongside books like *Long Walk to Freedom*, *Higher Than Hope*, and *Island in Chains*. Business was brisk, and I enjoyed it.

Kathy occasionally invited me to go with him to Mandela's

house, a property he bought for himself in Bishopscourt. One day, we walked into his lounge to wait for him, and I joked about sitting in his chair. Mandela liked a straight-back chair, and he would always take that seat, overlooking his guests who were on comfortable sofas in front of him.

Mandela walked in and told me: 'You are my special guest today. You must have my chair, please sit down.'

We did a sort of polite dance around the chair and sofa, while I protested that he must take his special place. In the end I sat in his chair. We had a sociable chat and I commented that he was still surrounded by police and guards, some of them even in uniform.

'You're still in prison,' I said. 'You have more security around you than ever before.' He said that was what happened in public life.

He seemed lonely to me. His marriage to Winnie was long over, and he had missed his daughters' childhood. I knew he prized family life and I began telling him about my sons. Riaan, the little boy he had met many times in Pollsmoor, was now 16. He was a lovely boy, a really soft-hearted person who could talk to anyone, and we were very proud of him. His younger brother, Heinrich, looked up to him greatly, and even though they were very different characters, he would often try to imitate him, even with his hairstyle. Mandela jumped up and found some notepaper. He wanted to send Riaan a message. He wrote it in front of me:

Dear Riaan, I am told that you are now 16 years old. Congratulations! If you work hard you are likely to rise and become one of the most important leaders of our country. Always remember that.
Sincerely, Uncle Nelson.

He couldn't find an envelope, but it didn't matter. I took it home to Riaan and told him to read it carefully and follow those words. I believed in his future too; he was a bright, active, caring boy.

Riaan was proud to have a letter from his uncle Nelson who also happened to be the president. He wanted to take it to school but, of course, we wouldn't allow it.

Mandela had told me he wanted to see Riaan after his matric exam and talk to him about further studies. When I saw him again, I said Riaan had decided on civil engineering. We weren't sure how to go about this, although I had an insurance policy taken out especially to fund his career. Mandela said he wanted to take care of my son's future. He called his secretary and told her that he wanted to arrange a scholarship course in New York, where he believed Riaan would have the best possibilities. A week later, Mandela called me and said the New York course would not be starting till the end of the year, and I should find him a way to keep busy till then.

Riaan was by now regularly diving for perlemoen (edible sea snails) at our favourite weekend spot in the fishing resort of Gansbaai and really enjoying himself. He was interested in all aspects of diving and beginning to change his mind about a career. I thought it would be difficult to explain to Mandela, and I didn't want to seem ungrateful. I went to see him to explain, leaving Riaan at home. But Mandela said: 'I want to see the boy myself. Can you fetch him here?'

So I sent for Riaan and stood with him at the door to Mandela's reception lounge, waiting to hear we could come in. When he heard we were there, he stood up and hurried out the newly appointed Archbishop of Cape Town, Njongonkulu Ndungane, before he had even started his cup of tea. Mandela had a way of just standing up and extending his hand, smiling all the while, to let a visitor know he should go. It wasn't quite the same as me telling him there were five minutes left for his prison visits, but it wasn't far off.

He was so happy to see Riaan. He actually asked me to leave them together, so I sat outside on the stoep while they talked. When I was called back in, Mandela told me: 'You know, Mr Brand, we can't tell children of today what they have to do. We have to respect their wishes. We can't impose our will on them. Your son is very serious about being a commercial diver, and I think we should encourage him to do that. I will arrange courses and equipment for him. You can leave it to me.'

There was an opening in Westlake, not far from our home, with a diving company willing to train him. He loved it from the first day and took naturally to the technology of handling construction materials under water.

Later, I found a company looking for divers and Riaan started his first paid employment. They had taken on a big excavating contract on Robben Island, so my son was to go to work with me. His job was to work with a team installing a new harbour wall, which had been built on the mainland and was being floated out to the island. Concrete blocks made by some of the political prisoners – huge solid squares weighing several tons each – had to be lifted by crane and dropped into the sea outside the harbour to protect boats from the rough seas. Riaan was taking part in the dangerous process of guiding the blocks into the sea.

As the concrete blocks were being retrieved, the divers were told to examine them for graffiti carved into them by prisoners. There were some names and dates and prison numbers, although the seawater had eroded a great deal. Some of the blocks dated back to the 1930s and '40s. Riaan's job was to chain them and guide them out of the water. They were to be exhibited as part of the island's prison heritage.

We used to travel on the staff ferry together out to the island. Sometimes he stayed in staff quarters overnight for the week to be constantly on call. Like me he loved to fish, and he took a spear-gun with him for the big species. He caught a small shark once, and he and his team hauled it up on the slipway and barbecued it.

Riaan always talked enthusiastically about his workmates, and it was good to hear him mentioning black and coloured guys as if those friendships were normal now among young people. All of them knew that he had met and talked to Mandela since childhood. I had put Mandela's birthday letter into Riaan's CV when he first applied for the job.

By now Mandela had remarried. He had known Graça Machel for many years. She was the widow of his fellow revolutionary Samora Machel, president of Mozambique, who died in a plane crash in 1986. She was to bring much-needed love and comfort into his later years.

He was happy again. They married on his 80th birthday, when he was well into his retirement but still actively working for the Nelson Mandela Foundation and the Nelson Mandela Children's Fund, his two passions. He wanted every detail of South Africa's troubled past to be documented and catalogued by the Foundation, including the Rivonians' part in it, and he wanted to improve education and career opportunities for the country's children.

When the Nelson Mandela Gateway was built as a grand edifice on the quayside in Cape Town's Waterfront, he was there to declare it open in December 2001. It was to be the embarkation point for tourist ferries to Robben Island and also housed an exhibition and a curio shop. Mandela gave a speech saying how delighted he was to have this monument named after him. That was funny really – after all, who else could they possibly name it after?

Today, his name embellishes landmarks all over the world. A total of 23 schools, universities, and institutions are named after him as well as 25 halls, buildings, monuments, and housing developments; 13 stadia, squares, plazas, parks, and gardens; 91 streets and boulevards; 32 bursaries, scholarships, foundations, and lectureships; and 14 statues, sculptures, and artworks. He received around 250 international awards, of which the most important to him was the Nobel Peace Prize, which he received in 1993.

At the Gateway that day, there were lovely flowers around the place, beautiful roses and lilies. The next morning, I saw the cleaners preparing to throw away some apricot-coloured roses on long stems and I stopped them. My mother was a superb gardener who might be able to get them to grow. She planted several in our garden and two of them are still thriving, bearing many flowers every year. I don't know their real name, but we call them our Mandela roses.

I was enjoying a useful life imparting my memories of the prisoners and the island to thousands of tourists coming through the museum and shop. Many of them were overwhelmed to find themselves with someone who was close to a man they had admired all their lives.

In 2002, the lawyer Priscilla Jana was organising a big event in Holland where the Queen of the Netherlands wanted to meet Mandela, and she invited me to be part of it. I travelled over with an African children's choir, and the Koninklijk Theatre in

Amsterdam was absolutely packed when Mandela walked in.

There were speeches and singing and dancing, with Mandela and the Queen and other members of the royal family in the front row. I had been asked to bring my prison uniform and cap, in hindsight a totally inappropriate idea. The event organisers had this notion that I would walk down to Mandela and 'arrest' him and bring him up to the stage. Thank God someone had the sense to cancel that mad plan.

I wore an ordinary suit as I walked out of the wings, and Mandela was astonished to see me. I walked down the steps to him and we hugged; he was very happy. I told him we had to walk together up to the podium, and he was so nervous about how he was going to get up the steps that I told him: 'Don't worry. I'll carry you if I have to.' Of course, I knew what was going to happen.

We walked up a couple of steps just fine and then I said, 'Let's stop here for a moment.' The step rose up from underneath him and he found himself centre-stage, slightly surprised but with his dignity intact.

He had to wait for a standing ovation to die down, then he gave a charming speech. Meanwhile, the young singers were clamouring around me to let them meet him somehow. It was easy. I just told him the boys and girls wanted to shake his hand and he instantly obliged, walking right down the line with a smile and a little conversation for each one. It must have been the thrill of their young lives.

Back in Cape Town, people were coming to the Robben Island exhibition at the jetty in their droves and buying hundreds of copies of *Long Walk to Freedom* and other books. They often asked me to autograph them. Ahmed Kathrada was then closely involved with the island and its new status as part of our cultural heritage, instead of a place of dread and fear. He often brought visitors, and people were excited to meet him and have him sign their books. Only recently I got talking to a woman passenger on the ferry boat and when I told her Kathrada was actually there, a few feet away from her, she could hardly believe it. I introduced her to him and he chatted to her, kindly as always.

Kathy brought many VIPs to Robben Island and involved me if I was around. Through him, I met Colonel Gaddafi and also Yasser Arafat, the Palestinian revolutionary. People have commented that these men were not exactly icons of liberation, but Mandela himself has said he needed all the support he could muster in the tense days between his release and the country's first election, when civil war or liberation were equally possible. That seems a good explanation to me, although I can't say I enjoyed either of those encounters.

On the other hand, there have been great stars – the American activist Jesse Jackson, singer and civil rights campaigner Harry Belafonte, and Gillian Anderson from *The X Files* were taken around by Ahmed Kathrada and myself, and it is gratifying to see that everyone, no matter what their status, is emotionally overwhelmed when they enter Robben Island prison and see for themselves the hardship Mandela and the Rivonians went through.

I was proud of the work my son was doing on Robben Island and went to find him every time I arrived at the harbour. He was in his fourth year working with the big construction company and still enjoying it every day, showing us photographs of what he was doing. I could see for myself the transformation of the quayside. He had a good social life with plenty of friends, and my wife and I were proud when he made a fine speech at his 21st birthday party. He was a real outdoor sportsman and had a great attitude to life and work.

But one night when he was at home on leave with us in Cape Town, he was out late at night, and I received the phone call every parent dreads with all their heart.

Riaan had been involved in a car accident and had died on the way to hospital. His girlfriend told me that some thugs – some drunken white guys – had been dicing with them in another car, playing at forcing them off the road. Eventually they sideswiped Riaan's car, sending it crashing into a lamp-post and a tree. Afterwards, they smashed the windscreen to get in and steal his cell-phone, in case there were photos on it revealing their number plate. They have never been found, never brought to justice.

It was 3 a.m. and I drove to Tygerberg hospital, a place I knew well, and saw my son's body. He looked serene and seemed to be almost smiling. I've had to keep that thought with me over the years as a small means of comfort.

I could not believe my Riaan was dead. That same day, I went to the police yard asking to see the car they had towed away. I wanted to see for myself what had happened. When I got there, they were busy siphoning the petrol out of it, and told me they were making it safe, which of course was rubbish. The next day, I had to do a formal identification. I was driving to the hospital mortuary with a heavy heart. My wife's brother was with me, and we were silent in the car.

When my phone rang, it startled both of us. I pulled over to take the call and heard Mandela's voice. He said: 'I heard about your boy. It is a terrible thing when a parent has to bury his child. I understand how it feels, because I lost my own son in the same way. I wish I could give you some strength to bear this.'

Mandela's oldest son Thembekile had died in a car crash in

1969, when he was 24 years old. Mandela was then incarcerated on Robben Island, before I worked there, and had been refused permission to attend the funeral. It remained one of the greatest sorrows of his life. Now he was telling me that I had to believe in something, I had to believe that Riaan was in a better place. He said: 'I was sent a message about Riaan's accident. Tell me what happened.' I explained to him about the car crash and said I was on the way to formally identify Riaan's body. Mandela was very emotional, very upset. He said: 'I know how you must feel, I have been through this myself. You must take comfort from the knowledge that you did your best for Riaan throughout his life and that he was happy and enjoyed life to the full. You saw him growing up, from a tiny baby to a big strong adult. And I saw him too. I know you did everything possible for him. I always saw that he was passionate about his career. But you can do nothing now. You must try to make peace with this and know that Riaan has gone to a better place. Your most important task is to stand with your wife and help each other get through this together.'

It was a long call, and as we were talking my phone suddenly cut out; the battery had gone. I saw that Mandela had talked to me for 22 minutes.

It helped my wife and me, and our younger son Heinrich, to know that people cared. We asked a retired priest we knew to do the funeral service, because he had known Riaan since he was a baby.

The Dutch Reformed Church in Ruyterwacht, near Goodwood, was packed for the funeral. There were family members and Riaan's many friends, and Kathrada with his partner Barbara Hogan. Dullah Omar's widow was there, and many colleagues of mine from Robben Island and the

Constitutional Assembly. Mandela had told me that he and Graça would be thinking of us. They were on holiday in Mozambique, and there was no time for them to return for the funeral, but they would be with us in spirit.

We had decided to have a cremation and to scatter Riaan's ashes at the harbourside on Robben Island, a place he loved and where he lived life to the full. We went across on the ferry, taking flowers with us to float in the sea, and we had a small ceremony where passages from the Bible were read and we said some prayers. Although it was totally heartbreaking, I felt Riaan was still there with us, and I have felt that ever since.

My wife and I continued to take flowers there every year for five years, but then we made a decision to stop. It was incredibly sad for us every time, and we felt strongly that we wanted to keep our happiest memories of him alive, not get trapped in a state of continual mourning.

It has been hard for my younger son Heinrich. He took his brother's death badly and dealt with it in silence, often on his own in his room. He had just finished his matric and, while trying to deal with the death of his brother, he couldn't decide what to do. He ended up with a casual job at Distell, a company that makes liquor. Later that year, he applied to the Cape Town Technicon to study as an interior designer but, unfortunately, that year they were only accepting applications from people of colour. It was another blow for him.

Fortunately, through some friends, we managed to find him a place in Damilin College and for the next two years he studied there. It was difficult for him to find permanent work. He worked for a guy for two years and even worked in Abu Dhabi – he had to travel there twice to finish a job he was doing. After that he was unfortunately jobless for one year but, eventually, he found a permanent job in Cape Town. He is a very clever guy, a talented interior designer who works endlessly on 3D drawings and plans on his computer. Like Riaan, he is also sporty and goes scuba-diving. He plays rugby with friends and took a martial arts course. He lives with us and my mother at home at present and one of the great joys of our life is his daughter, Mia. Heinrich and Mia's mother never married or stayed together, but they share the love of this delightful little girl, and we look forward to the weekends when she's with us.

One Sunday, our whole family was in Gansbaai, a couple of hours from Cape Town, when Mandela's granddaughter called to invite us over. Of course, we packed up quickly and drove over to Bishopscourt. Mandela was so pleased to see Mia, but she was very cautious about him and wouldn't go to him. We tried a few times but all we could manage was a photograph of her with him, something she now cherishes. Mandela was also happy to meet Heinrich, whom he didn't meet as an adult until this time; he knew how much it meant to me and my wife to have our son and his child with us as a family.

We spent more than an hour with him. Then he said he wanted to see me alone. By now, I was calling him by his clan name, Madiba, like all South Africans who love him. I said: 'Is there a problem, Madiba? What's wrong?'

He spoke to me quite severely. He said: 'I can see you are putting on weight. You need to get one of those exercise balls and use it every morning. And you need to eat more healthily. Discipline yourself, and you will get back in shape again.'

Even now, he was pushing me to improve myself. I laughed, but he was totally serious. When I went outside, I saw that one of his police guards was very fat. I said to him: 'Mr Mandela wants to see you. You'd better get ready for a lecture about your weight.' He looked terrified.

I often had spontaneous invitations to see Madiba. The last time I saw him was on his birthday. I told him: 'We all want you to reach 100, you just have a few years to go. Don't leave us.'

I had thought for years that he could not go on. I thought maybe he had a couple of years left. He was stiff with arthritis. But then I would see him doing that famous Madiba shuffle, and I realised I was wrong.

He asked me once about the Sisulu family. He missed Walter, his dear friend and mentor, so much since he had died in 2003. He said: 'How is Mama Sisulu? Have you seen her?' He meant Walter's wife, who has now also passed away.

Mandela told me: 'It's my turn next, for sure.' But he was probably joking. You could never really tell. At one of his birthday parties he told me the crowds of people there had only come because he was old. 'You know, they want a last look,' he said.

CHAPTER 16

As I write this, Madiba lies ill at home and it is feared that he may never recover. He has been plagued by the recurring lung infection that dated back to the onset of tuberculosis in Pollsmoor Prison, where he was put into isolation in a dark damp cell.

His 95th birthday came and went as he lay, intubated, in an intensive care ward in Pretoria's Medi-Clinic Heart Hospital. The window of his room was opened slightly for a brief time, so that he could hear African children singing for him outside the hospital. His family and close friends visited regularly and I know that Winnie and Mandela's new wife Graça Machel took turns to sit with him, to hold his hand and talk.

His daughter Zindzi kindly invited me to visit too. She told me: 'Come with us, Tata would like to see you.' But I felt that would be intrusive. This was a time for the family to be together as much as possible.

I received regular news and I knew that, at times, Madiba was strong enough to sit up and watch television, but mostly he was comfortably asleep. Winnie or Graça would wake him up to greet a visitor and he would open his eyes and appear to smile, though a tracheostomy tube meant that he could not speak.

I thought of him a great deal as I headed for Robben Island every working day.

Often I travelled on the old *Dias* ferry boat or the *Susan Kruger*, both still in service and used to transport staff there and back. I chose to descend the steep iron stairway into the hold, where I could lie full-length on one of the wooden benches and catch some sleep while the boat ploughed through the water for 45 minutes. Most people prefer the cabin with windows looking out to sea, or even the exposed top deck if the weather is good. But for me, the hold is a special place. It's starkly bare and there are no windows, but if the sea is rough I find it is the place where I'm least vulnerable to sea-sickness.

Actually, the real reason was that down there was where I belonged. So many, many times I would take those stairs down with Mandela and his comrades for the journey. They would be in leg chains, and we sat in a forlorn row on those hard benches. Today there are sturdy cushions to provide a little comfort, but in the Rivonians' day there was nothing but the bare wood, the dark steel of the walls, and either a medical appointment at one end of the journey or a grim return to Robben Island at the other.

There's no sunlight, so it can get very cold. All you can do is listen to the klap-klap-klap of the water as the boat hits the waves. When you lie down the wood is cold, the steel joints are cold. You are so cold you have to turn over and move your body in an attempt to keep warm.

The staff boat is often crowded with tour guides, maintenance and cleaning staff, security company workers, and people like me who run the tourist facilities. I was the shops supervisor, buying in historic books about Mandela, the apartheid struggle, and the island itself, as well as curios like posters and t-shirts. I dealt with the memorabilia from the prison cells and also ran the cafeterias with food and drink for visitors.

On one occasion I took with me to Robben Island Ebrahim Rasool, my ex-prisoner who became South Africa's ambassador to Washington. Like me, he wanted to be in the hold, no need for explanation. He even took his family members and children down there on the way back. The sea was rough, and he knew from experience the need to minimise that feeling of sea-sickness.

A little-known landmark in the cultural collection that commemorates Mandela's great sacrifice to his country is Jetty 1, where the *Dias* and the *Susan Kruger* are moored. It is tucked away along Victoria Harbour just off the busy thoroughfare where tourists throng. It is a National Heritage Site where the public can walk in free of charge. In its way, Jetty 1 is the saddest monument of all. It has not changed from the time when it was the only gateway to the sea and Robben Island.

It is a brick-built structure where prisoners and visitors once waited for the island ferries. I took Mandela there many times, locking him in a cell on the first floor, then escorting visitors into their separate waiting room. When the ferry arrived, the prisoners would be the last to board, hurried down the iron staircase into the bowels of the boat to sit there in misery.

Today, the ground floor contains memorabilia from those times, handwritten letters from families begging for permission to visit a loved one, and lists of names and dates drawn up by warders like me to denote whether a visit was allowed or not. There is a large painting of the handsome Xhosa chieftains in their tribal dress, banished to the island by colonial settlers in the 19th century and left there to die, disinherited of their land and their livelihood.

Anyone stepping inside the tiny museum would have to be made of stone not to weep at film footage of the last political prisoners coming home from Robben Island in May 1991. Their faces tell the whole story with broad smiles and unashamed tears, while their bodies sway to the spontaneous singing of celebration that breaks out as the ferry pulls into the jetty. Dozens of people lean dangerously over the roped-off quayside with outstretched arms, longing for the first embrace from men who are their sons, brothers, or husbands. Their joy when the men finally step ashore and walk into their arms is overwhelming.

It is extraordinary how Jetty 1 sits virtually unnoticed at the harbour's edge, just yards away from the bustle of tourist boats taking crowds of sightseers for a trip around the bay or a nighttime party cruise. Across the pathway, easily heard from inside Jetty 1, there is music and chattering from the glamorous restaurants and wine bars along the harbourside strip. The Victoria & Alfred Waterfront is Africa's most popular tourist attraction by far, drawing in millions of visitors every month. Yet the museum is hardly signposted and rarely filled with people.

At the immediate approach to it is the exact spot where I once stood, mystified, on that secret mission on my first night shift at Pollsmoor. It's the place where I saw the ferry coming in under cover of darkness and realised that Mandela, Mhlaba, Mlangeni, and Sisulu were emerging from the shadows, clutching their cardboard boxes of belongings.

There were no shops or restaurants or wine bars then, and no sightseeing cruise boats. It was a dark and soulless shipyard with harsh searchlights directed at us with our machine-guns and guard-dogs.

Of course, the tourists don't travel on the *Dias* or the *Susan Kruger*. We have a new modern ferry to accommodate crowds comfortably, and we don't go out to sea if it's bad weather. Tours go to the island several times a day at a round-trip cost of about £20 per person and less for children. They leave from the showy Nelson Mandela Gateway across the water from Jetty 1, next to the Clock Tower.

For me, though, the past never fades. How can it when I feel the boat engine slowing at the approach to Robben Island and go up top to see the harbour wall that my son helped to build? As I step ashore, I sometimes close my eyes briefly and I can see Riaan there, waving and smiling to greet me and getting on with the job he loved.

I walk across the landing-stage, and I can still see the prisoners in my mind's eye. I can see them and hear them. The warders are watching sternly as they kick a football around the soccer field for a few minutes of freedom and exercise before lockup. The pitch is neglected and overgrown now.

The whole island is full of ghosts for me. I am actually one of them, trudging up the track to my dismal quarters that stank of old fish or hurrying Mandela towards the visitors' centre, stopping only to let him pick a daisy for Winnie.

All the single warders' quarters are empty now, and I think it's a shame that visitors can't stay overnight in some sort of residential centre developed from these historic buildings. The island's only residents are ex-prisoners – many of them from the Soweto uprising – who take people around B Section and describe the daily life they once led there. They live in the former married warders' quarters. The guided tour takes a bus trip right around, to include the lepers' graveyard, the little church built for them with no pews – many of them were limbless – and the mosque. At the north end, there is a magnificent view of Table Mountain from the hard shingle on the beach, the spot where

DOING LIFE WITH MANDELA

Mandela and the others waded into the cold sea to pull out the giant seaweed plants.

The island school stands empty and, like the deserted houses, it is now inhabited by birds. A desalination plant has been installed nearby, ironically, now that most of the people have gone. In my time, there was just the brackish, virtually undrinkable water from the island's borehole, discoloured and strange tasting.

The overgrown sports field looks sad. But it strikes me that all these facilities could be brought back to life easily. There are conference facilities for workshops, and Robben Island could become a vibrant centre of education. Mandela's dream of a Robben Island university could be a reality.

Recently, I had to stay over after working late. I went outside on the stoep in the late-night darkness and saw the twinkling lights of Cape Town city in the distance and the looming shape of Table Mountain. I thought about all those evenings jogging around the limestone road. There were fewer twinkling lights then, but Mandela and his friends would have known that real life was just seven kilometres away, so near and yet so far.

Many times I am called in to talk to visitors who want to know about my days with Mandela. They listen teary-eyed and they will often tell me Mandela has been their lifelong inspiration. He is their hero, their role model of tolerance and goodness.

Yes, I tell them, but I am the only one among you who can say he was my prisoner and my friend.

It was soon after dawn on Sunday, 15 December 2013 when Christo Brand walked through the ancient fields of Qunu village and past the river where Mandela played as a child, on his way to a sad but fitting ceremony, the last goodbye to the great Nelson Mandela. Security guards noted his damp and muddy shoes and insisted on brushing them clean for him. He continued alone right up to the burial place and looked into Mandela's empty grave.

'I thought to myself how he would now be able to look over the whole of that green valley he loved so much. Madiba had come home, just as he always longed to,' he said.

Christo was greeted warmly by a group of military generals, every one of them an ex-prisoner from Robben Island. Film producer Anant Singh, whose *Mandela, Long Walk to Freedom* had recently received huge critical acclaim, persuaded Christo to sit nearby, along with actor Idris Elba, who took the lead part.

Mourners started up their beloved freedom songs dedicated to Mandela, and Christo felt proud. Close to tears, he listened to Mandela's grandson Ndaba giving his moving speech. 'I closed my eyes and I could hear the man himself, and see him in his youth', he said. Granddaughter Nandi was also impressive and talked of Mandela's warmth towards his family.

Daughter Zindzi saw Christo, gave him a special smile, and thanked him for being there. The singing stopped and everyone stood. It was the moment for Mandela's coffin to be carried solemnly past the mourners.

'The coffin was close enough for me to touch, but I didn't think that would be right,' said Christo. 'And it was enough to know that our lives had touched for so many years. I said a silent goodbye to the best, strongest and most honest human being I have ever known.'

Barbara Jones

Update: Life after Mandela

ANDREW RUSSELL

It was the news everyone had been expecting, but at the same time dreading. It was inevitable, I guess – not even he could live forever. And so on 5 December 2013, Nelson Rolihlahla Mandela passed away at his home in the Johannesburg suburb of Houghton, surrounded by members of his family. The world had lost an icon; a country had lost our hero; a family had lost their father, grandfather, great-grandfather. Christo Brand had lost a friend, someone who had become like a second father to him.

Christo was invited to attend the state funeral as a guest of the Mandela family. The funeral was to take place on Saturday, 15 December 2013 in the small Eastern Cape village of Qunu. How fitting that Mandela chose this small village as his final resting place, rather than a grand state cemetery in one of the country's cities. Here is what he wrote about Qunu in his autobiography, *Long Walk to Freedom*:

> We lived in a less grand style in Qunu, but it was in that village near Umtata that I spent some of the happiest years of my boyhood and whence I trace my earliest memories. ...

The village of Qunu was situated in a narrow, grassy valley crisscrossed by clear streams, and overlooked by green hills. It consisted of no more than a few hundred people who lived in huts, which were beehive-shaped structures of mud walls. ... The huts were generally grouped in a residential area that was some distance away from the maize fields. There were no roads, only paths through the grass worn away by barefooted boys and women. ...

From an early age, I spent most of my free time in the veld playing and fighting with the other boys of the village. ... I was no more than five when I became a herd-boy looking after sheep and calves in the fields. ... It was in the fields that I learned how to knock birds out of the sky with a slingshot ... to drink warm, sweet milk straight from the udder of a cow, to swim in the clear, cold streams, and to catch fish with twine and sharpened bits of wire. I learned to stick-fight – essential knowledge to any rural African boy – and became adept at ... parrying blows. ... From these days I date my love of the veld, of open spaces, the simple beauties of nature, the clean line of the horizon.

At the funeral, Christo sat directly behind Mandela's daughter Zindzi. This was a time for him to reflect on the journey he had walked with his friend. One day when Mandela was president, Christo had visited him in his office and told him he had something on his mind. Christo told Mandela that even though he was now the president, to Christo he still did not seem like a free man. He said that on Robben Island he had been guarded by warders, when he was released he was guarded by private security, and now that he was the president he was guarded by the presidential guards. Mandela paused, then slowly said to Christo: 'Mr Brand, you are right. But now this prisoner can tell the security in which direction to walk.'

A few weeks later, Mandela called Christo into his office and told him that he had recently come back from holiday in the Bahamas. One morning while there, he had remembered what Christo had told him, so he told his security guards he did not want to see any of them; he wanted to walk alone on the beach that morning. He hadn't walked very far when a young couple approached him. The lady looked at him and asked, 'Excuse me, sir, are you not President Nelson Mandela?' Mandela said that in that moment, he was worried. He turned to the lady and said, 'Ma'am, I'm sorry. One day I would also love to meet that man.' The couple apologized and walked on, never realising that they had actually met Nelson Mandela.

Christo also recalled another occasion when he, Mandela, and Ahmed Kathrada had visited a junior school in Wynberg. During the break, the delegation had gone out onto the rugby field. Mandela called Christo over and commented: 'Look at those two youngsters, Mr Brand – one black and one white, playing together. Look, they're even sharing an apple.' Christo turned to Mandela and said, 'Yes, Mr President. Now that you are the president, schools are open to all races. Those young kids don't see a colour; they just play together.' Mandela paused and then replied: 'Yes, Mr Brand – that is the rainbow nation I want to see developing in our country. We tried to change Robben Island into a university. But my comrades are not always educated. Now is the time to educate those youngsters. They will be the future leaders of our country.'

When Christo's book was published in March 2014, the publishers flew him to London for the official launch at Waterstones Bookshop in Piccadilly. He had no idea what to expect. When he arrived, he was surprised at the number of people queuing outside the shop to buy a copy of his book. Not having spoken in public much before, he was nervous at the thought of having to address such a large crowd. Fortunately a woman approached him, gave him a hug, told him that he could not run away from her, and said that her father's last wish to her was that, if he could not attend the book launch, she would represent him. That was Zindzi Mandela. It was a wonderful occasion, and all present certainly felt Nelson Mandela's presence and blessing.

Christo continued his work as a shop supervisor on Robben Island and soon noticed an increase in the number of people interested in hearing about his journey with Nelson Mandela, purchasing a copy of his book and asking him to sign it. His frustration was growing, because he was now often being asked to appear at private events and functions and even host private tours of Robben Island – all of which were impossible for him as an employee of Robben Island Museum.

In April 2015 on Robben Island, Christo met a group from Ashbury College in Ottawa, Canada. They were on a rugby tour of the Western Cape. They returned in 2017 and this time, through myself as their tour operator, Ian Middleton, their tour leader, asked me to arrange for Christo to meet and chat to the group of boys, staff, and parents at their hotel. I remember the date: 16 March. It was my mom's birthday, so I could not attend Christo's talk. It was a wonderful event, and it planted the seed for the next chapter of Christo's journey. The next morning, my group told me how incredible his story was and what an impression he had made.

After their tour Ian invited me to visit Ashbury College, where once again he and his colleagues spoke about the impact Christo's talk had made on the boys. And so on my return from Canada, I met Christo and Estelle for the first time and we started chatting about opportunities for Christo and his storytelling. He had started to feel he was in a rut at Robben Island and that, with every request he received to talk to a group, he was losing out on another opportunity to share his unique story.

In March 2018 Professor Michael Slattery, who had met Christo in 2016 while on tour in South Africa with a group of students from Texas Christian University, invited Christo and Estelle to spend a week in the USA as his guests, giving a series of talks to different groups within his community. Mike and TCU are involved in a programme combatting poaching of endangered southern white rhino at Amakhala Game Reserve in the Eastern Cape. This visit to the USA was another defining moment for Christo and Estelle. They noticed how warmly they were welcomed wherever Christo spoke, and this opened their eyes to the potential for even more overseas storytelling trips in the future. After much deliberation and soul-searching, Christo took the bold decision to take early retirement from Robben Island and so, as of 1 July 2018, he was suddenly a full-time storyteller. The next chapter in his remarkable life had begun.

We set up a website and launched his new career on social media, and tour operators around the world soon became aware of Christo's story and what he could offer their guests: a unique experience to meet and hear about Mandela from someone who had known him as well as anyone still living. Before long, bookings started to stream in for him to share his journey with guests. From small group dinners to private tours and exclusive helicopter trips to Robben Island, to conferences and other public events, people started contacting us for their guests to have the opportunity to meet Christo and hear about his journey with the world's most popular leader.

The Nelson Mandela Foundation hosts an annual Nelson Mandela lecture. On 18 July 2018, on what would have been Mandela's 100th birthday, Barack Obama delivered the Mandela lecture at the Wanderers Stadium in Johannesburg. I was privileged to be in the audience that day with my daughter, Abigail, my tourism friend Charmaine Wardenberg, and Christo Brand. It was an overwhelmingly emotional day – I could not think of a more appropriate world leader to honour Mandela that day than the first black President of the United States.

In 2019 Christo and I were flown to the Indaba Tourism show in Durban as guests of Wesgro, where we had our own stand and were able to meet tour operators from all over the world. One of the highlights of the show was South Africa's then Minister of Tourism, Derek Hanekom, visiting our stand and warmly embracing Christo and posing for photos with him. Hanekom jokingly announced to the group surrounding the two men: 'This is the man who kept Mandela behind bars for so long!' It was a lighthearted moment shared by all present. We also attended World Travel Market that year at the Cape Town International Convention Centre, where Christo was invited to be one of the keynote speakers in the main auditorium.

Internationally, Christo was invited to many events. One of these was organised by the Bank of Brazil for their staff and families. Estelle, Christo, and I were sent our air tickets and looked forward to a week in Brazil, visiting both Sao Paolo and Rio de Janeiro. At the main event in the Sao Paolo City Hall, Christo was one of three international speakers on the programme. The other two were Agnes Furey and Yann Arthus-Bertrand, an environmentalist, activist, journalist, and photographer who has also directed films about the impact of humans on the planet. He is especially well known for his book *Earth from Above* and his films *Home* and *Human*.

Agnes Furey, a retired nurse who worked thirty years in addiction treatment, has a remarkable story to share. In January 2005, Agnes sought healing from the rage eating away at her heart and health. Two of her children had already died from AIDS and sudden infant death syndrome when, in March 1998, former cocaine addict Leonard Scovens strangled her forty-year-old daughter Patricia Reed in her apartment in Sarasota, Florida. Reed had met Scovens in drug treatment, and they had dated after leaving the facility. Furey's six-year-old grandson, Chris, hid in the closet but also was killed by Scovens. Scovens was found guilty and sentenced to life imprisonment.

When Furey decided to write to Scovens in prison, she learned that her daughter's killer was hurting too. They slowly built a bond cemented in a need to understand each other and to heal. They exchanged hundreds of letters and phone conversations. And after two years of tedious work, they published a 96-page book, *Wildflowers in the Median*, including a sampling of letters written by Scovens to Furey as well as Furey's poems and vignettes. 'Sharing the story is not all that uncomfortable anymore,' she said.

Yet writing the book had been a challenge. During the process, she had been reading and rereading about the hurt that no mother should endure. 'That was difficult,' Furey confessed.

Assembling the book was also hard work. Scovens, serving his sentence at the Apalachee Correctional Institution East in Sneads, Florida, was allowed to send and receive only fifteen pages at a time. Furey handled the typing, and Scovens, who had previously taught English and social studies in Baltimore, did meticulous line editing.

Furey, a community activist and self-trained expert on restorative justice, believes her daughter would be proud of the book and of Scovens's attempt to help other inmates achieve healing. 'I believe then, and I believe now, she would not have wanted him executed,' she said. 'I believe she would want him to be able to do something positive.'

It was a truly emotional moment when Christo and Agnes embraced each other, both of them parents who had lost children in devastating circumstances. The entire event was a beautifully crafted show, running for five hours without a host or narrator. Each presentation, song, speech, poem, orchestral piece, and dialogue flowed into the next with seamless continuity. A highlight for me was when the famous Brazilian actor Antonio Pitanga read some of Nelson Mandela's quotes before Christo shared his story with the audience. I don't think there was a dry eye in the hall as Christo spoke about aspects of his journey with Nelson Mandela. He received rapturous applause – it was truly an inspirational event.

Christo was also guest speaker at a wonderful event hosted by SA Tourism, where we got to meet many Brazilian tour operators who deal with the South African market. He also conducted interviews with Brazilian media organisations.

One day we were contacted by a Norwegian tour operator, Rune Engstrom, who wanted Christo to meet one of his groups in Cape Town. This was to be the start of a very close relationship with Rune, culminating in him arranging for Estelle and Christo to visit Norway to speak at an annual Travel Expo as well as at other events and functions. During Christo and Estelle's visit to Oslo in January 2018, Rune contacted Christo to say that the former prime minister of Norway, Kjell Magna Bondevik, had discovered Christo was in Oslo and would like to meet him. Prime Minister Bondevik had hosted Nelson Mandela on two occasions in Norway. So a meeting was arranged, and Mr Bondevik and Christo enjoyed some time together at the Nobel Foundation, chatting about their mutual friend and comparing stories. They found a copy of *Long Walk to Freedom* where they found the references Mandela had made to Christo, and Christo presented Mr Bondevik with a signed copy of his own book.

In June 2018 Christo, Estelle, and I were invited to the UK as guests of SA Tourism for a celebration of Nelson Mandela's 100th birthday. The head of SA Tourism in the UK, Tolene van der Merwe, arranged an intimate dinner at the The Rubens at The Palace Hotel, overlooking Buckingham Palace. Other guests included Xoliswa Ndoyiya, who had been Mandela's chef at his Houghton home, and Anna Trapido, author of the book *Hunger for Freedom: The Story of Food in the Life of Nelson Mandela*. One of the chapters in her book is about Estelle's famous fruitcake, which Christo had smuggled into Pollsmoor Prison for Mandela and his fellow prisoners to enjoy. The menu had been carefully planned by Xoliswa to include all of Mandela's favourite foods, and before each course she spoke to us about what we were about to eat. We enjoyed some fine South African wines, and the tables were adorned with protea flowers. It was a truly moving and humbling experience. At the end of the evening, Tolene thanked us all for attending the dinner –

and only then did she mention that there were 27 guests in the room, one for each year Mandela spent in prison. Each guest was presented with signed copies of Anna's and Christo's books. I went back to my flat with such an indescribable feeling of pride at having been able to attend such a special dinner.

The next day we were guests of the South African ambassador at a grand Mandela birthday celebration at South Africa House in Trafalgar Square. Once again, Christo was one of the guest speakers in a question-and-answer session on the stage, and we enjoyed many South African-flavoured dishes and wines.

We were also invited to share Christo's story in the Attlee Room at the House of Lords, where we were hosted by the Bishops College Old Boys Society and Lord Anthony St John, who took us on a private tour of the Houses of Parliament. We were privileged to visit Westminster Hall where, on 11 July 1996, Nelson Mandela became just the third foreign leader in history to address the joint Houses of Parliament. We had great fun visiting Mandela's statue in Parliament Square, where we bumped into some fellow South Africans and shared memories with them. The next few days we spent driving around the UK, sharing Christo's story at a number of schools. Christo was also guest speaker at a South African Chamber of Commerce function in London, where it was a privilege to meet Lord Peter Hain, who had been heavily involved in the anti-apartheid movement and played a major role in international sports boycotts of teams that played against South Africa.

Twenty-twenty was promising to be a really busy year for Christo. From January to mid-March he shared his story numerous times with different groups. And then suddenly, Covid hit the world and almost immediately the tourism tap was turned off. All of Christo's in-person events for the rest of the year were either cancelled or postponed, and there we sat, wondering what we were going to do without any tourists in our country.

Following the initial shock and our very strict first lockdown period, I decided to work on a remote presentation titled 'Lessons from a Warder and his Prisoner.' The idea was that I would engage in a conversation with Christo while sharing a slideshow showing photos of him and Mandela growing up, personal notes, letters, and other images, including landmark events such as Mandela's release from prison on 11 February 1990 and his inauguration as our first democratically elected president on 10 May 1994, as well as images of his funeral in Qunu. Slowly we started getting more and more requests to host sessions for school, university, and special interest groups all over the world.

It started to dawn on us that even in a Covid world, there are people out there who are desperate to hear the story of how it was possible for these two men from such different backgrounds to develop a lasting friendship based on mutual trust and respect. Surely the two men should have hated each other. One was a white, 18-year-old, Afrikaans-speaking jail warder representing the apartheid regime, the other a black, 60-year-old, Xhosa-speaking prisoner serving a life sentence.

And so this remarkable story of hope, trust, and respect in a world blighted by racism, hatred, and division started to gain traction. We always send some reading material and our own YouTube video to groups ahead of time, so the educators can help their students gain more insight and context around that time in our history. We are also offering a corporate leadership session around lessons to be drawn from Mandela's life.

Nelson Mandela ends his autobiography with these words:

I have walked that long road to freedom. I have tried not to falter; I have made missteps along the way. But I have discovered the secret that after climbing a great hill, one only finds that there are many more hills to climb. I have taken a moment here to rest, to steal a view of the glorious vista that surrounds me, to look back on the distance I have come. But I can rest only for a moment, for with freedom come responsibilities, and I dare not linger, for my long walk is not yet ended.

Similarly, Christo's walk continues as he keeps alive the legacy of his friend and assumes the responsibility of sharing Mandela's wisdom with people from all over the world. After all, Nelson Mandela belonged to us all. So it is only fitting that the man who knew him so intimately from his dark prison days, through to his freedom and his presidency, should be the one tasked with keeping his vision alive. And Mandela certainly can rest in peace in the knowledge that Christo has taken on that mantle in a way which would make Madiba incredibly proud of him.

Christo Brand spent his early years on a farm called Goedvertrouw. The family had no luxuries and no electricity, but Christo enjoyed carefree primary school days surrounded by family and friends

When Christo was 12, his father developed pneumonia and the family were forced to leave the farm and move to his uncle's house in Parow Valley, Cape Town.

After finishing school, Christo made the life-changing decision to become a prison guard and, at the age of 18, was sent to work on Robben Island.

The visiting booth in the visitors center on Robben Island where Winnie Mandela sat when she came to visit her husband, Nelson, and brought their grandchild to the island.

One of Christo's daily tasks at Pollsmoor Prison was to hoist the South African flag each morning and lower it each evening. One particular day he was told to lower it for the last time; there was now a new South African flag to raise. This was the very last time the old South African flag flew at Pollsmoor.

Christo's boss during the years he worked in the constitutional assembly document printing centre, Cyril Ramaphosa, later became President of South Africa.

Christo developed a close friendship with Ahmed Kathrada, one of the Rivonia trialists banished to Robben Island with Mandela. Kathrada wrote the foreword for the first edition of Christo's book. Kathrada was also instrumental in arranging a job for Christo back at Robben Island in 1997, when it was declared a World Heritage Site.

During the twilight years
of his life, Nelson Mandela
would often invite Christo's
family to visit him. Here are
a few photos of Mandela with
Christo's son Riaan (above
left); Heinrich (above right); his
wife Estelle and granddaughter
Mia (right); and Christo himself
with Mia (below).

Christo was invited to attend the funeral of Nelson Mandela as a guest of the family. He sat with the family at the graveside and met dignitaries from all over the world, including Prince Charles, whose photo he took the opportunity to snap.

Two houses where Christo accompanied Mandela to meet visiting officials were the guesthouse at Pollsmoor where Mandela met with the Eminent Persons Group in 1985 (near left) and the house at Victor Verster Prison in the winelands where Mandela spent the last 14 months of his imprisonment.

RIGHT: During the Indaba travel show in Durban in 2018, Minister of Tourism Derek Hanekom came to visit Christo at his stand and tease him about being the one who kept Mandela behind bars for so many years!

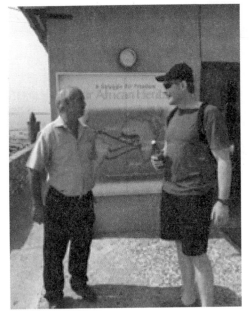

LEFT: In July 2015 Andrew Russell arranged a rugby tour to South Africa for Ashbury College from Ottawa, Canada. On their Robben Island trip, purely by chance they met Christo and Ian Middleton, the master in charge, bought a copy of *Doing Life with Mandela: My Prisoner, My Friend*. In July 2018, Christo resigned from Robben Island and asked Andrew to be his business manager as they set out on an exciting adventure into the unknown, sharing Christo's amazing story with the world.

One unique way guests can meet Christo is to take the Freedom Flight with NAC Helicopters which includes a private tour of Robben Island, a visit to Drakenstein Prison (formerly known as Victor Verster), and lunch at Richard Branson's wine farm, Mont Rochelle. On one such visit in 2019, Branson saw Christo in the garden and came out to chat to him and reminisce about the last time he had seen him, at Mandela's funeral.

On a speaking tour of the UK in 2018, Christo and Andrew met Lord Peter Hain, who had been an anti-apartheid activist, in particular in enforcing the international sporting boycott on South Africa.

Christo was invited by the Bishops College Old Boys to address them in the Atlee Room at the Houses of Parliament. On a tour of the buildings, Christo and Estelle were taken to the Westminster Hall, where Nelson Mandela had addressed the combined houses in 1996. We also visited the statue of Nelson Mandela in Parliament Square.

Christo was interviewed live on Sky News by Adam Boulton to talk about the 100th birthday celebrations of Nelson Mandela.

During November 2018 Christo, Estelle, and Andrew were invited to Brazil as guests of the Bank of Brazil. Christo was one of three international speakers at their annual staff event in the São Paulo City Hall. The other two were Agnes Furey and Yann Arthus-Bertrand, an environmentalist, activist, journalist, and photographer. It was an emotional moment when Christo met Agnes, both parents having lost children in tragic circumstances.

One of the other guests that day was the famous Brazilian actor Antonio Pitanga, who read some of Nelson Mandela's quotes before Christo shared his story with the audience. There wasn't a dry eye in the hall as Christo spoke about aspects of his journey with Mandela. He received rapturous applause – it was truly an inspirational event.

During Christo and Estelle's visit to Oslo in January 2018 organised by our good friend Rune Engstrom, the couple were invited to the Nobel Peace Centre, where Christo had an open breakfast meeting with Liv Torres, the executive director (above right). It was well attended by diplomats, including H. E. Selaelo Ramokgopa, South African Ambassador to Norway. The couple also met up with former Prime Minister Kjell Magna Bondevik, who had hosted Nelson Mandela on two occasions in Norway, and reminisced about their mutual friend. They even found the two references Mandela made to Christo in *Long Walk to Freedom*. Christo presented Mr Bondevik with a signed copy of his own book (above left).

Christo with Liv Torres and Ambassador H. E. Selaelo Ramokgopa.

Christo now offers private tours of Robben Island, sometimes with the assistance of former warder colleague Michiel Vosloo and former Robben Island Museum guide Yasien Mohamed.

Since retiring from Robben Island Museum in July 2018, Christo shares his story with guests from around the world in a variety of ways – private boat charters and tours of Robben Island, dinners, conferences, and talks to visiting tour groups. A popular excursion with tourists is to take a helicopter ride to Robben Island with NAC Helicopters and enjoy a private tour of the Island with Christo.

Tourists also enjoy meeting Christo at Jetty One at the Victoria & Alfred Waterfront – the building the prisoners used to leave from to the Island on the Susan Kruger ferry. Today Jetty One is part of the Robben Island Museum.

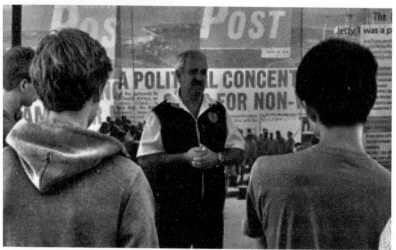

RIGHT: A chance meeting with Rune Engstrom, owner of Destination Africa, and Charlotte Ehde Eliassen, owner of Jomfrureiser, sparked a close friendship with Rune, who has become one of South Africa's hardest-working and most passionate tourism ambassadors.

In March 2020, just before lockdown, Christo celebrated his 60th birthday surrounded by family and close friends. Two of these were Viyassen Govender, who worked on Robben Island, and Igshaan Amlay.

Also at Christo's 60th birthday celebration, here are Christo and Estelle with their son Heinrich, his wife Veronica, and granddaughter Mia.

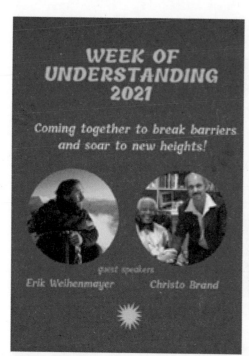

WEEK OF UNDERSTANDING 2021

Coming together to break barriers and soar to new heights!

guest speakers

Erik Weihenmayer   Christo Brand

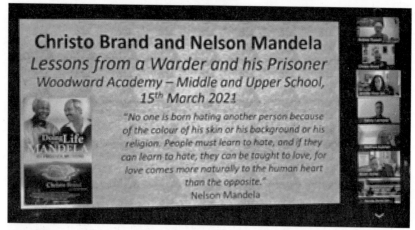

Christo Brand and Nelson Mandela
Lessons from a Warder and his Prisoner
Woodward Academy – Middle and Upper School, 15th March 2021

"No one is born hating another person because of the colour of his skin or his background or his religion. People must learn to hate, and if they can learn to hate, they can be taught to love, for love comes more naturally to the human heart than the opposite."
Nelson Mandela

After the pandemic broke out, we started sharing Christo's story remotely with schools, universities, special interest groups, and corporates in a session called 'Lessons from a Warder and His Prisoner'. The response has been amazing, and we have been able to reach new audiences all around the world. One of these sessions was a talk hosted by renowned author Dr Dean Allen on 18 July 2020, Nelson Mandela's birthday.

SPECIAL SECTION:
Witnesses to Friendship
and Forgiveness

Contents

Introduction

ANDREW RUSSELL

In March 2020 the Covid pandemic struck South Africa, and our tourist and event numbers dropped to zero overnight. Christo's speaking engagements went from just about one a day, to none. Our borders were closed; the planes stopped flying; life as we had known it ground to a halt.

After a couple of bewildered months wondering what we were going to do, we started to explore the idea of offering Christo's story remotely in a question-and-answer session with myself, which we called 'Lessons from a Warder and His Prisoner.' While Christo and I chatted, I would share slides showing pictures, personal letters, and events from his and Mandela's lives.

As the number of requests for these remote sessions increased, I soon realised that Christo's story on its own, documented in his 2014 memoir *Doing Life with Mandela: My Prisoner, My Friend*, needed some more context and understanding for our new audiences around the world. Many of them had heard about Nelson Mandela, Robben Island, apartheid, possibly even the Truth and Reconciliation Commission. But this was now the ideal opportunity to provide some more depth and insight into that remarkable period of our history. Many of our new audiences were school and university learners and educators – and after each session, I was struck by the depth and quality of the questions posed to Christo.

In fact, it was clear that we were merely scratching the surface. Many of our new audiences wanted to know more, ask more, learn more, understand more. Not just about Christo and Mandela, but about the themes and lessons from their journey together: trust, humility, friendship, honesty, mutual respect and understanding, reconciliation, forgiveness, healing. In a world torn apart by racism, division, and now Covid, this story was proving to offer a glimmer of hope – an inspirational tale of two friends.

That was when I came up with the idea of asking a wide range of people to write pieces on their own experiences of that time, their personal recollections of their journeys, their involvement with Christo and Mandela, and the role that each of them played in the birth of the new, democratic South Africa.

Lionel Davis was sent to Robben Island for seven years in 1964 for sabotage. He returned to work on the Island in 1997 and lived there for the next ten years, working first as a guide and then as the Education Officer. He is an acclaimed artist and storyteller. His piece included here is adapted from a book-length memoir he intends to publish.

Vusumzi Mcongo spent twelve years on Robben Island for incitement, sabotage, and terrorist activities. He was released in 1990 and returned to work as a guide on the Island when it was declared a World Heritage Site.

Igshaan Amlay was one of the Wynberg Seven, arrested in 1985 during a student protest and sentenced to a year in Pollsmoor Prison from June 1987 at the age of 18. In prison, Christo Brand befriended him and took care of him. The two men remain close friends.

Mario Meyer was born in the winelands region of the Western Cape. In 1984 he was sent to Pollsmoor Prison on criminal charges. During his time there he met Christo Brand, who introduced him to Nelson Mandela. Since his release from prison, Mario has remained close friends with Christo and Estelle.

Mary Burton was one of the commissioners on the Truth and Reconciliation Commission. She was appointed by President Mandela to serve for three years, from 1995 until 1998.

John Carlin was a journalist who reported on the historic events that took place in South Africa between 1990 and 1995. He became a celebrated author, writing the book *Playing the Enemy*, which was turned into the movie *Invictus* directed by Clint Eastwood, starring Morgan Freeman as Nelson Mandela and Matt Damon as Springbok captain François Pienaar. John also wrote a book called *Knowing Mandela*. He has always been very fond of Christo and writes about him in both of his books.

Yasien Mohamed was a drama teacher involved in the struggle against apartheid. In 1996 he was appointed to work as a guide on Robben Island. He is now retired but continues to share his story with interested groups.

Marcellette Williams met Christo in the Island shop in 1999. A simple bottle of water set off a remarkable friendship and cemented the already strong links between her University of Massachusetts Boston and South Africa. In fact, the U.S. launch of the first edition of Christo's book took place at UMass Boston.

Makaziwe Mandela is Nelson Mandela's eldest daughter with his first wife, Evelyn. She grew up in Soweto and was educated at the University of Fort Hare and the University of Natal before earning a Ph.D. in Anthropology from the University of Massachusetts Amherst.

Marjolein Westerterp, a Dutch journalist and travel writer, first met Christo on the Robben Island bus in 2014. She is an ardent fan of South Africa and in fact owns a holiday home here. After meeting Christo and Estelle, she invited them to join her on a roadshow in Holland, offering talks at a range of venues. She often visits them at their home in Cape Town.

Ian Middleton, a history teacher at Ashbury College in Ottawa, came across Christo on the Island in 2015 while he was on a school rugby tour. Ian was so taken aback to have met Mandela's prison guard that he insisted Christo speak to their touring group when they returned in 2017. It was then that I first met Christo, and we started to explore the opportunity for Christo to resign from Robben Island and take up his storytelling on a full-time basis. So a chance meeting between Ian and Christo on the Island in 2015 completely changed both our lives.

South African-born Michael Slattery met Christo in Cape Town in 2016, while leading a group of students from Texas Christian University. (That meeting was made possible by Ethan Casey, whose Blue Ear Books is the publisher of this new edition. Ethan was introduced to Christo by his brother Aaron. It was Aaron and Ethan's mother, Judith Casey, who first struck up a conversation with Christo on the Robben Island ferry in 2004.) Mike Slattery is a professor of environmental science at TCU and has maintained close contacts with his country of birth by supporting a rhino initiative at Amakhala Game Reserve in the Eastern Cape. He often brings groups of students to work on the project, and he has hosted Christo and Estelle at TCU on a speaking tour.

Rune Engstrom first met Christo in 2017 while visiting Cape Town. Rune is one of South Africa's favourite adopted sons. He adores traveling here and bringing Scandinavian tourists to our shores. He has twice hosted Christo and Estelle in his home country of Norway, a country that played a huge part in the anti-apartheid movement.

Annette Nobuntu Mul first met Christo in 2017. Since then she has become a close friend of Christo and Estelle and also published a book on Ubuntu, an ancient African word meaning 'People are people through other people.' Annette is the founder of the Ubuntu Society and chairwoman of the Ubuntu Netherlands Foundation.

William Ntebe lives in Hermanus on South Africa's southern coast but grew up in Cape Town, with a mom and dad who were actively involved in the underground anti-apartheid movement. He was one of the first intake of black students to be admitted to the country's oldest previously whites-only government school, South African College School, known as SACS.

Sam Hodson is my oldest friend; we met when we were just seven years old. Since 2015 Sam has been executive manager of Camphill Farm Community in Hermanus, the hosts for Christo's last in-person speaking engagement in March 2020 before Covid locked our country down.

Each of these remarkable people is a global citizen who could not help but be moved by the story of how a country could pull off a peaceful transition from being held captive under a repressive, racist system to a free and democratic society where the rights of every citizen would be upheld in a new constitution.

I then approached Ethan Casey of Blue Ear Books in Seattle, USA, who had met Christo before and heard his story, and asked if he would assist with the editing and publishing of this new edition. Ethan was only too happy to get involved. And so we started to receive some remarkable pieces, and it soon became clear that every one of these beautifully handcrafted articles deserved a place in a second edition of Christo's book. Each of them offers remarkable insights, and each, in its own personal way, acknowledges the immense roles played by these two remarkable South African heroes, Nelson Mandela and Christo Brand.

Very Young and Fighting Back
LIONEL DAVIS

I was born in District Six (D6), a municipal housing area between the foot of Table Mountain and the Table Bay foreshore and bordering the central business district of Cape Town.

When I was four, my family – my mother, my two sisters, and myself – moved into a tenement building in D6, and for many years we lived in a single small room. It was our kitchen, bedroom, lounge, even toilet at night. We lived from hand to mouth and could not preserve food, because we did not have an icebox or fridge. Our food was cooked on two oil burners (a paraffin stove and a Beatrice stove).

I was born into an overcrowded community of people of varied origin. D6 was culturally diverse, including residents from many parts of the world. There were former slaves, Indian and Chinese former indentured labourers, Black migrant workers, and Whites. However, the vast majority of D6 residents were classified 'Coloured,' meaning in apartheid terminology of mixed race.

In the mid- to late 1800s, thousands of Jews fled Eastern Europe to escape persecution and oppression. Many came to South Africa, and some settled in D6. During colonial times and, more pointedly, during apartheid, Whites were regarded as superior to those regarded as non-White. Whites had access to better jobs and education, and as they flourished, they left D6 for wealthier areas, yet they retained ownership of the properties and shops in D6.

At the age of 13, it was my duty to buy small items of food and fuel for our stoves from the local grocery shops. One Saturday morning, I was tasked to buy a few eggs at a local shop owned by Maisel, a Jewish man. When I got to the shop, he had his back to me and was standing at the edge of the pavement watching a street parade. I entered and waited for him. When he turned, he was surprised to see this Black boy. He eyed me suspiciously, thinking that I had sneaked in to steal. I bought my eggs, but he was eyeing the cloth bag I held in my hand, insisting that I give it to him. I refused. He got angry and threatened me. So I gave him the bag—which was empty! He just shrugged his shoulders and turned away from me. No apology! I was furious, grabbed one of the eggs, launched it at his head, but missed, and ran.

As I grew older and started working for a living, I went from job to job as a labourer. I continued to encounter White prejudice while travelling by bus or train and even at work. Aged 18, I was a labourer at a printing firm on their delivery van, transporting printed material. At lunchtime one day, we stopped for a short break in Woodstock, a suburb next to D6. My fellow worker, a Xhosa-speaking man, went to a shop to buy a loaf of bread. Our driver, in a hurry, asked me to see why this fellow was taking so long. As I entered the shop, I was witness to a huge confrontation between the shopkeeper and my colleague, who was arguing that he had been over-charged for the bread. I tried to explain to her why he objected, but she turned her wrath on me. I had to lift my arms to protect my face as she attacked me. She then reported to the police that I had physically assaulted her. I had no means for a lawyer and pleaded guilty in court. As a result I was sentenced to receive seven lashes with a bamboo cane, which had deliberately been soaked in saltwater to exact maximum pain. Every stroke of that cane drew blood.

Every time I looked at the scars left by the lashes, it angered me, and I needed to know why people not classified White were treated with disrespect by White authority. The sense of unfairness and callousness I had experienced at the hand of Whites drove me to attend protest gatherings. I started attending night school, hoping to find better work and earn a decent salary.

Also at night school in 1959, I met students belonging to a political organization, APDUSA, the African Peoples' Democratic Union of South Africa, and I joined them. Theoretically they were sound, but I longed for action, physical confrontation with the apartheid regime. Some of the APDUSA members were similarly dissatisfied and decided to break away and form the National Liberation Front (NLF) to engage in armed conflict against apartheid by means of guerrilla warfare. Unfortunately, because of our inexperience we recruited unreliable people, and some who were working for the Security Police. At this stage we were still reading about armed struggle in other countries and discussing ways of implementing similar actions in South Africa. Information from our meetings was leaked to the Security Police, and we were arrested. As a result eleven of us, seven men and four women, had to appear in the Cape Town Supreme Court. On April 14, 1964, we were sentenced for 'conspiracy to commit sabotage and violence in

South Africa', receiving sentences of between five and ten years. The seven men were sent to Robben Island, and the women were jailed at the Kroonstad Prison in the Free State.

On Robben Island, as in other South African prisons, food and clothing were based on racist discrimination. For example, while Coloured and Asian inmates received two level teaspoons of sugar with their maize porridge, Black prisoners received only one. The same petty discrimination of food rations applied to bread. A daily quarter loaf of bread with jam was allocated to Coloureds and Asians for supper, but not to Blacks. In warped apartheid thinking, it was argued that bread was not their staple food, so they had to eat maize porridge again. Three times a week we got a small ration of meat, with Blacks receiving half as much.

No political prisoner received underwear. Asians and Coloureds were given thick long pants, a shirt, a jacket, hat, shoes, and socks. Black prisoners had to wear short pants and sandals, a shirt, a jacket, and a fez-like cap. Every other aspect of our lives was the same: harsh labour under harsh conditions.

As political prisoners, we came from very different political organisations, some of which were opposed to and antagonistic towards each other. In jail, we had a common enemy and had to learn to stand together to bring about change. With the help of fellow South Africans belonging to anti-apartheid organisations, sympathetic countries, for example the Scandinavian countries, and international organisations like the UNO, the International Red Cross, and Amnesty International, conditions on Robben Island started to improve.

Two of the most fundamental changes were in education and sport. I had tried to further my education at night school but, with the help of fellow prisoners, I obtained my Grade 12 (Standard 10) certificate in 1969. Regardless of the many obstacles that made it difficult for everyone to study, the determination of prisoners to be educated allowed some who had come in illiterate to leave prison able to read and write. Many obtained degrees while on Robben Island.

Sports, especially soccer and rugby, were organised. Prisoners would disregard their conflicting political ideologies and join whichever team they wanted to. Prison guards leading a boring life on the Island looked forward to these games over weekends.

They were also astounded by the educational progress made by the prisoners. Amazingly, some of these prison guards were motivated by the prisoners to improve their own education. It was not unusual for one of them to appeal to a political prisoner for help with the guard's studies. An unwritten code existed among political prisoners that if one of the prison guards asked for help with his studies, one would not hesitate to help him. By doing this, one was making a friend.

One can now begin to understand the friendship between Christo Brand and Nelson Mandela.

We Cannot Live with Broken Hearts

VUSUMZI MCONGO WITH CHRISTO BRAND

Published by the Forgiveness Project

Christo Brand: The first time I saw Vusumzi was on our way to Robben Island. We both arrived on the same day in 1978. I was a warder. He was a prisoner in chains, on his way to maximum security. We did not speak to one another. The first time we spoke properly was nearly twenty years later, when we were both applying for jobs at the Robben Island Museum. We embraced each other warmly. Now that we work together, we talk about what was wrong in the past. Sometimes we have a laugh about things that happened then. There is no bitterness between us.

When I started on Robben Island, I was told that the men we guarded were no better than animals. Some warders hated the prisoners and were very cruel. But I could never hate, because these political prisoners were far more polite and friendly than any prisoner I'd met before.

Eventually I was put in charge of the educational studies of Nelson Mandela and a few other prisoners. Mr Mandela was determined to turn Robben Island into a university. It meant that prisoners who arrived with no education at all left as powerfully educated men. He kept saying that as long as you're alive, they can't take away your education. He was even determined to learn how to speak and write Afrikaans.

Mr Mandela is the epitome of forgiveness, able to reach out to all people. While he was in prison, the man who was the architect of apartheid, Hendrik Verwoerd, died. When Mandela was finally released, one of the first people he visited was Verwoerd's widow, Betsie. She received him with open arms in their house in a white suburb.

Vusumzi Mcongo: I was arrested in 1976 for being a member of the South African Student Movement (SASM) during a school boycott in Port Elizabeth. The charges laid against me under the Internal Security Act were for incitement, sabotage, and terrorist activities. I was detained for six months, during which time I was interrogated and tortured. I was lucky to survive. Many died in detention.

In prison I noticed Christo, but prisoners didn't talk to officers. I tried to keep out of his way, as it was my job to carry information from one section of the prison to another. It was a risky job, and to be found out would have meant having my studies curtailed. For us prisoners this was the ultimate punishment. Broadening our knowledge was about broadening our future.

Our relationship with the warders at Robben Island was often a stumbling block. We had to convince them we weren't violent men. But I never hated these warders. They were working for a system, and the system was brutal. The people I hated were those who had tortured and interrogated me in detention. I used to dream of revenge.

And yet, after I was released, that hatred diminished. All I wanted was to meet these people again to show them that I'd survived. And what's more, survived with a smile.

By chance, during Steve Biko's hearing at the Truth and Reconciliation Commission (TRC), I met some of the security officers involved in his case. I greeted them and reminded them that they'd also interrogated and tortured me. Then I wished them luck in their case. I bore them no ill will. I knew then that the experience of Robben Island had not brutalised me. We had all learned different lessons in different ways.

We cannot live with broken hearts. In time we have to accept that these things have happened to us, that those years have been wasted. To stay with the past will only bring you into turmoil.

No nation can survive without forgiveness.

Preaching reconciliation has become part of my daily task. For me this is a voluntary change, one that comes from within, even though the government has made me no reparation. But some former political prisoners are still very angry. They are not prepared to forgive. It's not hatred against the white man they feel, but anger at the government that has done nothing for them.

The Wynberg Seven

IGSHAAN AMLAY

When I was growing up in the 1980s, we were not allowed to share anything with our white counterparts. When travelling by bus, the whites sat downstairs and the coloureds sat upstairs. The people of colour could only visit certain beaches. The malls, schools, churches, hospitals, and communities were all divided into whites-only and non-whites-only facilities and areas. We were not allowed to have white friends. We were not allowed to study anything we wanted to. You either studied to become a doctor or a teacher, otherwise you would do an apprenticeship or just become a labourer. As a person of colour, you grew up in a restricted area. We were dictated to as to how we should live, according to the apartheid system generated by the minority.

In October 1985, I attended a rally at Wynberg High School with many of my comrades. During the rally the police dispersed us, and we all marched up Park Road towards Batts Road in Wynberg. When we approached the intersection, we were surrounded by police and Security Police in armoured vehicles called Casspirs. I remember throwing a petrol bomb under an unmarked powder blue Ford Escort police vehicle from behind a wall at the Luxurama next to the house we ended up in, where we were arrested. As the police stormed us, a group of about thirty of us ran into the house of friends of mine, the Pandys. The police surrounded the house, entered, and arrested ten of us and took us to Wynberg police station.

After a lengthy trial of lies and deceit, we got charged and seven of us, five men and two women, were sentenced to imprisonment. At that time, I was the youngest political prisoner. During our trial we became known as the Wynberg Seven, with support coming from around the world. We appealed our sentence but lost our appeal in May 1987 and started serving our sentence on Monday 8 June 1987. Our arrest was on the same day the Trojan Horse Massacre took place in Athlone. On the day we entered Pollsmoor maximum security, we were introduced to Warrant Officer Christo Brand. He took us to A Section, where we would stay for the duration of our sentence. When we applied to study, Warrant Officer Brand was the officer in charge of assisting us. He was at that time in charge of Nelson Mandela and all other political prisoners who entered the prison. Nelson Mandela was in a section right next to our section, and we could see him sitting under heavy security in the courtyard.

When speaking to Christo, I realised that he was not just a white prison warder but a man of integrity and compassion. I befriended him and asked him if he could do me some favours, which he ended up doing without hesitation. I think he also felt sorry for us as youths under those circumstances. During one of my visits arranged by Christo, he allowed my mom to have a contact visit with me and also allowed her to give him things illegally. We became very good friends, and he ended up visiting my mom's house to pick up or drop off letters, cigarettes, and luxuries. On one occasion he brought me a chip roll from Aneesa's, a fast food outlet in Wynberg.

My late father ended up making burglar bars for Christo's house in Ruyterwacht, which he always reminds me about whenever I visit him. He often took five of us to the roof section where Jeremy Veary, Anwa Dramat, Peter Jacobs, and many others were held. I remember one day when we went to the hospital section for our visits, we found Ashley Forbes and Ebrahim Rasool lying on beds with drips attached to them. I then gave Christo a letter, which he had to take to my mom, telling her to let their parents know that they were being held in Pollsmoor Maximum hospital section under section 29.

On one occasion Christo took me to the visiting rooms for a contact visit with my mom, where he introduced me to Nelson Mandela, a secret I had to keep until long after my release so that he would not be found out. Since my release in 1988, I have remained in contact with Christo up until today. In 1998, he got me to work on Robben Island with him. I visit him regularly and became family friends with his mom, wife, and son. I also attended his eldest son's funeral a few years later.

If only people knew the risks Christo took during those dark days, they would appreciate him much more. In recent years I have joined him in talks, and many a time get goose bumps when he takes me back in time. It is an honour to know Christo for his sacrifices and what he stands for, and we will remain friends.

Mandela's Pollsmoor Prison Cell Cleaner
MARIO MEYER

I was born in 1961 in the Paarl Valley. I spent my entire youth in Paarl, and from there I went to Stellenbosch, where I finished school. After school I stayed with my mom and dad on the farm called Nuwe Tuin. On that farm were a lot of workers, including my father. He worked as a driver on the farm. My mom and dad then moved to Mitchells Plain in Cape Town on the Cape Flats. While we were living on Nuwe Tuin I was chased away from the farm by a white guy called Mr Flip with a gun. He said he did not want me on the farm anymore. So I had to leave the farm without my family, and I went to my aunt in Paarl and stayed with her. I did a welding course there and started working as a welder in Paarl, at a place making buckets for chickens.

From there I went to work at a place in Blackheath called Leyland – a motor plant building cars like Minis, Jaguars, Range Rovers, Land Rovers. With a very good friend called Deon Jafthas, I started to do crime, stealing tapes and these kinds of things. I was the one hoarding the stuff, he was the one stealing it. And we survived a long time with this kind of crime. After he was arrested, I was not staying in Paarl anymore. He showed the police where I was staying, and the police came to arrest me. The two of us were in incarceration, and he made a confession that I was the guy who was with him and keeping the stuff.

After that I was sentenced to three years in prison, and he was sentenced to five years but released after 18 months in Paarl. Then we were arrested again and I was sentenced to eight years in prison and this time, in 1984, I was sent to Pollsmoor Prison. I was put in B section, in room number 18. I stayed there for a long time.

I was a guy who liked to train – every day I had to train in the yard. Sometimes I would train alone. On a specific day I was training in the yard alone. I am the kind of guy who, if I am training, I don't want to be disturbed by people. So while I was running and someone called, I never listened to their nonsense because the guys sometimes just called for no reason. But that specific day someone called me – I did not know who he was, because he was not from our section. He was sleeping on the ground section. I did not know anyone from the ground floor. So this guy called me, and I saw he was a kind of old man, and he spoke nicely to me in an English accent. The first thing he asked me was if I was a teacher. I told him I was not a teacher. I told him I was a prisoner there. He asked what I was in for, and I explained to him. He asked me if I wanted newspapers and by that time we were not allowed newspapers, watches, radios, those kinds of things. So I was very keen to get newspapers and see what was going on in the outside world, and especially the adverts showing sausages and nice kinds of food. We just memorized these kinds of things and told ourselves we wanted to buy these kinds of things when we got out of prison.

As time went by that day, he called me and said I must come

around. I didn't know where I must go, so I went to try and find out. One day he sent Mr Brand to find me in my room. Soon I discovered these guys were in isolation, and I had to go around past the prison kitchen, and then I was facing a gate where a warder was sitting behind these bars. He instructed these guys to open the gate so I could come inside. Inside that section of the prison was a passage. He introduced himself actually and said his name was Nelson, Nelson Mandela. He asked me if I knew him. I said I did not know him. He asked my name. I told him my name. He invited me into his home. I wanted to know who was this guy. He explained to me who he was. Then we went inside and I saw three big cupboards. He opened them. The one cupboard was full of luxuries, the one with groceries, and the other filled with butter beans. These guys clearly liked butter beans. He told me I can take some and packed them in a box. So we sat and chatted. He told me he was a politician fighting the government. To cut a long story short he asked me if I was interested to work in his room as a cleaner, iron and wash his clothes and clean his room every day. So I agreed to that.

Every day he received peanut butter and syrup and butter, but he never ate that kind of thing. He stacked it up. I told him he must put them in empty peanut butter pots I brought him. And the sugar and powdered milk. It was actually nice for him to do these kinds of things – it kept him busy. What I noticed was this guy had three cells. I wondered why he had three cells and he was staying alone – three big rooms with a capacity of 80 people. One was the gym room, one was a sleeping room, and one was where he showered and had a toilet. I used the gym a few times, lifting weights and these kinds of things.

Every day I spent a lot of time there and we became good

friends, talking about a lot of deep things, his objectives, the reasons why he didn't want them to release him; they said he must just die there; all he had to do was sign and he would be released. They even tried to get me to persuade him to sign. On the roof where Mr Brand was working – I worked a lot with him – there was a one-way mirror; we could see Mandela but he couldn't see us. And we were carrying plants – and these half drums with sand. He had a garden on top of that roof where Mandela grew tomatoes and things. We enjoyed this kind of stuff – it was his garden. What I noticed about this guy was that the police were very afraid for him. At one time while I was playing a library film for him, because I was the film projector operator, they told me I could not leave it unattended. During that time I got to learn and hear all about him. He explained everything to me – about his first wife, what his objectives were. A lot of things happened there. There was one guy who was nearly caught with a camera who was supposed to take photos of Mandela. There were even people who asked me to take photos of Mr Mandela, but at that time if I was caught it was a life sentence or death sentence; he would be arrested for high treason because he was a high-profile prisoner.

Mr Brand started doing many things for me. Even though I was not allowed visits, he would get stuff for me. Later on he arranged for me to move to B section. Warders were not allowed in there. The door had a lock with a special key. Only Mr Brand had that key to that section. The other prisoners didn't know him as Mr Mandela, and I was the one who went back to tell the guys about him. One day a guy called him and swore at him in Afrikaans. The next day they put a screen on the windows – it was dark – and we couldn't see Mr Mandela anymore. But I was the one working with him every day. I was also tasting the food alone which they brought him – he always made his own food. I saw he had a TV.

We shared a lot of stuff there. I also met Mr Brand there – he had been working there a long time. When Mandela wanted to see Mr Brand, he had to come immediately to see him. 'I want to see Mr Brand now. Not tomorrow; I want to see him now!' Maybe his clothes were not right or something. We escorted him to visits. Then I also met his co-accused like Ahmed Kathrada, Walter Sisulu, guys like Govan Mbeki, a lot of the high politicians like Anwa Dramat, Tony Yengeni. I was meeting all these kinds of guys, supporting them and doing all kinds of things for them like transferring letters for them. Each letter was sealed with red wax. One day I saw how they wrote the letters, but I could not make them out. It was all in code: some days like a bird or a stick; each word had a different meaning.

I was also allowed to go to the shop to buy things for the political prisoners. One day I was caught with money in my pocket. One warder took the money away from me despite me telling him I had permission. Eventually they listened to me, and it was put on my ticket that I was permitted to buy stuff for them. I was the one they trusted deeply, and I was working after that with all the politicians. I was also the mediator. I was the one they trusted, because I was allowed to sit in on the meetings, and Mr Mandela was the one who was doing a lot of things for them; he put his head on a block. One day he was nearly arrested because he brought a tape to me to play.

One day when Mr Sisulu was released, he gave me his watch. That night I slept with it in my hands, because if I was caught I would be sentenced to thirty days with less food. The next day I gave the watch back to him and told him I was scared to keep the watch. One day we were looking at a show in a stadium in London for Mr Mandela's 70th birthday. He gave me the films, and I gave them to Mr Brand. He also gave me a 16 mm film, *The Last Emperor*; I also gave that to Mr Brand. I even have a cassette of Mr Mandela where he was talking in prison – I still have it in my possession.

I was friends with Mr Brand. I met all Mr Mandela's family, his children as well. After my release from prison Mr Brand supported me in many ways with things I need in my life. We are friends now for over thirty years. He was even the one who took me to Robben Island with the boat and allowed me in the cockpit and to take photos. We are often in contact with each other.

Truth and Reconciliation: What Can Be Learned from Christo's Experience?

MARY BURTON

The discussions which led to the establishment of a changed system of government for South Africa after 1990, known as CODESA, the Congress for a Democratic South Africa, lasted for three years. Representatives of nearly all political parties, assisted by teams of experts, wrestled to create an Interim Constitution which would carry the country through to the election of 1994, when all adult South Africans would vote together for the first time.

There were many stumbling blocks and times when it seemed agreement could not be reached, but eventually the only one left was whether amnesty should be granted for past violations of human rights. For many representatives of the previous apartheid government, this was a non-negotiable demand, protecting people in the security services who might have committed serious offences. Finally, in late 1993, agreement was reached that 'there shall be amnesty'.

Many human rights organisations, community structures, and individuals who themselves or whose families had suffered gross violations of their human rights were outraged. During those years of negotiations, parallel discussions had been held in small and large groups, preparing themselves for the new constitutional provisions, and making public comments and direct representations to CODESA. There was widespread belief that trying to hide the incidents of killings and torture of the past would be disastrous for a new society.

Nevertheless, the agreement had been reached, and the elections would proceed. Amnesty had been the price paid for peace.

On 10 May 1994, Nelson Rolihlahla Mandela became the first democratically elected president of South Africa. Enormous challenges lay ahead. The whole system of apartheid legislation had to be dismantled. No longer would people be classified from birth into an assigned racial group, no longer should education, health, welfare, and the provision of services be based on such differences. Laws had to be repealed or drastically amended, and new systems of governance introduced to make up for past discrimination.

It was not until 1995 that the government turned its attention to the matter of amnesty. In the meantime, a great deal of thought and discussion in civil society had produced some further suggestions, and these were seriously considered by the new Government of National Unity.

If amnesty had been the price paid for the peaceful outcome of the election, there was still a need to ensure that amnesty should not be cheaply granted, in a sweeping blanket amnesty that pushed all violations out of sight. The price for receiving amnesty should be the revelation of the truth. Each person seeking amnesty should make a full disclosure of what he or she had done, in what circumstances, and with what objective.

At the same time, there should be a mechanism for people who had suffered gross violations of their human rights, or who had lost family members, to tell all they knew about the circumstances and seek further understanding.

The Promotion of National Unity and Reconciliation Act was passed in July 1995, the Truth and Reconciliation Commission was established, and the Commissioners were appointed by President Mandela in November.

For almost three years the task of the three main committees of the TRC worked constantly to fulfill that mandate: to hear the stories of the people defined as 'victims of gross human rights violations'; to consider applications for amnesty and to grant it, if the conditions were met; and to prepare recommendations to the government for ways in which to grant reparations and foster healing and reconciliation. A large team of staff with a wide variety of skills, experience, and knowledge of languages was quickly appointed, and the work spread out to the whole country from the four regional offices.

The formation of the Commission and the way in which it carried out its work marked a new step forward in the history of transitional justice mechanisms. None that came before it had held public hearings of 'victims' telling their stories, which became a marker of the TRC. None had requested public testimonies from the different political parties, the judiciary, the media, and numerous other sectors. The media covered these events, on radio and television and in the newspapers. No-one could say they had not heard the stories of deep human suffering.

In October 1998, Archbishop Desmond Tutu personally delivered the first five volumes of the TRC report to President Mandela. The final two volumes, dealing mainly with the

Amnesty Report, followed later. Despite criticisms and challenges, the report remains an important record of a period in South Africa's history which will be remembered for severe and brutal treatment, including killings, of thousands of people. It remains too as an indication of paths which could be followed towards a process of reconciliation, some of which have been pursued, but many of which have fallen away, leaving a country which continues to be bedeviled by what we have left undone.

Among the reparations which were recommended was a financial grant, to be made to every person who had been found by the TRC to have been a 'victim' in terms of the act; also for further reparations to be made to communities which had been ravaged by violent conflict. After a delay of several years, the government announced that financial reparations would be granted, but in a much lesser amount. Recipients felt a sense of betrayal, and angry voices were raised. Other groupings stepped forward to argue that they too had suffered the same violations, but had not been able to be heard by the TRC.

The amnesty process also elicited criticism and disappointment: Seven thousand applications had been received, and of these two thousand were granted. Far too many people failed to take the opportunity to make a claim for amnesty and reveal their actions. Much of the truth remains hidden by their silence.

It was anticipated that in matters where amnesty was refused, or where no application for amnesty was received, the natural course of the law would follow, and alleged perpetrators of gross human rights violations would be brought to trial. In all the past two decades, hardly any prosecutions have taken place, despite the efforts of families and their lawyers.

Worse still, the economic situation in the country, now exacerbated by the coronavirus pandemic, has left an enormous number of people suffering extreme poverty, while those who were able to benefit from the peaceful outcome of the transition process continue to do so. Ideas of a wealth tax, and the provision of adequate social protection for the most impoverished, remain only in the realm of possibility.

Given these problems, can one say that reconciliation has become a reality in South Africa? Many young people are angry and despairing. Inequality and aspects of racism persist.

In such circumstances, the inspiring example of some of the stories told before the TRC remains a shining light of hope: stories of regret, apology, new understanding, and forgiveness demonstrate that these are not idle dreams. In those early years of the new South Africa they provided a model of how a people can unite and work together to overcome the past, so that we could live together in peace.

The story of Nelson Mandela and Christo Brand – unlikely, unexpected, gradually built into trust and mutual respect – provides such a model. We can be thankful for it.

Mandela's First White Convert
JOHN CARLIN

P olitics is the art of persuasion. It means convincing people to identify with your vision and to follow the course you set. Nelson Mandela was the prime exponent of this art. He was a genius.

For ordinary political leaders, winning over your own natural constituency is hard enough. There are always differences of opinion within every large national grouping, as within every family. Mandela succeeded in uniting the vast majority of black South Africans, a fractured people despite the bonding factor of apartheid. They followed his lead and voted in overwhelming numbers for his African National Congress (ANC).

For most politicians, that would have been job done. But Mandela went further. He attempted the impossible: turning his enemies, capturing the hearts and minds of those who felt they had the most to fear from him, the white South African minority.

He began small and ended big. He first set about his mission impossible within prison and years later crowned his triumph, as free man and president, on the vast stage of the 1995 Rugby World Cup.

Robben Island, where he spent 18 of his 27 years in prison, was the laboratory where he conducted his first experiments.

The challenge was to see if he could win over his warders. Mostly Afrikaners, mostly individuals unthinkingly committed to the apartheid cause, they represented a challenge so seemingly insurmountable that if he did, in fact, succeed, he would own the template with which to go on and win over the white population at large.

The secret, he discovered, was to act on the words of Abraham Lincoln and appeal to the 'better angels' of people's natures. Mandela understood that it was by an accident of birth and other circumstances over which individuals had no control that they aligned themselves with a particular belief, be it political or religious. What he endeavoured to do was to burrow beneath the ideological surface and reach into the generous feelings that lurk in every human heart.

In Christo Brand he found a warder with an abundance of generous feelings. Brand had the bigness of heart to see beyond Mandela 'the terrorist', 'the communist', the convicted prisoner. Seeing that Mandela treated him with kindness and respect, he responded in kind. Brand may be seen as a milestone in Mandela's political mission: his first white convert.

Once out of Robben Island, but still behind bars, Mandela set about the more difficult challenge of persuading the most powerful, most sinister members of the white state apparatus, people far more wary than Brand, that he was a man of peace, that he desired to see a peaceful transition in South Africa from apartheid to democracy, that once in power he would rule on behalf of everybody, irrespective of the colour of their skin.

He held secret talks with apartheid's minister of justice, Kobie Coetsee, and with Niel Barnard, the head of national intelligence. Not only did he persuade them that on the day of his liberation he would not issue a call to arms against white

South Africans, he made them – almost – fall in love with him. It may sound like an exaggeration, but it is not far from the truth. Speaking to them in their language, Afrikaans, revealing a knowledge of and respect for Afrikaner history, demonstrating a sensitive understanding of white fears, he appeased and wooed them both. Interviewed years later, Coetsee would weep in recollection of what he called Mandela's dignity, nobility, and gravity; Barnard, a colder fish, did not weep, but he referred to Mandela continually as if he were his father. Apartheid's chief spymaster described Mandela affectionately as 'the old man'.

Once freed, Mandela had to appeal to white South Africans without the advantage of face-to-face contact. In private, Mandela's charm was almost irresistible. Now he had to test his seductive powers from the more impersonal terrain of his country's news media. From the very day he was freed he began working on the press, focusing his energies on the Afrikaner journalists. Again, he appealed to their 'better angels', again he drew out their nobler instincts.

When faced by the cameras he never missed an opportunity to reach out to the white population at large. Guileful as well as forgiving, he staged made-for-TV events where he mingled happily with the widows of former white leaders or, on one occasion, with the prosecutor who had argued in favour of condemning him to death in the famous Rivonia Trial of 1964.

In May 1994 he became president. But that was not the end of the story. It was the beginning of what the ANC have called 'a new phase of struggle'. Democracy in South Africa was new, young, and fragile. Dark forces within the extreme right plotted to undermine Mandela's vision of peace and stability. Civil war, or at the very least a campaign of far-right terrorism, remained a possibility. A year into his presidency the Rugby World Cup was staged in South Africa. Most ordinary politicians in Mandela's shoes would have feared the worst. Rugby was the white man's game and, as such, was loathed by the majority of black South Africans. The South African national team, the traditionally all-white Springboks, were a particular focus of black rage. But Mandela saw an opportunity. Rather than hide away during the tournament and pray that tensions between the races would not escalate, he set himself the biggest challenge of all: simultaneously to seal the legitimacy of his presidency among white South Africans and to persuade his black compatriots that the Springboks represented the pride and hopes of the entire nation, irrespective of race.

Once again, Mandela plotted skillfully. He met the Springbok captain, François Pienaar, and, sure enough, got him on his team, as he had done with Brand, Barnard, and Coetsee. Through Pienaar and the Springbok manager Morné du Plessis (both lifelong Mandela devotees), he convinced the rest of the Springbok team to see themselves not just as rugby players but as political players, united in the drive to use the World Cup as a force for national unity. Meanwhile, President Mandela addressed black audiences in rallies far and wide, each time conveying the message that the Springboks were no longer their enemies but their allies and friends.

It worked. Come the day of the World Cup final against New Zealand, South Africans of all races were more united than they ever had been since the arrival of the first white settlers in 1652. For the first time they all shared a common purpose: victory for the Springboks. On the day of the final Mandela sealed his life's mission when he appeared on the field of Ellis Park Stadium wearing a rugby jersey in the colours of the old enemy, the Springboks. The crowd, overwhelmingly white, began a chant that echoed all around the stadium: 'Nel-son! Nel-son! Nel-son!' He had appealed one more time to white South Africans' better angels, and one more time they had responded with generosity, respect, and warmth.

The outpouring of affection for Mandela was such that, at a flourish, the threat of the far right vanished and all notion of civil war was put to bed. From now on Mandela's presidency would be stable and secure. When South Africa won the final match and Pienaar with Mandela by his side lifted the World Cup the entire nation, black and white and all shades in between, celebrated as one.

Robben Island Tour Guide Extraordinaire

YASIEN MOHAMED

I was born on 21 September 1947. In 1963 I joined the PAC (Pan Africanist Congress of Azania) at the tender age of 16. Because I was not 'black', I could easily slip in and out of the country without being noticed. And as a teacher I had many school holidays to my avail to service the camps of the PAC in neighbouring countries. This also gave me the opportunity to travel across Africa, Europe, and Scandinavia in search of support – at times without genuine passports, especially to the African states.

As a drama teacher, most of my plays were directed at the state, what we termed protest drama. For this reason, I was encountered many times by the then Security Police. I escaped being arrested when the police confused me with my brother; his initials happened to be the same as mine, and he was also a teacher. Unfortunately for him, my brother had to spend eleven months in detention on my behalf.

I also had the honour to have met two very great icons in our struggle, namely Nelson Mandela and the founder of the PAC, Professor Robert Sobukwe, who died in 1978 and was the only political prisoner kept in solitary confinement for six years on Robben Island. In 1990, after the unbanning of the PAC, I became its first General Secretary in the Western Cape. I also served as Chairman of the Board of Telkom Social Development.

In 1989, when I lost my post as a teacher, I became the CEO of a non-governmental organisation called the Foundation for Social Development, funded by the Ford Foundation and Mobil Oil Company and situated in the poorest location on the Cape Flats, Bishop Lavis.

In 1996, when President Mandela declared Robben Island a museum, I was seconded by my political party to take up a position on the Island to ensure that the PAC narrative was always well recorded. It is here where I have ended my political career. My storytelling technique, plus my drama experience, together with my political involvement, meant that I soon found myself inundated with requests from groups from across the globe to guide their tourists visiting Robben Island.

As a self-made historian, I have made a thorough research on the impact of international politics on Robben Island since 1588, when the first Portuguese boats were stranded here, as well as the history of many countries that influenced the history of South Africa. In my narration I join the dots provided by my guests' country and emphasize the great contributions each country rendered to our freedom. Since retiring, I have been busy with:

- Doing part-time private tours to the Island.
- Archiving the history of my political party.
- Lecture tours. In 2016 I did a lecture tour in Norway for three weeks.
- Addressing many schools on the Struggle in South

Africa, from the Sharpeville massacre in 1960 to the release of Nelson Mandela, plus the history of the Truth and Reconciliation period.

While I was in the trenches fighting against apartheid, thinking endlessly about those still in prison and in the torture chambers, one could never have dreamt that the day of reconciliation was in sight and that we would sit shoulder to shoulder with the old enemy. Christo Brand, former prison guard of Mandela, is a typical example of peace and love. In short, Mandela shook hands with his old guard, Christo Brand, and likewise I salute both of them.

A Bottle of Water

MARCELLETTE WILLIAMS

My first visit to South Africa occurred in August 1999. My destination was Robben Island. Not South Africa, but Robben Island.

Several months earlier, at an international conference, I had observed a former Robben Island detainee contort into a fetal position, prompted by a triggered memory of having been detained and tortured in a container too small for him either to stand up or to lie down completely. In order to make more coherent what I had observed, I knew I had to go to Robben Island.

I was well aware of the activities for which Nelson Mandela and several others were sentenced on 12 June 1964, to life on Robben Island for what the apartheid government called treason and sabotage. Despite the difficult and circuitous avenues for the flow of information either into or out of South Africa, the rest of the world learned what had occurred that day in Pretoria.

I have also been fortunate enough to work at the first two public universities to divest of holdings in South Africa, in 1977, and to advocate from afar for the release of the Rivonia trialists. But until 1999 I had not yet had the opportunity to visit South Africa.

So one morning at the Cape Town waterfront, at the site of what is now the Gateway to Robben Island, a World Heritage site, I was waiting for the fog to lift sufficiently for the ferry captain to signal the clearance for the ferry to head for the Island. Looking up the pier for a place to buy a bottle of water, I spotted a little shop. Running up the pier and into the shop, I greeted the clerk as I headed to the refrigeration unit in the corner. I grabbed a bottle of water and hurried to pay to return to my perch on the pier. But the clerk, having heard my accent, asked if I was from America. I answered that I was. He excitedly asked me if I knew Robert Vassen. In fact, I did, and told him that our offices had been on the same corridor when I was at Michigan State University.

Now the clerk was really animated, as he reached under the counter to produce a book called *Letters from Robben Island,* edited by my colleague Professor Robert Vassen. Just then the ferry whistle sounded, and I turned to hurry back down the pier to head for the Island. The clerk shouted to me that Mr Kathrada was going to be in the shop in just a couple of hours and would be happy to inscribe the book for me. My response was to continue in the direction of the ferry. The clerk was nearly in pursuit, so I turned and gave him too many rand in payment for the book and continued to hurry back to the ferry, bottle of water in hand. He shouted, 'What should I have him write?' I shouted back a response, climbing aboard the ferry just as the last ropes were being lifted.

The experience en route to and on the Island, with a former prisoner as my guide, was haunting, providing the scaffolding for my earlier experience observing the former Robben Island detainee.

There were perhaps eight of us that morning on the ferry. We learned on the return trip that the little shop at the end of the pier had some cassettes of the tour we had just experienced and other small memorabilia. When we docked and disembarked, I saw the clerk waving the book and my change. I approached him, with the other visitors following me into the shop. They all had questions and were eager for assistance. I thanked him and tried to leave—it was a very small shop – but he continued to try to engage me by showing me a newspaper. I could see that he was in the picture, but without my glasses I couldn't determine the content of the article. All the time I continued to back out of the little shop, thanking him for the book. I was really feeling guilty about monopolizing him when others wanted to be helped.

That evening at the hotel, I realized that Robert Vassen, my colleague and the editor of my newly inscribed acquisition, was probably on his way to South Africa for the launching of the book, just as I was leaving the following morning. Indeed that was the case, so it was nearly two weeks before I could phone Bob to describe the experience I had just had. In the interim, however, because I felt that I had been somewhat abrupt with the clerk, I wanted to apologize. The receipt for the book had the name, address, and phone number of the shop. I telephoned. A woman answered, and I told her I wanted to speak with someone who had helped me the previous week. She asked me to describe the person. I did, and she responded that the person was Christo Brand, who would be there the following day.

I phoned again at the appointed time the following day. He answered and greeted me as the person who had received from him the inscribed book. I apologized to him for having been abrupt, explaining that I was only trying to allow the others to be waited on. I shall never forget his response. He said, 'Oh no.

There is no need to apologize. We are all in this world to help each other in our humanity.' I was speechless, but thanked him again.

When finally I spoke with my colleague and told him this story, he said, 'You know who Christo Brand is, don't you?' I didn't. He said, 'He was one of the warders on Robben Island when Mr Mandela and the Rivonians were sent there to prison for life.'

A few months later I met Ahmed Kathrada, Barbara Hogan, and Laloo Chiba at my colleague's home in East Lansing, Michigan, where they were all gathered for the book launch at Michigan State University, where MSU Press had been the U.S. publisher for *Letters from Robben Island*. Of course, by then Christo and Bob Vassen had already told the story of my August visit. The bottle of water became the symbol for my serendipitous encounter with Christo at the waterfront shop.

Since 1999 I have visited South Africa nearly every year at least once, until the pandemic. I usually have an opportunity to spend time with Christo and his spouse, Estelle. They have become part of my South African family.

The University of Massachusetts has had a longstanding relationship with several universities in South Africa, as had Michigan State University where I worked for 25 years. In 2014, UMass facilitated the U.S. launch of Christo's book *Doing Life with Mandela: My Prisoner, My Friend*. He visited each of the five campuses of the University, speaking of his experiences and talking with faculty and students. Christo has become a member of the UMass family!

For a fuller context for the relationship between UMass and South Africa, the following story might provide insights:

The University of Massachusetts has had an enduring rich relationship with South Africa since the 1970s, when it became one of the first universities to divest of holdings in South Africa, an action that swelled a movement around the globe and contributed to the demise of apartheid.

The University has awarded honorary degrees to many of those engaged intimately in the struggle for freedom. In 1993, the UMass Boston campus awarded honorary degrees to key negotiators Roelf Meyer and Cyril Ramaphosa, in acknowledgement of their efforts to accomplish a successful outcome between clashing political parties during the transition negotiations.

Meyer was South Africa's Minister of Constitutional Affairs and Communications and the leader of the government's negotiating team working to bring about democracy and an end to South Africa's white minority rule.

As Secretary General of the African National Congress (ANC), Ramaphosa worked with Meyer to ensure that the negotiations moved forward, even after formal talks had broken down.

UMass Boston's 1993 commencement program notes the reasons for their honorary degrees. In honoring Meyer, the university recognised 'his humanitarian commitment to eliminating the inequities of South African society and to creating a new democratic foundation for a multiracial government in that country.' Recognising Ramaphosa, UMass Boston paid 'tribute to a man whose courageous and tireless pursuit of democratic ideals serves as a model for those who seek to carry on the struggle to achieve a free and equitable society.'

Together they delivered the commencement address.

In 2000, UMass Amherst awarded the degree of Doctor of Humane Letters to Ahmed Kathrada, one of the Rivonia

Trialists sentenced in 1964 to life in prison (narrowly escaping a death sentence) along with Nelson Mandela and seven others. He served nearly 26 years before being released a few months prior to the release of Mr Mandela.

In 2006, and with careful facilitation overseen by Ahmed Kathrada, a delegation of three trustees and University leadership traveled to South Africa to award honorary degrees to Nelson Mandela and his spouse, Graça Machel, at the Nelson Mandela Foundation in Johannesburg.

In 2011, UMass Lowell awarded an honorary degree to Barbara Hogan, the first white woman sentenced to prison for her efforts to overthrow the apartheid government. She served nearly ten years and was released shortly before the release of Mr Mandela.

There were also two earned degrees awarded to Makaziwe Mandela, Mr Mandela's daughter, who earned an MA in Sociology in 1989 and a Ph.D. in Anthropology in 1993 from UMass Amherst.

In addition, over the years, the University has had academic agreements with several South African universities, such as the University of Cape Town, the University of the Western Cape, the University of KwaZulu-Natal, the University of Witwatersrand, the University of Pretoria, the Medical University of South Africa, and Stellenbosch University.

The UMass Medical School pioneered the drug nevirapine, which is still among the most effective treatments for AIDS as part of a multi-drug regimen. It is also used worldwide as a means of preventing maternal-fetal transmission of HIV. UMMS professors and staff took the drug to South Africa, distributed it, and taught local health professionals to test for and train others in the prevention and treatment of HIV.

One of the now retired South African Constitutional Court justices, Albie Sachs, is a frequent visitor to the University, lecturing in constitutional law at the Law School in 2010 and coming to offer assistance at the Boston and Dartmouth campuses (those primarily affected) following the Boston Marathon bombing in 2013. Having been the victim himself of a car bomb in 1989 in Mozambique, where he was in exile (the South African secret service had targeted him for elimination), his connection to our students, faculty, and staff was unforgettably moving.

Each year the University has visitors from South Africa who were active in the struggle for freedom. They visit our campuses and always describe it as a privilege to talk with our students, faculty, and staff.

Some of our students have even had internships at the Amy Biehl Foundation in Cape Town, where they have had the opportunity to work in the townships along with two of the young men sentenced to prison for the murder of Amy Biehl and later granted amnesty with the testimony of her parents. They, too, have been on our campuses. In fact, Linda Biehl was the first Greeley Scholar (Peace and Reconciliation) on the UMass Lowell campus.

Of the many contributions that the University of Massachusetts has made in furthering the cause of peace and free societies, one stands out: The University of Massachusetts is the *only* university in the world to co-convene a conference with Mr Mandela (then President Mandela) when, in 1997, the University and President Mandela brought together the chief negotiators from Northern Ireland to Arniston, South Africa for four days, to meet with all the chief negotiators from the parties in South Africa that had achieved their breakthrough settlement in 1994. Mr Mandela and others to whom UMass has awarded honorary degrees were participants at this conference, which the Northern Irish themselves later described as a seminal turning point leading to the Good Friday Agreement in 1998.

So, as you see, the University of Massachusetts indeed has a long, substantive, and enduring relationship with South Africa.

A Good Judge of Character
MAKAZIWE MANDELA

Christo Brand came into our lives without invitation, against our every wish, indirectly forced onto us by the unjust system that tore our father away from his family home for almost three decades. He never bowed down to injustice, nor could apartheid silence him. For all those long and trying years we developed an image of the prison warders – an image fuelled by the ongoing strife we faced in our daily lives, an image as dark and treacherous as a child's fertile imagination could conjure up.

So when my father first introduced Christo to us and the world as his friend, I was as perplexed as the millions of those who endured the apartheid system. I wondered, almost in disbelief, how my father could introduce this prison warder, this oppressor, as his friend.

My father will not go down in history for the 27 years he spent on Robben Island. He will go down in history because he was able to draw from his soul all the poison of hatred accumulated by such unjust punishment. He will be remembered for his generosity and his wisdom, his awareness that the new South Africa would never be built on the foundations of hatred and revenge. He realised that he had to reach out to others, both black and white, to build instead of tearing down.

But my father was always a good judge of character. He saw beyond the titles that people are given. He sought to see the soul of the human being within. And it was the openness and frankness of Christo's soul that helped to form this everlasting friendship between prison warder and prisoner.

Throughout their prison years, there were some warders who were sympathetic to political prisoners; Christo Brand was one of them. He was young, but something within him felt that he had to treat these prisoners with compassion and empathy. The fact that this ongoing friendship endured the harshest conditions and continued unabated well beyond the prison walls is a testament to both men. It is also an example to us all of what is possible if we are prepared to open our minds and hearts to each other.

The Key Keeper of Nelson Mandela's Legacy

MARJOLEIN WESTERTERP

You were the sun and the rain
The heart and the soul
The earth and the blood
The hope and the dream
The past and the future.
You, Nelson Mandela, were and are
South Africa.

Thank you, Tata Madiba.

Mandela's first words to reach the world, his speech from the dock in the 1964 Rivonia Trial, included:

I have fought against white domination, and I have fought against black domination. I have cherished the ideal of a democratic and free society in which all persons will live together in harmony and with equal opportunities. It is an ideal which I hope to live for and achieve. But, my Lord, if it needs to be, it is an ideal for which I am prepared to die.

These were words that touched us in the Netherlands. Here was someone standing up against the great injustice of apartheid in far-off South Africa.

Mandela's mission was taken up, and a big star-studded Free Nelson Mandela concert was organised in honour of his 70th birthday in 1988 at Wembley Stadium in London. I traveled there from the Netherlands to stand up for his freedom and saw world-famous artists like Sting, Peter Gabriel, Whitney Houston, Neil Young, and Stevie Wonder carrying his message: Apartheid could not and should not be. The world showed South Africa that we did not accept it. More than a billion people in sixty countries witnessed the struggle for freedom and democracy of which Nelson Mandela had become the iconic face.

His release from prison in 1990 was world news. The man who did not look back in resentment, but faced the world with a smile, showed that the 27 years he had spent as prisoner 466/64 had been worth the immense sacrifice. He began his inaugural speech by saying, 'Our greatest fear is not that we are imperfect. Our greatest fear is that we are immensely powerful. It is the light, not our shadow that most frightens us.' And he fearlessly stepped into the light and showed so many others the way.

In 2012, I was in Qunu in the Eastern Cape. My mission was to walk in Mandela's footsteps, from Johannesburg through Howick and Qunu to Cape Town. After finishing his presidency, Mandela had retired to a house on a hill in Qunu, the village where he had grown up, in a beautiful landscape of rolling hills, scattered huts, fertile valleys, and thousands of streams that keep the grass green even in the blistering hot summers. He wanted to live among the villagers he had known all his life. And they wanted him back in their midst. I listened to the stories about the man who invited the children of the village every year and gave them toys and later books, because he thought it was so important that they learn something. After all, education was the gateway to a better life.

'Would you like to meet him?' asked our guide, a villager named Phikolomzi Habe.

'Is that possible?' My heart skipped three beats.

'Yes, we'll just visit,' he said nonchalantly.

I took an evening to think about what I would want to say if I actually met Madiba. I decided to at least write down the words he stood for to me: compassion, perseverance, humor, empathy, leadership. He had shown the world that you could change injustice, that you could really fight for freedom, with words, with wisdom, with a smile. For me, he was the symbol of hope for all humanity, because he had been able to forgive what seemed unforgivable.

The next morning, we stood in front of the entrance gate to the bungalow that had been built as a replica of the house in which Mandela had spent his last imprisoned years. The fencing consisted of an assemblage of the bottoms of tin cans. I looked at it and compared it to the bombastic fencing in front of my queen's palace in the Netherlands. Tin versus gold, a bungalow versus a palace, guards in a cubicle instead of a parade of troopers. Humility versus power. Mandela's wealth was his people, the children of his nation.

In his last speech as president, he had put it this way: 'I am the product of Africa and her long cherished view of rebirth that can now be realized so that all of her children may play in the sun.'

343

Madiba was not at home. I left my letter behind and asked if I could stand still for five minutes to feel his life, the sacrifices he had made, the smile he nevertheless showed to the world, the charisma that lit up the room when he entered, the warm hand he reached out to so many.

In my head echoed the sound of a key being turned grindingly in the lock. The distancing footsteps. Had he been rebellious at first? Had he felt he had been robbed? Certainly someone had taken away his time, his life, and how easily the men with the heavy key rings could feel like enemies. How much a power struggle lurked. After all, indifference and arrogance are tempting weapons against helplessness. How great the task had been for him to fill the void, to become his own best company, to transform himself from better to best, despite everything.

On that long road to freedom, one man had walked with him. His name Christo Brand – not a name that would conquer the world, you think. But the boy who became a prison guard on Robben Island at the age of 18 is the only one who experienced Nelson Mandela's prison years up close. He also remained Mandela's confidant during his stay at Pollsmoor and later Victor Verster prison. 'When he was released, the prison felt empty,' said Christo. 'Mandela was my prisoner, but I also considered him my father and my friend.'

Thanks to Christo's book *Doing Life with Mandela: My Prisoner, My Friend*, not only Mandela's mental struggles, but also the lessons Mandela taught Christo, have become available to the world.

It is also thanks to this book that I met Christo on a windy afternoon on Robben Island. It was my umpteenth visit.

On the bus, I wondered if then-President Zuma had also been imprisoned on Robben Island and, if so, how the great difference between these men could have come about. I asked the guide at the coffee stop at the bookstore on the Island. He didn't know the answer, but he returned a moment later with a man who told us that Zuma had indeed been imprisoned on the Island for ten years, but not among the well-known names. He greeted us kindly and left the bus.

'That was special,' said the guide.

'Why?' I asked in surprise.

'That man is Christo Brand. He used to be the warder of Nelson Mandela, and he is writing a book about their special friendship.'

Some months later, when I saw the book in stacks in a Cape Town bookstore, I decided to ask him for an interview. We met at 3.00 p.m. on the dot (the prison past is hard to brush away) at Jetty One, and during the interview I realized I was sitting across from the man who held the key to the real treasure chest of Nelson Mandela's legacy. The man who had befriended not only the entire Mandela family, but also the other now-famous prisoners of the Island, the man who had seen Mandela in his deepest despair and who had ensured that there were some happy moments for his prisoners as well.

Christo had one big wish: to return to the Netherlands, where he had visited with Mandela after his release. I made it happen, and for ten days Christo, his wife Estelle, and I crisscrossed Holland and Flanders to tell the story of this special friendship. Sometimes I interviewed Christo in front of a cheering audience, and it was in those moments that I felt that Mandela looked down with pride on the man he had come to know so well, whom he had appreciated and trusted.

And I understood why there was this mutual trust, because the more time I spent with Christo, the more I saw the similarities between the two men, both raised in rural South Africa. I saw the kindness of Mandela reflected in Christo's eyes, the humility and compassion toward others. Christo did not and does not have the desire to become the father of a rainbow nation, but he is the key custodian of the legacy of the human Mandela.

'Death is something inevitable,' said Mandela. 'When a man has done what he considers to be his duty to his people and his country, he can rest in peace. I believe I have made that effort and that is, therefore, why I will sleep for the eternity.'

Death ends life, but not a relationship nor a legacy. Mandela's portrait hangs in my bedroom. I get up with his smile beaming at me, and I end the day with that same smile. His prison years and his humanity remain with us, thanks to Christo Brand – another name we should never forget.

Christo Brand the Educator:
The Importance of Respect and Loyalty
IAN MIDDLETON

Two great passions in my life, the sport of rugby and the study of history, led to a sunny March day in 2015, and a chance meeting with Christo Brand on Robben Island. Since then, Christo and I have developed a great working relationship and, more importantly, a great friendship. As a result of both, my students have benefitted greatly.

In 2015 the Ashbury College boys' rugby team embarked on our first tour of South Africa. This was a much-anticipated destination, as we knew that not only would South Africa provide wonderful rugby opportunities (which it did, despite our often being on the wrong end of lopsided scores) but, more importantly, it was a country with a rich history, a wonderful culture, and amazing biodiversity. As a rugby coach and history teacher, it was a tremendous opportunity for me to share two of my great passions with my student-athletes.

On a visit to Robben Island, a colleague told me he had overheard that Nelson Mandela's former guard was working in the Island's gift shop. I wondered if that was the guard mentioned in John Carlin's book *Playing the Enemy*, who persuades Nelson Mandela to learn about rugby so that he would be able to communicate with the warden in language the warden understands, specifically with the goal of getting a hot plate for his cell. As the story goes, Mandela quickly learned all he could about rugby and soon was talking as one rugby man to another with a somewhat stupefied warden of Pollsmoor Prison. Though Christo was obviously busy, and I was reluctant to bother him, I went over and introduced myself, on the urging of my colleague. We had a brief chat in which I learned that Christo was indeed the guard I had read about, and that he also had written a book on his experiences working with, and becoming a friend of, Nelson Mandela.

I bought a copy of Christo's book and could not put it down on the flight home. I was absolutely amazed by his story, his relationship with Nelson Mandela, and how he was both an actor in, and witness to, some of the most important events of 20th-century history. I was also struck by the fact that a man with such an important story to share with the world was such a modest and hardworking man, still employed on Robben Island.

Ashbury's first trip to South Africa was such a success that we decided to break with the tradition of alternating our tour destinations and take a second rugby group to South Africa in 2017. We are always looking for new experiences to add to our trips and make them multidimensional, including sporting, cultural, and educational experiences, to create as great a shared experience between coaches and players as possible. With this in mind, I emailed Christo (I had recently found his business card, which I had forgotten he had given me), and asked if he could give us a tour, or at the very least meet the students and talk to them about his experience as a prison guard and his friendship with Nelson Mandela. Christo responded almost immediately, telling me how lovely it was to hear from me and how much he looked forward to seeing me again. He would not be able to meet the group on Robben Island, but he would happily come to our hotel to talk to the students. Much to my surprise he did not want to be paid, but simply reimbursed for his petrol. He also hoped some students would buy his book. The students were so moved by his talk that Christo's supply of books quickly ran out.

Since this second meeting Christo has spoken to Ashbury students several times, including via his first Zoom lecture, and has formed a great relationship with the school.

For most Canadians, and I would imagine many non-South Africans, their understanding of the history of South Africa is limited. Those of us who remember the 1980s recall the protest music of artists such as Peter Gabriel, the Specials, and Juluka, and how those groups brought South Africa into our consciousness. The news was filled with images of violence in townships and government forces cracking down. Domestically, Canadians marched for divestment and applauded Prime Minister Mulroney, who championed the end of apartheid as part of his foreign policy. We all remember Mandela's release from Victor Verster Prison and his casting a vote in the first free elections in 1994 and finally becoming the country's president.

Rugby fans will remember 'The Return Test' between the Springboks and All Blacks, and how the joy of the return of the sport was also tarnished by the actions of some fans who waved Nationalist flags and sang *Die Stem* in Ellis Park. More importantly, rugby fans will remember the 1995 Rugby World Cup and the iconic image of Nelson Mandela and François

Pienaar lifting the Webb Ellis Trophy together, in a tremendous moment of unity.

These are the big moments of history that have been well documented and written about many times. However, too often the study of history focuses on the stories of the great figures alone and fails to look at the equally important role played by common individuals in shaping history. There has always been a mass of people who blindly follow the party holding power or act with indifference to preserve their own safety when evil occurs, and a very small number of people who courageously follow their values, fight for the rights of the oppressed, and change the world for the better. This is where the power and importance of Christo's story comes in. His story provides a very personal touch to South Africa and Nelson Mandela. Sure, it is about Mandela and being a witness to some of the most important events in South Africa's history. But it is truly Christo's story, one that shows how a young man working for the apartheid state was not afraid to break the rules, show humanity, and do the right thing to make the lives of his prisoners more bearable while standing up against the system. It provides a lesson of the importance of the ordinary individual in actively challenging the system, doing the honourable thing, and influencing necessary change.

It also provides the valuable lesson that two men of different generations, races, backgrounds, and authority could put their differences aside, respect each other, and ultimately form a lifelong friendship, while shifting the balance of history. The authenticity of Christo's message, focusing on his personal relationship with Mandela, gives the listener an intimate understanding of both Christo and Mandela and how the two men formed a lifelong bond. This is what really resonated with my students and colleagues.

I am amazed by my first meeting with Christo. Here was a man who was a witness to some of the most important events of the 20th century, quietly going about his job on Robben Island and cheerfully engaging in conversation with tourists, casually and humbly mentioning his book. I am so glad that Christo is now a fulltime speaker, sharing this crucial story with the world.

Africa Never Leaves You

MICHAEL SLATTERY

I first met Christo Brand in July 2016. I was in South Africa with a group of my students as part of our Biodiversity and Human Development study abroad course. Christo had agreed to spend the evening with us in Cape Town talking about his relationship with Nelson Mandela. We were all mesmerised by this humble Afrikaner who, at the tender age of 19, had been given the responsibility to guard the world's most recognised prisoner, inmate #466/64. Growing up, Nelson Mandela was an enigma to me. I had heard his name but was too young to really understand what apartheid meant. He was branded a communist terrorist by the apartheid regime, and his 'evilness' was perpetuated through state propaganda and misinformation. I didn't even know what he looked like until he walked free from Victor Verster Prison on 11 February 1990.

Christo's story is not just one of friendship; it is also one of truth, transformation, reconciliation, and forgiveness. It struck a chord with me because I no longer wanted to feel guilty about my childhood under apartheid. I grew up in Johannesburg in the 1970s and '80s. As a young boy in the decidedly middle-class suburbs of Glenhazel, Highlands North, and Orange Grove, I had access to everything: good schools, movie theatres, golf courses, shops, arcade games, sweets, swimming pools, friends. We had the time and space to be children and spent more time outdoors than in. My parents let me play unsupervised in the streets, though my instructions were to return home when the street lights came on. I didn't need a passbook to go anywhere. It was a bubble of privilege and freedom (for whites), and I never really gave it much thought. That is, until I entered the University of the Witwatersrand in 1985 to begin my undergraduate studies.

In my second year at Wits, a large group of us drove from Johannesburg to Grahamstown for a geography club field trip. After an eleven-hour journey we arrived at the campsite tired and hungry, only to be told that we couldn't stay there.

'Why not?' asked our driver and tour leader, Sean.

'Well … you know…' mumbled the campsite owner, pointing to two of our group sitting near the front of the bus.

The two in question were both master's students (one, named Meshack, went on to do his doctorate at the University of Oxford), and both were, yes, black. I'll never forget how ashamed I felt, not just because these two kind, humble, and intelligent men could not camp with us because of the colour of their skin, but because I had spent years in a cocoon of naiveté without the slightest acknowledgement of the advantage I had been born into. I remember Meshack saying, 'Don't worry, guys, we can stay elsewhere.' We *all* left together, and we spent the night in a field on the edge of town.

I left South Africa in 1988, not for any political reasons but to continue my studies, first in Canada and then at Oxford where, quite remarkably, I ran into Meshack as he was finishing up his Ph.D. thesis. I then moved to the U.S. in 1994 and have spent 25-plus years carving out a career in the academy. But here is the problem: Africa never leaves you. Ever. The smell of the bush. The deep red soils. The cold highveld mornings. The people. Sure, I would go back often to see my family, who now lived in Cape Town and Port Elizabeth, but there was always that nagging feeling of wanting to not just go back but *give back*. Perhaps it is the guilt I sometimes feel from my childhood under apartheid, or perhaps, more simply, just an altruistic desire to help. Either way, that opportunity came in 2014 when I met world-renowned wildlife veterinarian Dr. Will Fowlds.

Will, who is also a landowner at the Amakhala Game Reserve in the Eastern Cape, introduced me to the rhino poaching crisis and visited Texas for a week to engage our community. I then started the TCU Rhino Initiative at my university in Fort Worth and brought our first group of students to South Africa in 2015 as part of that initiative. We stopped in Johannesburg and Cape Town before our ten-day field immersion at Amakhala, helping Will and his team with animal procedures such as collaring and relocations.

On our first morning in Johannesburg, we took our students to Soweto, the sprawling township southwest of the city. We stopped, as most tourists do, at the road sign that reads 'Welcome to SOWETO.' And then, the unexpected: my eyes filled with tears. I felt my chest tighten. I remember gulping for air, and it suddenly hit me: The last time I had been here was in a Casspir, an armoured vehicle, during my military conscription. I stood, completely frozen. Where had the time gone? Why had I not said anything? Why had I not *done* anything?

The end of apartheid was signalled by a great gesture of forgiveness and hope. It was Nelson Mandela, once viewed by most whites (me included) as a terrorist, who became viewed as miraculous for his lack of bitterness. He used his remarkable ability to forgive and to forge reconciliation to transform South Africa into a multiracial democracy. It is far from perfect; old scars run deep. But as I have listened to Christo discuss his personal transformation, as well as the wider transformation of South Africa from a state of oppression and hate to one of reconciliation and hope, I have also begun the process of reconciling my own past as well as embracing my responsibilities moving forward. Navigating racism and discrimination requires deep and serious conversations. It also requires action.

In the meantime, our rhino initiative has gone from strength to strength, winning the Senator Paul Simon Spotlight Award in 2017 for designing and implementing innovative internationalisation programs and initiatives. We continue to leverage the resources of my university and our community not only to help with the protection and management of rhinos, but also to uplift communities. We support conservation programs in local schools and an after-school community centre whose children have been affected by HIV/AIDS. Our initiative's slogan is 'Fighting from afar, but our heart is still there.' As I said, Africa never leaves you.

The Norwegian Connection

RUNE ENGSTROM

If, like me, you grew up in Norway in the 1960s and '70s, you could not avoid hearing about South Africa, apartheid, and Nelson Mandela. Most Norwegians have a strong belief in human rights and justice. Everybody remembered, or younger people had heard about, the Holocaust, the evil symbol of Nazi racism. Nelson Mandela became a symbol for the injustice in this world. The social democrat governments of the Scandinavian countries supported the African National Congress in its fight for justice and equal rights. So did churches and trade unions. A minority believed the ANC was a communist terror organisation, and that the South African government of those days was a buffer against Soviet communism taking over Africa. Those were the days of the cold war between the western and eastern blocs, with proxy wars around the globe.

The Nobel Peace Prize

The Nobel Peace Prize is awarded by the Nobel Committee. The members are elected by the Norwegian parliament, but the committee lives its own life. They give the prize to whoever they believe has worked in the spirit of Alfred Nobel. Some prizes have been criticised both in Norway and abroad, but they are fully independent of any government interference.

Chief Albert Luthuli was awarded the 1960 Nobel Peace Prize for his role in the nonviolent struggle against apartheid. He was the first person of African heritage to be awarded the Nobel Peace Prize. He was followed in 1984 by Archbishop Desmond Tutu, and in 1993 jointly by Nelson Mandela and Frederik Willem de Klerk 'for their work for the peaceful termination of the apartheid regime, and for laying the foundations for a new democratic South Africa.'

Christo Brand

The first time I heard about Christo Brand was around August 2017. I saw a post on Facebook where Andrew Russell wrote about this man and his incredible story. In November the same year I travelled to South Africa with a Norwegian tour operator, Charlotte Ehde Eliassen. We met with Christo Brand one sunny afternoon on the Victoria & Alfred Waterfront, and within minutes knew we had met someone with a unique story the world should hear.

Since that day, Christo has met with every single one of our groups visiting South Africa. His stories about life with Mandela, Sisulu, Kathrada, and the other political prisoners are unique. Christo is a quiet man from a humble background who never tries to brag about his experiences or make up stories to make his role bigger.

My company, Destination Africa, has invited Christo and his dear wife Estelle to Norway twice. He has told his story in churches, visited schools, and met with prisoners and warders in a Norwegian maximum-security prison. Absolutely everyone he meets is blown away by his stories and anecdotes. The highlight of Christo's visits to Norway must be the invitation to present his story at the Nobel Peace Centre and at the Oslo Centre led by our former Prime Minister, Mr Kjell Magne Bondevik.

A Real Time Witness

Human rights, and fighting racism, sexism, and all forms of discrimination, is an important part of education in Norway. At the ages of 16 and 17, tens of thousands of Norwegian students have traveled on so-called White Buses. They are taken to Auschwitz and other concentration camps in Germany and Poland. The tours have traditionally been led by what we call time witnesses. These have been survivors of the death camps, and they have told the students how it was and why it should never happen again. After all these years, there are no witnesses left to tell this important story about the cruelty of man. At the ages of 17 and 18 many spend a year in what we call Folk High Schools. These schools can be seen as something between a gap year and university. The school curriculum is often very liberal, and it can focus on sports, arts, politics, the outdoors, and travel. What they have in common is that they all travel for three to five weeks of the school year, many to South Africa.

Like every young white man in South Africa in those days, Christo had no choice but to go to the army or to the police/prison system. He is a very good example of a real time witness. He saw apartheid from the inside and met prisoners like Mandela. These meetings caused him, from day one, to question the system he was a part of. Slowly he got to know his prisoners, to respect them, and to become friendly with them. It was a very dangerous balancing act, as the system spied on everyone, including the prison warders. If he had been caught, Christo would have been convicted as a traitor and thrown in jail for many years. His story touches the heart of everyone who meets him. His story is not secondhand; he was in the middle of it.

When you listen to Christo's story, you get a feeling of a deeper understanding of what humanity is. This is extremely important, especially for the younger generations. They are growing up in a world where fake news and conspiracy theories flourish. Dark forces are trying to split our societies through social media and fake news. Even though no one can change the world alone, every small step can lead to a better world. Small steps they take can influence the world, and Christo is a prime example of this. Who knows if the world after apartheid would have been the same without people like Mandela and Christo getting to know and trust each other? An enemy can become your friend, if you listen to and respect the other side.

Being a Mensch

I have looked for a word to describe Christo and other ordinary people like him. The closest I can get is to use a Jewish expression: He is a Mensch. According to Leo Rosten in *The Joys of Yiddish*, a Mensch is 'someone to admire and emulate, someone of noble character. The key to being "a real Mensch" is nothing less than character, rectitude, dignity, a sense of what is right and responsible.' The term is used as a high compliment, implying the rarity and value of that individual's qualities.

Ubuntu: 'People Are People through Other People'
ANNETTE NOBUNTU MUL

'You can leave South Africa, but it won't leave you.' That was the text on a billboard at the airport in Cape Town. And that's what happened. From the very first moment I set foot in South Africa, in the year 2000, I experienced the spirit of *Ubuntu*, without being able to put words to it. As a white Dutch woman, with my intergenerational roots and my blood laced with 'I think, therefore I am,' I thought I was averse to spirituality. But here, in the land of Nelson Mandela, an intense urge to wallow in the red earth overcame me. South Africa, the country that still struggles daily with its torn past, but at the same time is a worldwide example of restorative justice, of forgiveness, of reconciliation.

How can a man who has been imprisoned for 27 years come out of prison without vengeance, unite a torn country, and become president? It was the crucial question that occupied me most when I first visited South Africa. I had read a lot from and about Nelson Mandela. In his book *Long Walk to Freedom*, the source of Ubuntu hit me right in the heart. *Umntu ngmuntu ngbantu*: People are people through other people. In all the years that followed, in all my encounters with South Africans, I learned that forgiveness is about healing the past in the present on the way to the future. Ubuntu is the flow of our existence. We, our ancestors, and our unborn children. Forgiveness is about healing the community, with the community.

Humanity in an inhumane system

I first met Christo Brand in January 2014. Christo taught me, in all the stories about his relationship with Mr Mandela on Robben Island, the essence of interconnectedness. It was Mandela who saw that Christo was also trapped in the brutal system of apartheid. By seeing this humanity in an inhumane situation, Christo was also able to admit his own humanity, to Mandela and to the other prisoners. Everything that happened on Robben Island was a reflection of society. Nelson Mandela called it 'the university of life'. That Christo was known for his humanity in an inhumane system, and that this was invaluable for survival, became clear to me in all my encounters with Madiba's fellow inmates. For example, Christo introduced me to Vusumzi Mcongo.

Vusumzi was a political prisoner on Robben Island for nearly twelve years and placed directly under Christo's charge. Bound together by the chains of the apartheid system, they became linked as friends. I tried to understand how this could be done without bitterness and hatred, and Vusumzi explained to me what dignified humanity can bring. He said: 'By accident, during the hearing on the death of Steve Biko before the Truth and Reconciliation Commission, I met some of the security officers. I greeted them and reminded them that they had also interrogated and tortured me. I congratulated them in their cause and their request for amnesty. I could do that without any feelings of revenge. Then I knew that the Robben Island experiences hadn't made me cruel too, hadn't dehumanised me.'

When we fight, we destroy their future

In 2017, again through Christo, I met ex-political prisoner Dumisani Mwandla. I asked him: 'How is it possible that you don't hate us whites?' Dumisani looked at me, tears in his eyes, pointed to a white man and a group of children, and said: 'When we fight, we destroy their future.'

But of all the stories Christo told me, Robert Sobukwe's touched me the most. Ubuntu means: 'People are people through other people.' All the prisoners I spoke to indicated how they had survived the physical and psychological torture: through music, through friendship and hope. Professor Robert Sobukwe was cut off from all human contact for nine years. Even his own guard was not allowed to talk to him, and was given a guard himself, to guarantee this inhuman form of non-communication. He eventually became depressed and ill. I try to imagine the slow psychological torture for him and for his relatives, and even for his guard.

To go the extra mile

On 5 December 2013, the day of Nelson Mandela's death, Archbishop Tutu said: 'Mandela would not want to be placed on a stone pedestal.' To go the extra mile for the sake of others is a pillar of Ubuntu, and what this means I experienced firsthand in my friendship with Christo at a crucial moment. It was November 2019, and I was back in South Africa with a Dutch delegation for the annual Ubuntu Leadership Program. On one of the evenings Christo was our guest of honour teacher. That very night, one of the participants had broken her back falling down the stairs and had to go to the hospital in Plattekloof. My co-trainer Babah Tarawally and I were leading the group and

362

the eight-day program. How should we reconcile individual necessity with group responsibility?

Christo saw and understood and came to me: 'You have a diabolical dilemma. I think you should continue with the group tomorrow. Estelle and I will unconditionally take care of Clara for the next week.' I am incredibly grateful to Christo and Estelle for that. 'Mr Mandela would have wanted it that way,' Christo said, calmly but firmly.

The power of storytelling

Storytelling helps people learn to listen to each other, and through listening comes understanding. Christo says:

> So many atrocities have taken place on Robben Island, but intense friendships have also been formed, allowed and not allowed. A part of my life is on the Island, a part that also asks for the 'apologies' of history. It has become a soul task for me: I must contribute to telling the full truth, the whole story. It is also a story of reconciliation. It is about the truth of history that is so important for our next generations. Apartheid must never happen again. Let Robben Island now be a monument to reconciliation.

That forgiveness can be a long path was made painfully clear to me by Thulani Mabaso, another political prisoner to whom Christo introduced me. The whole truth must continue to be told, with recognition of the pain. Thulani cannot (yet) forgive. He especially remembers his psychological torture. He waited in vain for more than a year for his father to visit. Months later, Thulani stole a newspaper to 'wipe' himself with. It was his father's obituary.

Christo lives Ubuntu, following the spirit of Madiba. He is not infallible or holy, but honest and sincere in his human struggles, thus an example of humanity. Through my encounters with Christo and through his stories, I am able to understand and internalise Ubuntu a little bit more and in turn pass it on in my own immediate environment, work, and country. But I also confront the realisation that, as human beings, we are all capable of both: apartheid and reconciliation.

Raised in a Family of Change Agents

WILLIAM NTEBE

My parents were both active agents for change in the road towards democracy in South Africa.

My mother Ann Ntebe (maiden name Tomlinson) was one of the founding members of the Black Women's Federation, together with Fatima Meer and Winnie Mandela and other black women from different professions. She was a recently qualified social worker and one of the youngest founding members of the Federation. This developed into her being custodian of the Mandela daughters when Winnie Mandela would come to the Cape to visit Mr Mandela on Robben Island.

Mr Mandela wrote a letter in February 1983 from Pollsmoor Prison congratulating my parents on their marriage the previous month and thanking them for the support provided to the Mandela family.

My father Solomzi Ntebe was a member of the Western Cape division of Umkhonto we Sizwe, the armed wing of the African National Congress (ANC), and provided research work for the intelligence branch. When Mrs Mandela was banished to Brandfort, my father was assigned to the Soweto home of the Mandelas to provide support for the family.

My parents believed and acted on the belief that we all must be active participants in the changes needed to bring democracy to South Africa.

In 1991, once the education system was opened for all races, I and my younger brother were privileged to be among the first non-white students to attend previously white-only schools. The school of choice was the South African College School (SACS), the oldest school in South Africa, situated in Dean Street, Newlands.

When the first person achieves what has not been achieved before, they really break a psychological barrier, which paves the way for the rest of us to follow. The next generation often are oblivious to the fact that there was a psychological barrier blocking progress in the first place.

As young students, we were threatening the way that the education system had been structured for many years. We were therefore treated a bit like lab rats: closely monitored, scrutinised, isolated, and treated with caution. It was an extremely confusing situation and environment to understand or navigate.

At that stage we lived in Settlers Place, the first bonded housing settlement within the township of Langa. This housing settlement was situated on the outer edge of Langa, being surrounded by the previous migrant labourer hostels. This human settlement arrangement was in itself a very new environment that created a very distinct class structure between the hostel dwellers and the owners of the bonded houses in Settlers Place.

Each morning, we would travel out of Langa to attend school in Newlands and see how the built environment changed along the journey. Our home environment and school environment existed in two completely different worlds. Navigating these two worlds became part of our educational experience, leading towards 1994 and the first democratic election.

A Timeless Ethos

SAM HODSON

Camphill was founded as a movement in the late 1940s with the intention of changing the way in which marginalised people, specifically the intellectually disabled, were treated. It was a revolutionary approach at the time – and in many ways it still is. The movement was founded on simple yet timeless principles, with the underlying ethos being one of believing that every person is a unique spiritual being with the right to a purposeful life, lived with responsibility, respect, and dignity.

Just before South Africa went into a hard Covid lockdown in March 2020, Christo Brand – Nelson Mandela's warder for much of his incarceration – was the keynote speaker at the International Camphill Dialogue conference held in Hermanus, South Africa. The telling of his story was immensely powerful and impactful. The delegates, both local and international, were mesmerised as Christo shared example after example of how he and Nelson Mandela interacted.

The relationship that started and grew between Nelson Mandela and Christo Brand over the years, both in prison and afterwards, was a living example of Camphill's ethos. As many people as possible need to hear their story of reconciliation and respect – perhaps now more than ever before.

Note: This was Christo's last in-person speaking event before the pandemic closed South Africa's borders to international tourists. In fact, his talk was the only event which the conference organisers managed to conclude before the delegates started heading for the airport to return home.

Further Reading

ANDREW RUSSELL

So many books have been written by or about Nelson Mandela. I have chosen my own selection, each unique in its own way.

Of course Mandela's own epic autobiography *Long Walk to Freedom* is the ideal starting point for anyone wanting to learn more about his life. What can I say about this book except that if you have not yet read it, what are you waiting for? The South African newspaper the *Sunday Tribune* called it 'an enthralling tale told simply, the story of one man's remarkable life and of a people which finally became free'.

Dare Not Linger by Nelson Mandela and Mandla Langa is the story of Mandela's presidential years, drawing heavily on the memoir he began to write as he prepared to conclude his term of office but was unable to finish. The acclaimed South African writer Mandla Langa has completed the task, using Mandela's unfinished draft, detailed notes that Mandela made as events were unfolding, and a wealth of unseen archival material. It tells the extraordinary story of a country in transition and the challenges Mandela faced as he strove to realise his vision for a liberated South Africa. Mandela had always intended to write a sequel to *Long Walk to Freedom*. He wanted to tell the story of his years as the first president of a democratic South Africa. For many years the project loomed large in his life, and he undertook the mammoth task under challenging circumstances. The demands placed on him meant that the project lost momentum, and eventually the manuscript lay dormant. Throughout the last years of his life he often talked about it, worried about the work he had started but not finished. It was left to Mandla Langa to take up the challenge of completing this book. It is a wonderful account of Mandela's presidential years.

Fatima Meer (1928-2010) was a South African writer, academic, screenwriter, and prominent anti-apartheid activist who knew Mandela since the early 1950s. In the preface to her 1988 book *Higher Than Hope: Nelson Mandela*, she wrote:

> In one of Nelson's letters to me in the early seventies, he expressed the opinion that an autobiography was an excuse for an ego trip. I wrote back disagreeing. ... In any case, what were his feelings about biographies? A few months later I was at a mass meeting. ... A message was whispered to me – from Nelson Mandela, I was told. ... He would like me to write his biography. ... I offer this book as an addition to Mary Benson's pioneering work on Nelson Mandela. At best it is my interpretation of him. ... I have tried as far as possible to interpret Mandela through Mandela's eyes.

Another book I can highly recommend is *Conversations with Myself* by Nelson Mandela. This book gives readers access to the private man behind the public figure, from letters written in the darkest hours of Mandela's 27 years of imprisonment to the draft of an unfinished sequel to *Long Walk to Freedom*.

It is an intimate journey from the first stirrings of his political conscience to his galvanizing role on the world stage. It gives the reader an opportunity to understand and appreciate much of what Mandela endured, the hardships as well as the victories. A truly inspirational book.

The best-known biography is *Mandela* by Anthony Sampson. Sampson became keenly interested in South African affairs in 1951 when, after leaving Oxford, he first went to Johannesburg to become editor of the black magazine *Drum*. This epic biography provides many insights into Mandela's story.

Mandela, edited by Mac Maharaj and Ahmed Kathrada, is a beautifully crafted and constructed coffee table book full of tributes from people all over the world and photographs, letters, and documents from Mandela's life, with a foreword by Kofi Annan and introduction by Archbishop Desmond Tutu.

John Carlin covered the fall of apartheid for the British newspaper *The Independent*. His book *Playing the Enemy* is a thrilling account of how Mandela deployed his sense of humour, charm, and political vision to pull off the most unlikely of miracles, South Africa's victory in the 1995 Rugby World Cup, which the country also hosted. But the book is not just about that famous rugby match. It offers fascinating insight into the years leading up to it, a time when civil war was a very real threat in South Africa. The book went on to be made into the movie *Invictus*, directed by Clint Eastwood and starring Morgan Freeman as Mandela and Matt Damon as Springbok rugby captain François Pienaar. My favourite quote from the book is:

For decades Mandela had stood for everything white South Africans most feared; the Springbok jersey had been the symbol, for even longer, of everything black South Africans most hated. Now suddenly before the eyes of the whole of South Africa, and much of the world, the two negative symbols had merged to create a new one that was positive, constructive and good. Mandela had wrought the transformation, becoming the embodiment not of hate and fear, but generosity and love.

John Carlin got to know Christo Brand very well during his time in South Africa, and he mentions Christo multiple times in the book, accurately describing him as 'a sweet-tempered man who came to regard his prisoner in a fatherly light'. Carlin also wrote a short second book, *Knowing Mandela*, which I absolutely adore. In it he writes at length about the relationship between Mandela and Christo's family. It is a stunning book, highly recommended.

A wonderful book which includes previously unseen material is *A Prisoner in the Garden: Opening Nelson Mandela's Prison Archive*. This book contains many fascinating documents, photos, and anecdotes from Mandela's life. There is also a section about Christo Brand and copies of both the letter written by Mandela to Christo's son, Riaan, on his 16th birthday, and the letter to Estelle Brand that he smuggled out of Pollsmoor in a chocolate bar. Nelson Mandela himself wrote the following in the book's foreword:

We have mandated the Nelson Mandela Centre of Memory and Commemoration to locate and document the many archives that contain traces of my life and those who have lived it with me. This book tells the story of that project, a story made up of many stories. Anyone who has explored the world of archives will know that it is a treasure house, one that is full of surprises, crossing paths, dead ends, painful reminders and unanswered questions.

One of Nelson Mandela's closest friends, sentenced to life imprisonment with him in the Rivonia Trial, was Ahmed Kathrada, the man who wrote the foreword to the first edition of this book (included in this edition). Kathrada's *Memoirs* is a wonderful insight into his life and contains some of the most descriptive and insightful writing on the life of the prisoners on Robben Island.

In her remarkable autobiography *When Hope Whispers*, Zoleka Mandela, daughter of Zindzi and granddaughter of Winnie, recalls from a unique perspective one of the seminal moments in the historic friendship between Nelson Mandela and Christo Brand:

Before I was a year old, my grandmother had already smuggled me into Robben Island on her back. She says that at the time it was the only gift she could give my grandfather, who by then had not seen a baby for many years. As it was, the law of the country stipulated that only one child could visit at a time from each family, and visiting children had to be 16 years and older.

Zoleka was the baby Christo allowed Mandela to hold in his arms in the visitor's centre. Her book is a story of healing and triumph and serves as a testimony to the strength of the human spirit in fighting against life's challenges, including drug and alcohol addiction and cancer. Who will ever forget the tragedy Zoleka suffered during South Africa's hosting of the 2010 Soccer World Cup, when her own 13-year-old daughter Zenani died in a car crash?

Neil Barnard's *Secret Revolution: Memoirs of a Spy Boss* reads like an espionage thriller! The first half is all about Barnard's spy life and his role in the murky world of the National Intelligence Service. The second half deals with the period from when his meetings with Mandela started – the full negotiation process – and offers fascinating insight into the life and dealings of this man who came to know and respect Mandela over the course of many years. Barnard ends his book with this sentence: 'I am immensely grateful to the Heavenly Father that I had the unique privilege, together with Mandela, of preparing the way for a political settlement in our fatherland, for which both he and I, two patriots, had endless love.'

There and Back is the fascinating autobiography of Eddie Daniels, born in the District Six neighourhood of Cape Town in 1928 and imprisoned from 1964 to 1979 on Robben Island in B Section with Mandela, Sisulu, Kathrada, and the other leaders. This book offers an incredible insight into the life of the political prisoners on the Island. I had to search far and wide to secure my copy of what should be essential reading for anyone interested in this period of South Africa's history.

One book I literally could not put down once I started reading it is *Rivonia's Children* by Glenn Frankel. I purchased it a few years ago when I visited Liliesleaf Farm in Rivonia, where Mandela's comrades were arrested in 1964. It sat on my shelves for several years before I picked it up and started reading it. The book offers a fascinating insight into the lives of true South African heroes, people who fought in the background against the apartheid regime without looking for any kudos or back-slapping. They were seemingly ordinary South Africans – but reading the book, you come to understand how important their roles were. They deserve to be highlighted and thanked for everything they did for our country. The sleeve describes the book as follows:

> This is the story of three families: Hilda and Rusty Bernstein, longtime communists so deeply committed to the cause that even the threat of life imprisonment did not stop them; Ruth First, a fiery activist arrested and held for 117 days without charge, and her equally committed husband Joe Slovo, eventually part of the ANC team responsible for negotiating the end of white rule; and AnnMarie Wolpe, an uneasy bystander, forced to decide whether to risk her own freedom and the life of her sick infant by helping her activist husband, Harold Wolpe, escape from prison, or to flee the country without him.

One Step behind Mandela by Rory Steyn and Debora Patta is a very honest and insightful look into the life of one of Nelson Mandela's bodyguards. Steyn was appointed team leader of President Mandela's personal protection unit in 1996. Patta is a highly respected broadcast journalist in South Africa. This combination makes the book a highly readable glimpse into the private and political world of Mandela.

Island in Chains: Indres Naidoo, Prisoner 885/63 is another book by a former Robben Island prisoner. As an activist for the African National Congress, Indres Naidoo was arrested for sabotage in 1963. *Island in Chains* is his account of the ten years he spent on Robben Island. First published in 1982, it reaffirmed that the fight against apartheid would be won. The updated edition I own follows the path his life has taken since his release and his subsequent appointment as a minister in the first democratic government. In 2001, *Island in Chains* was the runner-up for the prestigious Alan Paton Non-Fiction Prize.

Solitary by Albert Woodfox is the unforgettable story of a man who served more than four decades in solitary confinement – in a six-by-nine-foot cell, 23 hours a day – for a crime he did not commit. The fact that Woodfox survived this ordeal was a feat of extraordinary endurance. On a number of occasions he refers to Nelson Mandela and how he inspired him when he was in the darkest of places and losing hope. It is a tough book to read, but it once again shows how Mandela reached someone in a profound way.

More Than Just a Game: Football vs Apartheid by Chuck Korr and Marvin Close is the compelling story of how political prisoners on Robben Island turned football (soccer) into an active force in the struggle against apartheid. It is a remarkable book, a celebration of bravery and heroism that shows how sport has the power to unite and overcome adversity.

I'll end by recommending two other fascinating books that look at different aspects of apartheid. The first, a monumental investigation by Hennie van Vuuren called *Apartheid, Guns and Money*, lifts the lid on some of the darkest secrets of apartheid's economic crimes. David Welsh's book *The Rise and Fall of Apartheid* researches apartheid against the backdrop of a long history of conflict spanning the liberation movement's suppression and subsequent resurrection.

Foreword to the Original Edition of *Doing Life with Mandela: My Prisoner, My Friend* (2014)

AHMED KATHRADA

My lasting impression of Christo Brand is that he's a very good human being. He's not a politician; he's just a very caring man who took chances for other people, which could have brought him trouble.

While his book naturally focuses on his relationship with Madiba while he was a prisoner, I too experienced the humanity of Christo while I was in prison. I did not really encounter him on Robben Island where I began serving my life sentence, with Madiba, from 13 June 1964. It was only after I was transferred to the mainland, to Pollsmoor Prison in October 1982, that I really had a lot of dealings with Christo.

We all realised that this was a good man, someone who could help us, but we were warned by Madiba not to take advantage of young warders and get them into trouble. He was asking us not to use Christo for political things, like sending political messages and so forth, and so he didn't do that for us. But he did many other things.

One of my lasting memories of Christo's difference to the brutish warders we had been used to before was at the time I was allowed to start having legal visits from Advocate Dullah

Omar. We had been trying to see each other for quite some time and I got my chance when, after I had finished my two Honours Degrees through the University of South Africa, the prison authorities would not let me register for a Master's Degree. So I said I was going to take the matter to court and asked to see Dullah.

On one of his visits, Dullah brought samosas – two packets – one for the warders and, once the warders accepted theirs, he asked if I could have the other packet. Christo obliged. At this time, Dullah's wife, Farida, was running a fruit and vegetable stall at Salt River Market in Cape Town, so we then arranged for Christo to go to her and collect fruit from her for us – she also gave him fruit and vegetables for his own family. Next, Dullah started arriving for legal visits with his lawyer's bag packed full of food; not a legal book in sight. Christo knew it and he let it go.

Even better than that was the extra visits he allowed me to have. Christo arranged visits from people I was not ordinarily allowed to see, such as Professor Fatima Meer, other political activists, and extra family members. I will never forget the day when a niece of mine was married in Cape Town and Christo organised for virtually the entire wedding party to visit me, illegally, in prison. He set up a special visiting place upstairs and I saw them all, kids and adults. With the kids, it was one or two minutes I was allowed to see each of them. They filed into the room and brought with them laughter and light, a rare and glorious sight for a prisoner. I got to spend a little more time with the adults, again one by one.

He also took me to see political activists who were detained at Pollsmoor Prison, which was in a way more dangerous for him than it was for me. It was the 1980s and the time of the

State of Emergency, when thousands of anti-apartheid activists were detained throughout the country. Many of the Western Cape and even some Eastern Cape activists were detained at Pollsmoor. Their own families did not know where they were or how they were faring, but Christo let me see them. One day, he took me to see Trevor Manuel, who was not allowed any visitors at all. Trevor, who later became Finance Minister under Madiba and other presidents, had already been in solitary confinement for two years when Christo took me to his prison cell.

It was a big thing for Trevor to have me there speaking with him. In prison, we had been hidden from the world for two decades. Only old photos of us, much younger, were available and even then it was a criminal offense to possess them. One can imagine the impact of our visit to him during which I passed on greetings from Madiba and Walter Sisulu, among others; it really boosted his spirits. Christo also let me give him an inspiring poem at one stage. On another occasion, he took me to see Matthew Goniwe, an Eastern Cape activist who was killed by the security police after his release.

Isolated as we were in prison, we were very ignorant about AIDS, and Christo once told us seven ANC guerrillas who were HIV positive had been captured and brought from Angola. One day, when we were outside, they rushed to us and embraced us. We worried afterwards that we might have caught it from being hugged by them. Later, after we had been locked in our cells for the night, we happened to see Christo, walking with these fellows with his arm around them, up and down the courtyard. That image with Christo and the HIV positive prisoners, along with that of Princess Di when we saw her on television with an HIV positive child, broke our suspicions about HIV, especially when I saw how comfortable he was with these chaps.

Because of the difficulty of communications with the other activists in prison, we used to stand under their cells and talk, so that they would be able to hear what we were talking about. It was our way of passing on information to them. In another small show of humanity, Christo was aware of what we were doing and he didn't do anything to stop us. When we were eventually transferred to a Johannesburg prison in October 1989, just days before our release, I had two televisions. I left one with Christo for these prisoners and he gave it to them. The other he kept in his garage for me and gave it to me when I came back to Cape Town as a Member of Parliament, five years later.

One of the most important things Christo did for us was one day in 1986, some months after Madiba had been isolated from us, so that we had no idea of what was happening with him. Christo came to me and said, 'I've got something to tell you, but you'll go and tell Sisulu and them.'

I said, 'Well, don't tell me.'

But of course he told me anyway. He said, 'Last night we took Madiba to the house of the Minister of Justice, Kobie Coetsee.' And that was enough information for us, to let us know what was happening. We worked out that Madiba must have started discussions with the enemy. It was not long thereafter that Madiba was allowed to see us at Pollsmoor and informed each of us that the talks had started, at his instigation, to get the government to eventually talk to the ANC. Christo would also tell us whenever he took Madiba somewhere for a drive – often it was the only news we had of Madiba, and it was so important to us.

On weekends when Sergeant James Gregory, another warder, was not on duty, Christo would call me to show me letters that

Gregory had refused to pass on to me. They had them for years, along with a whole bundle of *Indicator* newspapers – a weekly anti-apartheid newspaper started by Ameen Akhalwaya, who had them sent every week. Christo would give them to me in bulk when he could.

And then, of course, his wife started baking Christmas cakes for me. Every Christmas she used to bake me a cake and Christo would bring it to me, a tradition that continues to this day.

It makes a tremendous difference to the life of a prisoner having someone like Christo as a warder. We first had warders who were brutes, like criminals themselves really – of course, they never touched us – but when the younger ones arrived things changed because they were not indoctrinated against us. Christo, though, stood out for his kindness and humanity – even from the younger chaps.

Our relationship continued after our release and, when he resigned from his job, I helped to arrange for him to fill a position at the Constitutional Assembly offices. Later, when he was ready for another job, I found him one at the Robben Island Museum.

He is the hardest worker, ready to help with anything, always willing to do overtime, which many of the other staff won't do. He ran our shop at the Nelson Mandela Gateway to Robben Island, at a profit. And not only was he making a profit, but also, as a public relations man, there was nobody better, because he likes to talk. For instance, once a woman stopped there on her way to the Island to buy a bottle of water, and Christo, being Christo, hears her accent: 'Are you American?'

'Yes.'

Without any further information, he asks, 'Do you know a man called Bob Vassen?' (He is my friend who then taught at

Michigan State University.)

She replied, 'Yes I do, we taught together.'

My book *A Simple Freedom* had just been launched and Christo had a big box – not yet to sell but of course he doesn't ask me – and so he says, 'Would you like to buy this book?'

'I'd love to buy it.'

'Would you like his signature?'

So I met this woman, and she turned out to be Professor Marcie Williams, and from that bottle of water developed a strong friendship with her which endures to this day. In fact, I received a doctorate from the University of Massachusetts, through that bottle of water.

I sincerely hope that Christo's book *Mandela: My Prisoner, My Friend* will receive the respect and attention it deserves because it's a valuable addition to the writings about imprisonment during the apartheid era, and it is written by a fine man. It is also unique in that it is the most honest account I have read by a warder relating their interaction with Nelson Mandela, and for that alone it deserves credit. I wish Christo all the success in the world.

Eulogy at Nelson Mandela's Memorial Service
15 December 2013
AHMED KATHRADA

The last time I saw Madiba alive was when I visited him in hospital. I was filled with an overwhelming mixture of sadness, emotion, and pride. He tightly held my hand until the end of my brief visit. It was profoundly heartbreaking. It brought me to the verge of tears when my thoughts automatically flashed back to the picture of the man I grew up under. How I wished I'd never had to confront the reality of what I saw.

I first met Madiba in 1946; that's 67 years ago. I recalled the tall, healthy, and strong man; the boxer; the prisoner who easily wielded the pick and shovel at the lime quarry on Robben Island. I visualised the prisoner that vigorously exercised every morning before we were unlocked. What I saw at his home after his spell in hospital was this giant of a man, helpless and reduced to a shadow of his former self.

And now the inevitable has happened. He has left us and is now with the 'A Team' of the ANC – the ANC in which he cut his political teeth; and the ANC for whose policy of a non-racial, non-sexist, democratic, and prosperous South Africa he was prepared to die.

He has joined the 'A Team' of his close comrades: Chief Luthuli, Walter Sisulu, Oliver Tambo, Dr Yusuf Dadoo, Jack

Simons, Moses Kotane, Bram Fischer, Dr Monty Naicker, JB Marks, Helen Joseph, Ruth First, Professor ZK Matthews, Beyers Naude, Joe Slovo, Lilian Ngoyi, Ma Sisulu, and Michael Harmel.

In addition to the ANC's 'A Team', Madiba has also joined men and women outside the ANC – Helen Suzman, Steve Biko, Alan Paton, Robert Sobukwe, Cissie Gool, Bennie Kies, Neville Alexander, Zeph Mothopeng and many other leaders.

We are a country that has been blessed by many great and remarkable men and women, all of whom played a critical part in this grand struggle for freedom and dignity. We have been blessed by the contributions of many different movements and formations, both inside and outside the country, each making an indelible imprint on our history. We have been blessed by a struggle that actively involved the masses of the people in their own liberation.

We have been blessed that under the collective leadership of the ANC, we can proudly proclaim that South Africa belongs to all who live in it, black and white. We were mightily, and unexpectedly, blessed when the old, oppressive, undemocratic order succumbed and bowed to the inevitable. And then, finally, we were truly blessed by the farsighted wisdom of our collective leadership – with Madiba at the helm – that took us into a democratic future. For all of this and much more, we are deeply grateful.

We are fortunate that today we live in a noisy and lively democracy. We are eternally grateful that dignity has been restored to all South Africans. We are forever grateful that the lives of many are improving, although not enough yet. We are deeply grateful for a constitution that encompasses all that is good in us and a constitutional order that protects our hard-won freedom. Finally, we are infinitely grateful that each and every one of us, whether we are African, white, coloured, or Indian, can proudly call ourselves South Africans.

Mindful of our gains, we nevertheless know that a long, long road lies ahead, with many twists and turns, sometimes through difficult and trying times. Poverty, ill health, and hunger still stalk our land. Greed and avarice show their ugly faces. Xenophobia and intolerance play their mischief in our beautiful land. Parts of the world out there find themselves in unhappy situations; economies falter and stagger; extremism and fundamentalism of all kinds are rampant; the Earth reels from climate change, and the poor battle to survive. Ferocious struggles for democracy unfold daily before our very eyes, and the numbers of political prisoners grow in step with rising intolerance. For instance, we think of the Palestinian Marwan Barghouti, who is languishing in an Israeli prison. All of these people and prisoners throughout the world will continue to draw inspiration from the life and legacy of Mandela.

And finally Mr President, I wish to address myself directly to Madala, as we called each other. What do we say to you in these, the last, final moments together, before you exit the public stage forever?

Madala, your abundant reserves of love, simplicity, honesty, service, humility, care, courage, foresight, patience, tolerance, equality, and justice continually served as a source of enormous strength to many millions of people in South Africa and the world. You symbolise today, and always will, qualities of collective leadership, reconciliation, unity, and forgiveness. You strove daily to build a united, non-racial, non-sexist, and democratic South Africa.

In this spirit, so exemplified in your life, it is up to the present and next generations to take up the cudgels where you have left off. It is up to them, through service, to deepen our democracy; entrench and defend our constitution; eradicate poverty; eliminate inequality; fight corruption; and serve always with compassion, respect, integrity, and tolerance. Above all, they must build our nation and break down the barriers that still divide us.

Xenophobia, racism, and sexism must be fought with tenacity, wisdom, and enlightenment. Anything that defines someone else as 'the other' has to go. Tolerance and understanding must flourish and grow. In all these actions we are and will be guided by your wisdom and deeds.

Today, mingled with our grief is the enormous pride that one of our own has during your life, and now in your death, united the people of South Africa and the entire world on a scale never experienced before in history. Remarkably, in these last few days, the masses of our people, from whatever walk of life, have demonstrated how very connected they feel to you; how the story of your life is their story and how their story is your story. Madala, you captured this relationship beautifully on the occasion of Walter Sisulu's death, when you said: 'We shared the joy of living, and the pain. Together we shared ideas, forged common commitments. We walked side by side through the valley of death, nursing each other's bruises, holding each other up when our steps faltered. Together we savoured the taste of freedom!'

To Mrs Graça Machel and the Mandela family, our love, respect, and support go out to you. We wish there was a way that we could ease your grief and pain. These last few months have been particularly hard, and we trust that in the ensuing weeks you will be able to find the rest and peace you need so much.

We mourn with you and wish you strength in this time of need.

Madala, while we may be drowned in sorrow and grief, we salute you as a fighter for freedom to the end. Farewell my elder brother, my mentor, my leader. With all the energy and determination at our command, we pledge to join the people of South Africa and the world to perpetuate the ideals and values for which you have devoted your life.

Hamba Kahle, Madala! Hamba Kahle, my dearest friend!

About the Cover Artist

My name is Madodana Cita, mostly known as Mardee Cita. I am a 24-year-old portrait artist, ceramist, painter, and sculptor.

I was raised in the rural parts of the Eastern Cape in South Africa but currently live in Zwelihle, Hermanus.

I realised at a very young age that I had a passion for artistic pursuits. I would use whatever material I could find to either draw or sculpt. I would even use my sister's face makeup to colour my artworks.

I would make my sculptures from clay dug from the earth near my home village, which I would bring home in a wheelbarrow.

I'm also heading an empowerment project with the help and guidance of Lillian Lloys Ellis, which has become the most encouraging platform for me to reach my art career goals.

I'm still at it since I began as a child, doing all I can to achieve my dreams of becoming a good and well-known artist.

I'm so privileged to have been chosen to create an artwork which will be used on the cover of Christo Brand's new book, sharing his wonderful experience with our former president Nelson Mandela. I have painted for the cover of the book his home where he was raised in Qunu in the Eastern Cape where I too was raised.

I hope with this opportunity of my story being included in the book to reach many people who will follow up on my works of art and support me to reach higher heights than I have ever imagined.

I'm so grateful, and hope each and every reader of the book enjoys and learns so much from it.

Mardee Cita

Email: madodanacita@gmail.com
Facebook: Mardeeafricahats
Instagram: mardeedesigns

THE HUNTER HUNTED

Caleb Black was not only a preacher but a bounty hunter whose deadly power with the gun was known throughout the territory. He arrived to an unfriendly reception at the small town of West Ridge, carrying with him flyers on two outlaws, Pete Coyne and Al Gates. The reward money would be a welcome boost to his meagre income. Nothing was quite what it seemed, however, and Caleb found he had to face the gang responsible for the deaths of five bounty hunters. Cold-shouldered by the town and its sheriff, Caleb wondered whether he would live to collect the reward money.